COMBAT AND CARNIVAL

HACCOMBE

✝COMBAT AND CARNIVAL

PETER CAREW

CONSTABLE · LONDON

LONDON
PUBLISHED BY
Constable and Company Ltd
10–12 Orange Street, W.C.2

INDIA
Orient Longmans Ltd
BOMBAY   CALCUTTA   MADRAS

CANADA
Longmans Green and Company
TORONTO

SOUTH AND EAST AFRICA
Longmans Green and Company Ltd
CAPE TOWN   NAIROBI

First published 1954

Printed in Great Britain by
BUTLER AND TANNER LTD
FROME AND LONDON

CONTENTS

Part One

THE SOLDIER-GROOM

Part Two

THE BARONET

ILLUSTRATIONS

ACKNOWLEDGMENTS

THE author wishes to give due acknowledgment to *The Taylor Papers* for the helpful assistance gained therefrom, to Messrs. Longmans, Green & Co. Ltd. for their permission to refer to *The Greville Memoirs*, and to Mr. James G. Commin, of Exeter, for permission to consult *A Memoir of the Rev. John Russell.* He also desires to express his indebtedness to Messrs. Horace Marshall & Son Ltd. for permitting him to consult *The Life of Sir Stamford Raffles* which has been out of print for many years.

Finally, the author wishes to express his gratitude to Messrs. Wm. Blackwood & Sons Ltd. for their helpful suggestions regarding the publication of certain articles which have appeared in *Blackwood's Magazine.*

FAMILY TREE

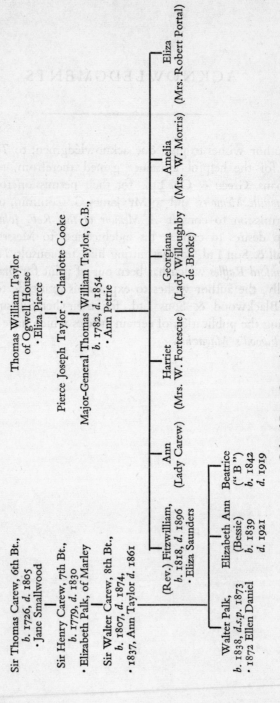

Thomas William Taylor
of Ogwell House
· Eliza Pierce

Pierce Joseph Taylor · Charlotte Cooke

Major-General Thomas William Taylor, C.B.,
b. 1782, d. 1854
· Ann Petrie

Sir Thomas Carew, 6th Bt.,
b. 1726, d. 1805
· Jane Smallwood

Sir Henry Carew, 7th Bt.,
b. 1779, d. 1830
· Elizabeth Palk, of Marley

Sir Walter Carew, 8th Bt.,
b. 1807, d. 1874,
· 1837, Ann Taylor d. 1861

Ann
(Lady Carew)

Harriet
(Mrs. W. Fortescue)

Georgiana
(Lady Willoughby
de Broke)

Amelia
(Mrs. W. Morris)

Eliza
(Mrs. Robert Portal)

(Rev.) Fitzwilliam,
b. 1818, d. 1896
· Eliza Saunders

Walter Palk,
b. 1838, d.s.p. 1873
· 1872 Ellen Daniel

Elizabeth Ann
(Bessie)
b. 1839
d. 1921

Beatrice
("B")
b. 1842
d. 1919

Colonel Peter Carew is great-nephew to Sir Walter
Carew, 8th Bt, and grandson of Rev. Fitzwilliam Taylor.

FOREWORD

THE characters in this narrative, all of whom have long since departed, were members of the author's family and were closely interwoven. His great-grandfather on the paternal side, Sir Henry Carew, gives place to his great-grandfather on the maternal side, Thomas Taylor. His great-uncle and great-aunt (see Family Tree), with their children, take the next place and finally his great-uncle and great-aunt (see Family Tree) of lesser vintage figure in the story.

He pleads forgiveness of their shades for any inaccuracy or for any seeming aspersions on their characters which may transpire.

The material for this book has been gathered from family diaries and letters and from a heterogeneous mass of old papers. Since one member of the family fought at Waterloo and wrote an account of what he personally saw of the battle, and a later member of the family was a Captain in the 4th Light Dragoons, the famous Light Brigade that charged at Balaklava, and survived to write the story of it to his mother, these old letters and journals have more than a pious interest.

What is most likely to strike the modern reader, apart from the ineptitude with which England seemed to conduct her wars, is how little these wars affected the life of the people at home. The privileged classes continued to enjoy their privileges, to shoot their pheasants, eat their six-course dinners and generally to enjoy themselves. The young men went to war with something of the insouciance with which they would go to a meet, and it is startling to find that pleasure cruises for the wealthy

were run from England to Scutari during the Crimean War
and that ladies were taken on sight-seeing expeditions to the very
battlefields.

Throughout all this period, from the French Revolution to
the Crimean War, hardly a ripple seems to have disturbed the
smooth and glittering surface of the social life of the people who
move through this story, in spite of allusions to the Bristol riots,
the Chartist Petition and the Irish famine.

PROLOGUE

TUCKED away in that happy valley of Devonshire, between the estuary of the Teign and Torbay, stands Haccombe, the centuries-old ancestral domain of the Carew family. The great sandstone mansion, of no intrinsic architectural merit, flaunts its ugliness down the undulating park sloping to the river Teign. A stone's throw away is the little fourteenth-century Church of St. Blaise, a gem in its way, with the tombs of Crusaders inside and horseshoes on the door to mark the victory of a Carew over a Champernowne when, for a wager, they swam their horses over Teignmouth Bar. The dose of salt imbibed probably cooled their overnight enthusiasm, but the horseshoes remain to this day. The little church, moreover, is unique in another way, for its incumbent was an Archpriest, a relic of pre-Reformation days. This dignitary, with his lawn sleeves and fur stole, paid a grudging allegiance to the Archbishop of Canterbury, but had no truck with the Bishop of the diocese or with his visiting Rural Deans; and the patron of the living has been known to see them off the premises.

Towards the end of the eighteenth century, the reigning magnate of Haccombe was the sixth Baronet, Sir Thomas Carew. Sir Thomas at that time was one of the largest landowners in Devonshire, his estates in North and South Devon extending to well over 300,000 acres. His son Henry later increased this family wealth by marrying in 1806 Elizabeth Palk, the daughter and heiress of Walter Palk who had amassed a fortune in India by means best known to himself and seldom discussed. On the death of Walter Palk, the Marley estate, twenty miles from Haccombe and comprising a good part of Dartmoor in which there were lucrative iron mines, was inherited by his daughter and later added to the Carew properties.

A few miles to the West of Haccombe lay the Taylor estates of Ogwell and Denbury. Old Thomas Taylor lived at Denbury Manor and the Reynell property of Ogwell had come to him through his wife who had died in 1776. The Carews, Taylors, Reynells and Courtenays formed an integral part of the Devon landed aristocracy and for untold years had dined, wined, and on occasions married each other. Since the death of his wife, who was an exceedingly good business woman and had kept the estates together, old Taylor had fallen on evil days and was plagued by creditors on every side. Nothing daunted, however, the old man was starting to rebuild Ogwell House for his son Pierce, then a Captain in the 21st Light Dragoons. But in 1783 Pierce transferred to the 3rd Dragoons and put paid to his military career which in any case had not been marked with any special distinction, and in the next year the 3rd were disbanded. Pierce and his wife Charlotte, who was the daughter of Dr. William Cooke, Dean of Ely, then settled down to farm at Coombe Royal, which old Taylor had persuaded Sir Thomas Carew to let to them. There they remained for ten years. Sir Thomas was glad enough to oblige old Taylor, of whom he was very fond, although the chances of obtaining any rent were problematical as he suspected that Pierce would prove to be no greater success as a farmer than he had been as a soldier.

Pierce Taylor, though he did not improve the agricultural production of Coombe Royal to any appreciable extent, was productive in other directions. His efforts to provide for an increasing family effectually prevented any rent being handed to Sir Thomas which, as things were, did not worry the baronet to any great extent. Thomas, the eldest Taylor son, with whom this narrative is mainly concerned, was born in 1782 and became the special favourite of his grandfather, who did everything within his means—which were fortunately limited—to spoil him. In 1794 old Taylor, finding himself unable to cope with his accumulating debts, handed over the Ogwell estate to his son, who with his household moved from Coombe Royal to Denbury Manor until Ogwell House should be completed. Charlotte Taylor, who had found housekeeping for her father-in-law a mixed blessing, was thankful when they finally moved into Ogwell and young Thomas was removed from the fond clutches of his grandfather.

Sir Thomas Carew and Pierce Taylor continued to be the best of friends. Pierce and his eldest son often went to Haccombe during the shooting season, where the deep sunk valleys and precipitous hills provided some of the best pheasant shooting in the West of England. Young Thomas Taylor was allowed to join the beaters, shouting "cockover" with the best of them, but the shooting, due to the high elevation of the birds and the poor marksmanship of the best performers, was disappointing. When the shoot was over the gentlemen would adjourn to the dining-room to warm themselves with a succession of hot toddies. This was apt to be a protracted entertainment and young Thomas was sent to the housekeeper's room where Mrs. Marks, who was in charge of the Haccombe household, dispensed tea. There came a day when the gentlemen's refreshment was so prolonged that young Thomas tiptoed into the dining-room to find out the reason for the delay. All the guests had gone and only Sir Thomas, Pierce and old Taylor remained. To young Thomas's inexperienced eyes it was something of a shock to find the three tipplers in a comatose state. Old Taylor had slipped under the table and was snoring peacefully, whilst Sir Thomas and Pierce Taylor were disposed in various attitudes on the floor. Thomas had perforce to spend the night at Haccombe since his father and grandfather were quite incapable of taking him home. Despite the uncomfortable night which they must have spent, Sir Thomas and the Taylors were up betimes next morning.

Sir Thomas Carew had promised old Thomas Taylor that in due course he would present his grandson to the living of Haccombe, which was worth the not inconsiderable sum of £1,500 a year. Pierce had no objection and old Taylor, who foresaw eventually a comfortable home for himself, was bent on the project. It was thought that in order to prepare him for Holy Orders an early religious grounding would be of advantage to the young proselyte, and so, when he was eleven years old, the boy was sent to the grammar school at Ottery St. Mary where he boarded with the Vicar. Thomas unfortunately did not respond to the reverend gentleman's treatment and at fifteen he was sent to his father's old house at Eton, then under the Rev. Mr. Codrington, who found his pupil sadly intractable. Thomas Taylor was not attracted by the thought of entering the Church and he determined as soon as he was old enough to take up his father's old profession. Mr. Codrington wrote to Pierce Taylor in despair :

" I have endeavoured to direct young Taylor's footsteps into the path of that most honourable profession of which I am a humble member ; I regret to say that he is unresponsive and is bent on following your footsteps into the army. As you suggest I have entered him for St. John's at Cambridge and trust he will be a worthy student."

Taylor went up to St. John's College in 1800 as a Gentleman-Commoner, and it was here that he made friends with two men who were afterwards to become Prime Ministers of England : Henry John Temple, later Viscount Palmerston, and Frederick John Robinson, who was ultimately created Earl of Ripon. Both were Harrovians and Taylor, with the innate snobbishness of the time, was at first inclined to consider himself on a higher plane. Eventually, however, they sank their differences and Taylor and Temple formed a friendship which was to last for life. The undergraduates let themselves go when the Peace of Amiens was signed in March 1802, and on this occasion Taylor's footsteps seem to have strayed still further from the path which leads to Holy Orders. In a letter to his father, he writes :

" I am sorry to tell you that on this day the wine or the devil or both entered into me. I fell in with some boisterous fellows from your old regiment, the 21st L.D., who are billeted here ; they were making merry in a tavern, and it was decided to make a pyre of Boney in the market place. It was past midnight and most of the worthy burghers seemed to be asleep. We marched to the market place making a fine to-do and had got the fire going lustily when a party of constables appeared. There was a scuffle in which several persons were hurt, amongst them being yours truly who got a bleeding head. I got clear away, but an interfering bulldog spied me. Next morning I was before the Proctor, who gave me no very encouraging words and gated me for a month."

Pierce Taylor, recalling his own shortcomings as a young man, received this news calmly but old Taylor, realizing that his hopes of a comfortable old age with an adequate income were rapidly disappearing, affected to take a grave view of his grandson's fall from grace. He threatened to remove the delinquent from Cambridge and force him to become a parson willy-nilly. Since his fees were paid by Sir Thomas Carew, a fact of which young Thomas was well aware, he accepted his grandfather's bluff for what it was worth.

In May 1803, when war broke out again between England and France, the university became more or less disorganized and friendships were broken up. Frederick Robinson had entered Lincoln's Inn and was studying law ; and Temple, who had succeeded to his father's peerage, found it necessary to attend to his estates in Hampshire. Taylor decided to go home and settle once and for all the dispute between his grandfather and himself regarding his entry into the Church. Pierce Taylor evinced no great pleasure at the prospect of seeing his son and told him that he and his grandfather were staying at Haccombe, warning him to look out for squalls as his grandfather was furious at his obstinacy and was in no mood to be argued with.

Thomas Taylor spent an unhappy hour with his grandfather and with Sir Thomas Carew. Pierce, always one to avoid unpleasantness if possible, kept discreetly out of the way. Old Taylor opened his batteries first. He rated his grandson for his unbelievable impudence in setting up what he called his ill-judged ideas against Sir Thomas and himself, who had been at pains to secure him an honourable future. He taunted him with being a pauper (which, in truth, applied to both of them) dependent on other people's bounty for an expensive education which appeared to have profited him but little. He then went on to demand his reasons for disgracing the family by endeavouring to enter the army, which was now the resort of every ne'er-do-well in the kingdom. Then, with the complete selfishness and limited vision of old age, he asked who would support him if he threw away the £1,500 a year which went with the Haccombe living. Thomas listened patiently to this tirade and then had his say. He told his grandfather that he refused to perjure himself in order to gain a house to live in. He reminded old Taylor that he had lived in peace and plenty all his life ; he admitted to having received an education for which Sir Thomas had paid, and for which no thanks were due to his father or his grandfather. He concluded with some heat, and reminded his grandfather that from all reports a French invasion was liable to take place at any moment and accused him of wishing his grandson to evade his responsibilities to his country by the cowardly method of donning a parson's garb. "In truth, sir," he said, "it seems that you have strange notions of what a gentleman should do." He announced as his final decision that he intended to join the army by hook or by crook and have a go at Bonaparte. Sir Thomas, who had listened with lazy indifference to the sparks flying, suddenly came to life and said to old Taylor : "Flummoxed by Gad, Thomas, the young renegade has the better of you. I will give him £500 to go to the devil in his own way."

Taylor considered that he had emerged pretty well from the encounter; moreover he was richer by £500, which was the largest sum of money he had ever possessed. The Government, in view of Bonaparte's preparations at Boulogne for the invasion of England, had issued an urgent summons for men to join the various yeomanry and volunteer regiments; and Sir Thomas, who was a friend of Lord Clifford, who commanded the Teign-bridge Hundred squadron of the South Devon Yeomanry Cavalry, used his influence to obtain Taylor a commission of cornet in his squadron. The training does not appear to have been of an arduous nature, and opened with a ball at the Teign-bridge Club which was attended by most of the neighbouring rank and fashion. Taylor, well pleased with himself in the Teignbridge Hundred uniform of scarlet with black facings and white breeches, made quite a personable figure at the ball, and attracted considerable attention from the young ladies present. The débutante of the evening, in Taylor's eyes, was Miss Elizabeth Palk, who was there with her father, Walter Palk of Marley, a disagreeable old man in the last stage of decrepitude, worn out by the combined effects of good living and the climate of India. Mrs. Palk had given up the unequal contest and had died out there. Miss Elizabeth, however, who was five years older than Taylor, was full of vivacity and charm and, having an eye to a good-looking young man, she allowed him to be her partner in an endless succession of gavottes and mazurkas. So well did they get on that at the end of the evening she extended an invitation to Taylor to stay at Marley. This news, when com-municated to Walter Palk, did not meet with his approval as he had other views for his daughter. He had no use for penniless young cornets of yeomanry hanging round, and he re-minded his daughter that they had received an invitation to stay at Haccombe with Sir Thomas Carew. This clinched the matter, and the young people parted with a promise to meet again.

Taylor, however, was forced to dismiss fair ladies from his mind, for soon after the ball ugly rumours of riots appeared in the Exeter *Flying Post*, and the Teignbridge Hundred squadron was called out to assist the civil power. The people of Exeter had taken umbrage at the depredations of the press-gang, who had been set upon by an organized body of townsmen who had rescued their captives and had raided the bakers' shops. They then proceeded towards the prison with the intention of liberating the prisoners. A troop, commanded by Taylor, was sent to intercept the mob, which they were successful in doing by using the flats of their sabres. The tumult increased, however, and Taylor drew off his troop and went to the Town Hall to report to Lord Clifford for orders. The Mayor and Magistrates were assembled there and the Riot Act was read. Meanwhile, the Yeomanry Cavalry had been reinforced by a squadron of the 6th Dragoon Guards and the combined force, having been ordered to disperse the mob, charged down the High Street. The malcontents were unwilling to face the charge of the regulars, who did not use only the flats of their sabres, and the affair was over. Taylor overheard one member of the crowd saying, " We would have faced up to the Yeomanry, who were afraid to use the edge on us, but they dragoons was proper devils."

The Yeomanry training did not extend beyond an occasional field-day on Haldon and an inspection in Ugbrooke Park by General Simcoe, a hard-bitten old veteran of the American War. It was from General Simcoe that Taylor learnt that there was a vacant cornetcy for disposal in the 6th Dragoon Guards, who were quartered in Exeter. Taylor called on the Colonel, and with part of the £500 given him by Sir Thomas Carew he purchased his commission in March 1804. The 6th Dragoon Guards were under orders to proceed to the Mediterranean almost immediately, but owing to rumours that Bonaparte was proposing to start on his much-heralded invasion, General Simcoe was unwilling to sanction Taylor's release from the Yeomanry for the present, and the 6th Dragoon Guards sailed without him.

By September 1804 the invasion still showed no signs of materializing and General Simcoe recommended to Lord Fortescue, the Lord-Lieutenant, that in view of Taylor's appointment to the 6th Dragoon Guards his resignation from the Yeomanry should be accepted. He was granted two months' leave to buy his uniform and to make his final arrangements before joining his regiment. Meanwhile, Walter Palk had died at Marley, leaving his daughter Elizabeth sole heiress to his enormous fortune. Many disinterested ladies with marriageable sons were anxious to help Miss Palk in her unprotected loneliness and old Thomas Taylor, who had known Walter Palk and who usually had an eye to the main chance, persuaded his son's wife Charlotte to invite her to Ogwell. Charlotte Taylor, being only human, saw no reason why her son should not have his chance before he went abroad, and she wrote to him telling him of the arrangement. Young Thomas, who had not met Elizabeth Palk since the Teignbridge Club ball, was wildly excited and lost no time in writing to his mother informing her of the date and time of his arrival by the accommodation coach at Newton Bushel.

He arrived on 6th November, expecting to be met by his father in the tandem. He was surprised, therefore, when a footman, an unknown quantity in the Taylor household, approached him and asked if he was for Ogwell. On replying in the affirmative, the man took his baggage and led him across to a closed barouche, both windows of which were shut. The footman let down the window, opened the door for him to enter, and then closed both the door and the window again. Taylor was delighted to find that the only occupant of the carriage was Miss Palk, who explained that she was on the way to Ogwell and had heard from Mrs. Taylor that her son was arriving by the coach. She was apparently a chilly person, and preferred to be hermetically sealed. Taylor was delighted at the chance of sharing the intimacy of a closed carriage with the lady of his choice, and this was enhanced by her perfume which pervaded the atmosphere. During the hour's drive to Ogwell Miss Palk told him of the unreasonable and tiresome behaviour of her father before he died ; how he had forbidden any young men to come to the house, but had encouraged Henry Carew in what she described as his "clumsy efforts" to make himself agreeable to her, and how she had put him in his place. Encouraged by the rebuff to Henry Carew, Taylor, with the audacity of youth, asked Miss Palk if she could ever care for him. In the next moment his arms were round her and she submitted unresistingly to his embrace. She disengaged herself as the carriage drew up and the footman came to open the door. Taylor went into the house well pleased with himself, but was somewhat damped when Miss Palk told him that evening that they had had a very amusing time in the carriage and warned him not to take it too seriously.

Taylor, however, thoroughly enjoyed basking in the young lady's presence during the remainder of his leave, though his pleasure was marred by the repeated appearances of Henry Carew under one pretext or another. He realized soon enough that Elizabeth Palk was Henry's quarry, and came to the conclusion that the lady had merely found him "very amusing" but was after higher game. She had obviously inherited the mercantile instincts of her father. On Taylor's last night before going abroad there was a farewell dinner at Ogwell House at which all the family were present, including the ubiquitous Sir Thomas, who was not sorry to see Taylor depart as he had suspicions that the young man was interfering with his plans. "I propose," he said, with a quizzical glance at old Taylor, who was looking glum, "a toast to the gallant young man who with £500 is going to save our bacon."

Sir Thomas, who had a cousin, Captain Thomas Carew of the *Pheasant*, a sloop of eighteen guns which was sailing from Plymouth Dock, had procured a passage for Taylor as far as Gibraltar, and she was due to leave on 22nd January. Miss

Palk, who was returning to Marley the next day, had offered to take Taylor to the Quicksilver coach at Newton Bushel. Foreseeing another "amusing time" in the carriage without the presence of Henry Carew, Taylor gratefully accepted the invitation. Elizabeth Palk, having issued her warning, was most amenable and responded to Taylor's advances wholeheartedly.

Taylor was relieved that he had got his own way in the matter of not becoming a parson, and that he had struck out a line for himself and was now a full-fledged cornet of dragoons. The recollection of Elizabeth Palk waving good-bye to him from the window of her carriage carried with it nostalgic yearnings, although by degrees he realized that her response to his endearments was inspired by love of excitement rather than by any deeper feelings. This was brought home to him when a year later he learned that she had married Sir Henry Carew, who had become the seventh Baronet on the death of his father. Two years later Lady Carew fulfilled her destiny by presenting her husband with a son and heir. This son, in the course of time, was to be inextricably connected with the persons and events with which this narrative is concerned.

Part One

THE SOLDIER-GROOM

Chapter One

THE A.D.C.

TAYLOR was held up for some time in Gibraltar owing to the escape of the French Admiral Villeneuve from Toulon and the consequent scarcity of ships to convey him to Malta. It was not until the 27th July 1805 that he disembarked from the filthy old fly-boat which had landed him at Valletta. The crew were verminous, the ship's biscuits full of weevils and the water on board was impregnated with animal matter. To add to the discomfort a violent sirocco had sprung up which agitated the Mediterranean and the equilibrium of Taylor's stomach, which was unaccustomed to the tack provided by the *Swallow's* cook. When this misguided individual out of the kindness of his heart came to Taylor's cabin with a plate of cold rancid pork and fly-blown biscuits, the invalid was not disinclined to believe the current tale that murder was excusable in a sirocco. On landing he hailed a carozzi and drove to Floriana Barracks, the headquarters of Sir James Craig's expeditionary force; the courtyard was full of sweating, scurrying soldiers who were man-handling stores and baggage off wagons, Sir James Craig and his headquarters staff having only arrived two days previously. The chattering of the Maltese hangers-on was varied by oaths of the British variety, the usual accompaniment to the work of the soldier.

Taylor's diary describes his entry on the scene.

"As I arrived," he wrote, "an officer in undress uniform strolled out of the fort and made himself unpleasant to an

3

artilleryman who seemed to do little but add to the discord. He warned him to have done with this babble of talk and that the Colonel expected the stores to be unloaded by five o'clock ; if not, there would be the devil to pay. When he saw my gharri, he welcomed me effusively and seemed surprised at the arrival of a heavy dragoon. He introduced himself as Lieutenant Tomlinson of the 58th Foot, and informed me that he was on the staff of Sir James Creaker, as he called him. He then affected to be shocked by my dilapidated appearance, which was not surprising considering the agonies I had suffered aboard the *Swallow*, and he took me into the mess-room for a glass of wine."

In spite of the bustle and hurry in the courtyard, the officers seemed to be taking things very easily. One aged gentleman whom Taylor at first took to be the General, but afterwards discovered was the surgeon, greeted him with a loud belch, saying, " Your pardon, sir, but the wine of this country has an adverse effect on the intestinal ducts ; take my advice and beware of it." Taylor put him down as a tippling gas-bag, and registered a vow to keep out of his clutches. Taylor describes his intro-duction by Tomlinson to Colonel Bunbury, the Adjutant-General, whom he describes as " A vastly civil person." He writes :

" A sudden emptying of the mess-room warned me that some-thing was afoot, and then I saw a tall, impressive looking man who could not have been more than thirty enter. He seemed annoyed with my friend Tomlinson, and told him he had been awaiting his report that the stores were unloaded. Tomlinson, looking on me, I suppose, to get him out of a mess, introduced me as having just arrived to take up duty. Colonel Bunbury then told me he had my appointment in a despatch from Lord Castlereagh, the Secretary-at-War, with a high recommendation. For the life of me I could not understand this tribute to my ability, as I had never set eyes on Lord Castlereagh, until I remembered that he had been a friend of Palmerston's father. It seemed to be an odd way of doing business, but I thought it very civil of Henry all the same."

Taylor met his Commander-in-Chief, commonly known as
" Old Creaker," in the mess next morning. The General was
presumably not at his best at breakfast, for he was abusing the
Maltese servant who had brought him a dish which obviously
was not to his liking. Taylor, hoping to improve matters,
wished the General a cheery good-morning. The rough and
ready Sir James, perhaps scenting a world of which he knew
little, determined to put the callow cornet in his place. " The
mornin's all right, young man," he said, " depends on the
cornets you meet." Taylor, not to be outdone in politeness,
replied, " I trust, sir, that this one at least will do you credit."
Sir James became a little more human, and having learnt Taylor's
name told him that he had heard about him from Colonel
Bunbury, who had said that the Secretary-at-War had spoken
well of him. Sir James apparently did not take a high view of
Lord Castlereagh's recommendations, for he told Taylor that
he had the most idle set of young ruffians on his staff who had
all been sent with good reports—chiefly, as he said, from their
colonels, who no doubt wished to be rid of them. Taylor did
not regard this as a hopeful beginning, but he thought the least
said soonest mended.

Taylor's first interview with Sir James Craig was not without
result. Two months later he was sent for by the Adjutant-
General, Colonel Bunbury, and much to his surprise was told
that the General had been favourably impressed by him and
that he would be appointed A.D.C. to the Commander-in-Chief.
Taylor, whilst acting in that capacity, made himself indispensable
to Sir James Craig and succeeded in lightening that old man's
burden by evolving some sense out of the farrago of nonsense
which Lord Camden, when Secretary-at-War, had sent him in
the form of orders. Taylor and Sir James Craig were on the
best of terms when finally the latter, broken down in health by
fever and by remedial doses of port wine, handed over the command to Sir John Stuart.

Taylor had no opinion of Sir John Stuart, to whom he had

5

been passed over as A.D.C. "The whole situation savoured of comic opera," he writes, "with Sir John Stuart as the chief buffoon." Sir John was apparently incapable of making any preconceived plan and was content to lounge in his tent dreaming of military glory. When in 1806 the British troops were withdrawn to Messina, the one encouraging factor was the brilliant little expedition to the Calabrian coast, culminating in the action of Maida on 4th July. But Taylor has some acrid remarks to make about the action. "Sir John Stuart, of course, received the credit for the defeat of the French General Reynier, but there is not the slightest doubt, and I was a close onlooker, that Colonel Bunbury and General Kempt, commanding the Light Infantry, were mainly responsible for the victory." As Colonel Bunbury wrote at the time :

"But where was Sir John Stuart and what great part did he play in this action ? He formed no plans, and scarcely did he give himself the trouble to give an order. He was cantering about indulging himself with little pleasantries and was highly gleeful when a Sicilian Marquis, whom he had brought as an extra A.D.C., took himself hurriedly to shelter from fire behind a haystack. After the charge of General Kempt's Light Infantry and the utter rout of the French left wing, he was an altered man and full of the visions of coming greatness. He dawdled about breaking into passionate exclamations : ' Begad, I never saw anything so glorious as this, it is the finest thing I ever witnessed,' as though it had been all his work."

Taylor finally gave his general up as a bad job ; he writes :

" As his A.D.C. I did my utmost to persuade Sir John to observe the most elementary rules of war, of which I had lately learnt a good deal, but he seemed to be incapable of making up his mind about anything. We were getting nowhere and I was very surprised but very thankful when I heard from my old General, Sir James Craig, that I had been promoted Captain in the 24th Light Dragoons and seconded to be Military Secretary to Lord Minto, the Governor-General of India."

Chapter Two

FACING THE MUSIC

INDIA was in a state of great unrest when Taylor joined
Lord Minto as his Military Secretary in 1807. Two strong
Governors-General, Lord Cornwallis and Marquis Wellesley, had, in the face of great difficulties and often in the teeth of
opposition from the Board of the East India Company, cleansed
the British administration of much corruption and inefficiency,
established procedure and defined jurisdiction. But after the
recall of Wellesley, policy in India was uncertain and fumbling
and followed the disastrous course of leaving the Native States
to weaken each other by perpetual fighting. As a result, central
India was in a state of chaos. There was a mutiny of Sepoys
at Vellore, in the State of Madras, in which they killed a number
of British soldiers and officers. Among British officers, also,
there was a great dissatisfaction with their conditions, which
almost threatened a mutiny on their part.

The Sepoy mutiny was quelled and the fear of the Sepoys that
they would be forced to become Christians was allayed ; the
grievances of the British officers were removed ; the turbulent
Rajah of Bhurtpore was defeated by Lord Lake and the Sikhs
were impressed by a display of British military strength.

In these circumstances, the post of Military Secretary was no
sinecure, as may be well imagined. But towards the end of
1809 the situation had improved and Lord Minto was contem-
plating operations further afield, no less than an attack on the
French possession of Mauritius.

7

Before this adventure took shape, however, the Military Secretary had had time to fall in love. Lord Minto and his staff happened to pass through Madras where the Governor, William Petrie, put them up for a night or two. Petrie's three nieces had just arrived from England. The young ladies were no strangers to India, since their father, John Petrie, had begun life in the army there and had made a considerable fortune. On his return home, he purchased Gatton in Surrey and returned himself to Parliament. He also owned land in Tobago, on the strength of which he sat as a deputy in the French Assembly and was thus a member of the English and French Parliaments at one and the same time. But these days of prosperity did not last long. John Petrie, through heavy losses, became a poor man and in 1803 retired with his family to France, where he fell into Bonaparte's hands. His daughters, who had managed to reach England, accepted an invitation from their uncle and sailed forthwith for India. Lord Minto, who had been interested in the story of the Misses Petrie by a friend, invited them to stay at Government House in Calcutta, and here Taylor very soon became engaged to Ann, the second of the three sisters.

The wedding was fixed for 14th January 1810, and on that day Government House was in a festive mood. Lord Minto gave the bride away and it was altogether a most splendid affair. Taylor makes a passing allusion to the event in his journal :

" My wedding day and a vastly cheerful one in spite of Nabobs within and Bonaparte without. Lord Minto as usual was all kindness and gave us his blessing for a fortnight's felicity, which is all he can spare me for reasons known only to himself and me. George Elliot (Minto's son) supported me nobly and did all that was expected of him, and to my mind rather more when he insisted on kissing Ann who, I am bound to say, submitted with a tolerably good grace."

Taylor's shortened honeymoon was, as expected, followed by a month of intensive planning for the operation that was to secure a rich plum for Britain—Mauritius. Lord Minto decided on the island of Bourbon as his first objective. He had, as his Military Secretary well knew, received definite instructions from the home Government through the medium of the Secretary-at-War, Lord Castlereagh, that under no circumstances should any expedition be undertaken to Java or any place eastward of India. But Lord Minto, who was of a perverse disposition, told Taylor in the privacy of his office that he had no intention of obeying the dictates of Lord Castlereagh or of anyone else, and that as soon as the Company's finances permitted he would go ahead. " I will risk being called out by Castlereagh," he said, " if he ever returns to office, and maybe will fare better than George Canning when they crossed swords last year."

The supreme command of three thousand men who were to capture Bourbon was vested in Admiral Bertie, but the spade-work was performed by Taylor. The commander of Bourbon surrendered on 8th July 1810, after a nominal resistance. Taylor was quite prepared to co-operate with the navy on land, but as a soldier, he was inclined to be sceptical of amphibious operations unless the landing force was under military control. When, after the easy capture of Bourbon, Admiral Bertie announced his intention of pushing on to Mauritius, Taylor felt bound to advise Lord Minto of the risks involved unless further reinforcements were available. An express letter was sent to Admiral Bertie to this effect, but it was too late ; the Admiral's desire to secure what he thought would be easy prize money having outweighed his discretion. Confident of the ability of the British navy to sweep all before it and unmindful of the devastating effect of red-hot shot propelled by the coast batteries on the Ile de la Passe, he allowed Captain Pym, the senior naval officer, commanding the *Sirius*, to sail into Grand Port Harbour on 10th August. The Commander-in-Chief had a rude awakening and was forced to make an undignified retreat, leaving four of his frigates sunk in the harbour. Taylor, whilst refraining from saying " I told you so " in public, made a confidant of his journal.

" Lord M. is furious and fully upholds my contention. I solaced myself by conveying his Lordship's disapproval in no uncertain terms to that puffed up old sea-dog who will now drink small beer. I know something of General Decean who commands the French force in the Mauritius ; he is capable of outwitting three Admiral B's. Lord M. is determined to have the Mauritius and we have asked for the force to be increased to 10,000 men with, I am thankful to say, a soldier in command, Sir John Abercrombie."

General Decean, recognizing that the odds were now against him, surrendered the island on 2nd December 1810.

The news of the surrender reached Calcutta towards the end of January 1811, and the Military Secretary's office immediately became a hive of activity. It was the signal to implement the plans already drawn up for the invasion of Java, for which Lord Minto had received from the home Government a grudging sanction hedged round with impossible provisos. The views of the directors of the East India Company, which according to Taylor, " did not extend beyond their cheroots," only allowed for the liquidation of the Franco-Dutch authority, after which we were to evacuate the island and hand it " over lock, stock and barrel to the natives."

" The Honourable Lunatics must have been seized with a palsy to think that I would be party to such absurdity," Lord Minto said to Taylor, who replied, " Well, sir, I hardly thought you would stomach their nonsense, but as you know, Mr. Raffles and myself have collected some valuable information in the last four months which should be of help in the expedition."

The Military Secretary's war diary records the progress of events to date :

" *January 27th.* This day a long despatch arrived from Mr. Raffles at Malacca of whom Lord M. thinks very highly, and rightly so, though he is a trifle self-opinionated as I own I am myself. Raffles reports that Java is likely to prove a stiffish fence. Bonaparte has recalled Marshal Daendels and superseded him by General Janssens, who surrendered the Cape to us. Bonaparte apparently warned Janssens that since he was now a French General, a second surrender would not be tolerated. We shall see. According to all accounts, Janssens has a force of about 20,000 men and has strongly fortified Weltevreeden and Fort Cornelis. If we can raise half that force, we shall be lucky. Captain Greigh of the *Minto* has confounded the Navy's pessimism regarding the Caramata passage and reports it is perfectly feasible and Borneo may be made through the Strait of Singapore. Dr. Leyden, a friend of Raffles, and a protegé of Lord M., has been a very useful channel of communication owing to his knowledge of Malay. Leyden is a curious mixture of apothecary, poet and scholar. He bled me for a fever when assistant surgeon of Madras, though goodness knows, I was bloodless enough already ; having done so, he solaced me with porter and poetry. He is to accompany us on the expedition as interpreter and general adviser, and will work well with Raffles whom we meet at Malacca. No one save myself has an inkling that Lord M. is coming in person."

Lord Minto had his own reasons for waiting until the last moment before making known his intention of personally directing the Java expedition. He was well aware, as was his Military Secretary, that his activities as Governor-General were not always regarded with favour in Government circles. The pundits considered that it was his duty to " stay put " and obey orders rather than issue them. Lord Minto held different views, and his Military Secretary, being young and enthusiastic, naturally endorsed them. Taylor, moreover, had a secret ally in his old friend Lord Palmerston, now Secretary-at-War, whose views on expansion were even then beginning to take shape. The two had kept up a private correspondence and in a letter to Taylor, Palmerston writes : " You may rely on me to support you in any way possible, your Patron's views correspond very closely with mine own, though it is not always politic to air them."

Lord Minto gave the busybodies little chance of interfering with his plans. He launched his bombshell at a Council meeting in Calcutta on 8th March, and almost immediately afterwards embarked with his staff on board the Company's ship *Mornington*. On the 11th the vessel quietly shipped her moorings and sailed for Madras. Taylor, describing the departure, says :

" His Lordship gave the bigwigs at the seat of Government a terrible shock. They threw up their hands in horror at the Governor-General demeaning himself over a paltry place like Java ; would not believe that he really intended to go there ; and comforted themselves that he was merely going to quell an insurrection in Madras. More fools they ! When I told Lord M. he said, ' Let them think what they please, it makes no odds to me.' "

The *Mornington*, according to Taylor, was no credit to her owners ; nor apparently was the Captain, " who preferred East India sherry in his interior to wind in his sails." The sherry seems to have beaten the wind, for the voyage to Madras took well over a month. Taylor says of it :

" The voyage was tedious in the extreme. Our small cabin party, consisting of Lord M., Dr. Leyden, and myself, might be termed select were it not for the Captain who had to be tolerated. Leyden and Lord M. got on pretty well. Leyden is a sort of clansman of the Elliot family, coming as he does from Teviotdale, and having helped Walter Scott to write it, keeps Lord M. happy by constant recitals of the *Minstrelsy of the Scottish Border*. I, being a mere Sassenach, have to grin and bear it (the *Minstrelsy*, not the sherry !) "

On arrival at Madras, Lord Minto came to the conclusion that a month of the Company's hospitality aboard the *Mornington* was more than sufficient, and he and his party exchanged into the *Modeste*, a fast-sailing frigate commanded by his son, Captain George Elliot. Taylor writes :

" The change to a King's ship from a lumbering old tub was very pleasant. A further addition to our party is Mr. Seton, who is to be Governor at Penang, our next port of call. Less welcome, but unavoidable, was a party of the 59th Regiment, highly perfumed with arrack after a farewell celebration on shore. George is a highly efficient Captain and being under parental supervision is on his best behaviour."

The *Modeste* reached Penang on 18th April after, as Taylor says,

" a harmonious voyage of a week or so disturbed only by the incessant disputations between Leyden and Seton on oriental languages of which no one except themselves knows anything and cares less. Even Lord M. became very bored, and when we dropped Seton at Penang, said, ' Thank God for a calm before the storm.' "

The calm continued until the *Modeste* reached Malacca on 18th May, the time being passed pleasantly playing deck games and charades, at both of which Lord Minto proved himself an adept.

Taylor, writing on the last day of the voyage, records :

" *18th May, 7 a.m.* Now running into Malacca Roads. The *Amboyna* corvette met us with despatches for Lord Minto, who was much put out by one from the Board of Control putting all responsibility for the expedition on him and saying that as Governor-General he should have remained at the seat of Government. Maybe the Marquis Wellesley has a finger in the pie, sour grapes perhaps. Directly we came to anchor, Sir Samuel Auchmuty and Mr. Raffles came on board and the first Council of War was held. Lord M. is highly impressed with Sir S. Auchmuty as a C.-in-C. ; unlike the Duke of York who Palmerston tells me is likely to be reinstated in his high office, thanks to his brother. Birds of a feather ! "

Mr. Raffles reported that according to the latest intelligence Marshal Daendels had left orders that, if necessary, operations in Java should be carried into the mountains and jungle. Sir Samuel Auchmuty therefore wisely ordered that whilst in Malacca the troops should be exercised in guerilla tactics. The Sepoys proved themselves efficient in this type of warfare, having practised it with some success on us at Vellore and Seringapatam, but the European troops had a lot to learn. The officers were not helpful, hide-bound as they were by textbooks and parade-ground movements.

Taylor writes :

" The sham fights were very comical, the elderly Colonels vieing with each other in stupidity. Colonel M'Cleod of the 59th Regiment was particularly obstinate and foolish, and Colonel Gillespie, who luckily has arrived and is directing operations, determined to teach him a lesson. The 59th was ordered to attack a redoubt and was advancing in column in the jungle without flankers or rearguard. Colonel Gillespie, unknown to M'Cleod, had stationed a troop of the Madras Horse in the jungle behind and said to M'Cleod : ' Look to your rear, Colonel.' M'Cleod angrily replied : ' Damme, sir, a British soldier never looks to his rear,' whereupon Colonel Gillespie ordered the Madras Horse to charge from behind, which they did, pulling up short of the 59th. The men of the column were tumbling over themselves in hopeless confusion, much to the amusement of the onlookers and the fury of Colonel M'Cleod."

After a month or so of this sham warfare, Sir Samuel Auchmuty decided that the troops under Colonel Gillespie's tutelage were sufficiently well versed in the elements of guerilla tactics to undertake the great adventure. On 11th June, 11,000 men, the most formidable Anglo-Indian expedition ever despatched from India, began to leave Malacca for Java. Troops, guns and stores were embarked without a hitch under the capable direction of Sir Samuel Auchmuty. The army was extremely fortunate in its commander ; the same could not be said of the navy, whose senior officer was Commodore Broughton, an elderly sailor whose energy had long since been exhausted by fever and port wine. The Commodore, whose timidity as a navigator was

proverbial, mistrusted Captain Greigh's report and ordered
Captain Elliot to go ahead in the *Modeste* and survey the passage
to the rendezvous. The Military Secretary, who resented the
lack of respect shown to his chief, was highly indignant and gave
vent to his feelings with easy familiarity to Lord Minto. "The
impudence of this old dummy decked out in a blue coat," he
said, "is only equalled by his pusillanimity ; he prefers that you
should go to the bottom rather than himself. What is the
Navy coming to ? "

Lord Minto took the matter lightly. "I would much prefer
this arràngement," he said. "George is by far the most competent navigator in the fleet, and the *Modeste*, being the fastest
sailer, can overtake any vessel."

Thanks to the masterly inactivity displayed by Commodore
Broughton, who was "left to dree his own weird in the rear,"
the transports conveying the troops, consisting of eighty-one
sail, arrived intact off the coast of Java on 3rd August. The
Modeste, with Lord Minto, Mr. Raffles and Taylor on board,
closely followed by the *Minto*, commanded by Captain Greigh,
with Leyden as a passenger, arrived at Chillinching, the rendezvous, a point on the coast ten miles east of Batavia, well ahead
of the fleet. Commodore Broughton, still playing for safety,
came in a good last in the *Phoenix* and then fades out of the
picture. Taylor sarcastically remarked to George Elliot, "We
shall no longer be in charge of a dummy ; Admiral Stopford in
the *Scipio* is come from the Cape to supersede the Commodore ;
what a pity ! "

It was uncertain what opposition would be encountered at
Chillinching, and Sir Samuel Auchmuty, knowing the limita-
tions of some of his troops, was taking no chances. "Zero
hour" was fixed for 6 p.m. on 4th August, and Colonel
Gillespie, with his brigade of seasoned troops, was ordered to
secure a bridge-head. This was accomplished without difficulty,
the operation, according to Taylor, resolving itself into opera-
bouffe.

" It was extremely comical," he writes, " to see our heroes, soldiers with muskets and sailors with cutlasses, leaping into the water preparing for a fight to the death. Leyden, who loves acting a part, was dressed as a pirate in a red-tasselled cap, a cutlass round his waist and a pistol in his belt ; he was first ashore and bore the brunt of the attack which came from a flock of barn-door fowls headed by an aggressive rooster. A Master-at-Arms sliced off the rooster's head in fine style, and there was a mighty destruction of fowls. Colonel Gillespie came up in a fine pet and ordered Captain Hayes of the Navy to get to the rear with his rabble and cook fowls whilst the army tried to kill Dutchmen ; exit the Navy ! "

Lord Minto and Sir Samuel Auchmuty went ashore soon after the landing. Sir Samuel made his temporary headquarters in a comfortable Dutch house and " hoped that the Governor-General would do him the honour of joining him." His Excellency much appreciated the invitation, but preferred to make do with his Military Secretary since, as he said, they were both volunteers merely serving under Sir Samuel. Taylor, who liked comfort even if he was a volunteer, for once criticizes his chief's action. Writing to his wife, he says : " Lord M. insisted on going with Gillespie to the outposts ; he has a right to cut capers if he likes, but it strikes me it would have been more dignified in his position to accept Sir Samuel's invitation. As it was, we were very uncomfortable for no reason." Taylor was nothing if not a realist.

General Janssens, accustomed to the bracing climate of South Africa, was under no delusions about Batavia as a health resort. He had therefore withdrawn his forces to previously prepared and strongly fortified positions on a line of hills seven miles south of the town. Colonel Gillespie, who looked for trouble and usually found it, was somewhat surprised when he was able to occupy the place without a shot being fired. Janssens was a student of human nature and he had not only declared Batavia an open town, but, with a subtle generosity, had left it well

stocked with wine and provisions. The invaders swallowed the
bait with results that fulfilled the Dutch General's anticipations.
Taylor certainly found his comforts, but at a certain cost to himself and to others.

" We set to with a will," he writes, " on the good things
provided after days of hard tack. The men gorged themselves
with food and wine and I'm afraid there was a good deal of
drunkenness. The officers were more restrained, but to celebrate the occasion drank toasts to the King, Lord Minto, Sir
Samuel Auchmuty and even General Janssens, who must have
laughed in his sleeve ! Most of us felt very seedy next morning
and a large number of men were unfit for duty. Gillespie was
the only one who felt really well, and in consequence was very
much put out with everyone else."

General Janssens, in his role of unlicensed victualler, under-
rated the recuperative powers of his customers, and on 9th August,
within two days of the celebrations, a composite force of 6,000
men under the command of Colonel Gillespie moved out of
Batavia to attack the enemy's advanced position at Weltevreeden.
The Franco-Dutch advance troops were approximately of
equal strength, and were strongly entrenched behind elaborate
earthworks. Taylor, who had received permission from Lord
Minto and Sir Samuel Auchmuty to accompany Gillespie, was
enthusiastic about the dash and gallantry of our troops in their
first engagement. Writing to his wife after the action, he says :

" The men behaved magnificently ; they left their ' Dutch
courage ' in Batavia and displayed something far better, British
pluck. The 89th Regiment was in the van and drove the enemy
helter-skelter out of their entrenchments with the bayonet, and
the 22nd Dragoons followed hard on their heels. They were
making, I suppose, for their main position at Fort Cornelis,
which will be a tougher nut to crack ; meanwhile we have
established ourselves on high and healthy ground. I do not
envy Lord M., Sir Samuel Auchmuty, Raffles and Co., in the

poisonous air of Batavia. Lord M. has issued a beautiful proclamation to the Dutch inhabitants promising peace and protection to those who ' pass cordially ' under the British Dominion. It is signed by Lord M. and Mr. Raffles who, I believe, is to be Lieut.-Governor."

It is, of course, inevitable that in military operations major campaigns should overshadow subsidiary ones ; and so, in 1811, the lines of Torres Vedras in Portugal attracted considerably more attention than the lines of Cornelis in Java. Nevertheless the battle of Cornelis was a striking example of a victory won in quick time over an enemy enjoying superior numbers and holding a strongly entrenched position. General Janssens's force at this time consisted of 13,000 men including a battalion of French Voltigeurs and 280 guns of heavy calibre. Sir Samuel Auchmuty in his official report says :

" The enemy, greatly superior in numbers, was strongly entrenched between the great river of Jacatra and the Sloken, neither of which was fordable. The fort of Cornelis was in the centre and the whole of the works were defended by a numerous and well-organized artillery. Our numbers were insufficient to admit of regular approaches. To carry the works by assault was the alternative, and on that I decided."

The command of the assaulting column was entrusted (as usual, when there was a stiff proposition to be tackled) to Colonel Gillespie, and Taylor, with Lord Minto's permission, accompanied him as staff officer. For bulldog courage Gillespie had no equal, but as a tactician his capability is open to question ; and the art of reconnaissance does not appear to have come within his purview. Taylor, as his staff officer, suggested that a preliminary reconnaissance of the position and its approaches would be advisable, but Gillespie would have none of it. Taylor writes :

" It was a case of kill or cure, and so far as we were concerned, it was nearer kill than cure. On the evening of 25th August it was decided in the most secret manner to storm next morning. Everything was so secret, in fact, that we knew little of where we were going or the nature of the works we had to storm. We had to rely on a German deserter to guide us, and I suspect he knew about as much as we did. At 12 midnight the column was formed, the Bengal Pioneers with scaling ladders and Colonel Gillespie's brigade leading. Colonel Gibbs, with the 59th, 14th and 5th Bengal Volunteers, followed. Major Yule, with the 22nd Dragoons and two Horse Artillery guns, was to make a diversion on the left, and Colonel M'Cleod, with the 69th Regiment, was intended to make a flank attack on the right, whilst Colonel Gillespie attacked the centre."

The dispositions on the face of it were sound enough, but the operation did not quite work out according to plan. Taylor, continuing his narrative, writes :

" For four hours we went in single file through dense jungle without much sense of direction, until day began to break, when we found ourselves four hundred yards from the enemy's main works. We then received the agreeable intelligence that part of our Brigade and the whole of Colonel Gibbs's had lost their way, leaving Gillespie with five hundred men. Suddenly firing broke out on the right ; Colonel M'Cleod was making a flank attack on us instead of on the enemy ! M'Cleod, in spite of his lesson at Malacca, was at his old games again and was neglecting his rear, for Colonel Gibbs was attacking him behind ! I bent my sword over the backs of some Sepoys who were firing with enthusiasm on both of them. By the mercy of Providence I retrieved the lost sheep and Gillespie gave the order to charge, and one redoubt was carried after the other. Colonel M'Cleod, sometimes lacking in sense but never in courage, carried the last with the 69th in fine style and completed the victory when the Dragoons and Madras Horse took up the pursuit. Gillespie and I were entering the fort and were nearly blown to kingdom-come by two French officers who had fired the magazine. The enemy lost over 4,000 killed and wounded, and we took at least 3,000 prisoners."

19

Taylor, in a chatty postscript to his wife, says :

" General Janssens has fled to Buitzenborg, leaving his carriage and horses behind with a much bedizened lady of uncertain complexion in possession. We presented the carriage (but not the lady) to Lord Minto, who was highly delighted with the whole affair."

With the capture of Fort Cornelis, opposition in the island ceased, although as Taylor says :

" General Janssens made a nuisance of himself for a time, aided and abetted by the lady he had left behind with his carriage, who had followed her lord and master to Samarang. We found out that she was a Java chieftainess and had collected about 1,500 of her ragamuffins, armed with stolen pikes and muskets, to help Janssens against the ruthless invaders."

Sir Samuel Auchmuty was standing no nonsense of this sort and personally directed " mopping up " operations in Samarang, and on 24th September Taylor, who was at Buitzenborg, writes :

" 7 a.m. Gillespie has just waked me to say that he has an express from Sir Samuel to inform him that he has arrived at Batavia with Janssens, who has made his second surrender in spite of Buonaparte's warning. *Vae victis !* "

By the middle of October Lord Minto decided that he could safely leave the administration of Java to Mr. Raffles, whom he had duly appointed Lieut.-Governor, and made his preparations for his return to India. On 17th October Mr. Raffles gave a dinner party at his official residence in Batavia at which Lord Minto and Sir Samuel Auchmuty were the guests of honour. To avoid ill-feeling General Janssens and two other Dutch generals were invited. Taylor describes the ordeal without enthusiasm.

" An ineffably dull affair, not made more cheerful by the lugubrious expression of our host, who was feeling the death of his friend Leyden. He died of fever and was not executed as a pirate ! Lord M., who was fond of him, was also affected and not as cheerful as usual. Janssens has the manners of a gentleman and speaks tolerable English, though he scarcely opens his mouth except to eat the food which he had generously provided. The silence was oppressive, broken only by noisy ejaculations from de Koch, one of the Dutchmen, whose zeal for food outran his discretion. The room was still covered with decorations in honour of Buonaparte's birthday ; it was quite agreeable to spoil all this by drinking the King's health, which Janssens did with a good grace, seeing it was no longer a case of shouting ' vive L'Empereur ! ' "

On 19th October Lord Minto and his Military Secretary left Batavia for Calcutta. On the return journey the satisfaction felt at the success of the expedition was tempered by reflections of how it would be viewed by the Court of Directors whose express order not to set up an administration had been disregarded in every particular. Taylor remarks : " Lord Minto was very easy about the matter, hoped for the best and expected the worst. As he said, we must now go back to face the music."

The music proved to be of a mournful variety, and for Lord Minto took the form of a Nunc dimittis. Taylor took the recall of his chief to heart more than did Lord Minto himself, and in a final summing up, he writes :

" And so ends what will perhaps be the happiest five years of my life, in which I have gained a perfect wife and the friendship of a great Chief. Lord Minto cares little for the loss of position. Although he was entitled to look for gratitude from the great ones of his country, he found instead the jealousy and malice of petty Nabobs. Sic transit gloria mundi."

Chapter Three

WATERLOO

ON Lord Minto's recall, Taylor's staff appointment came to an end, and he took his wife and his two sons, who had been born in Calcutta, to England. It was in 1814 that he became acquainted with the Duke of Clarence, later to become the Sailor King, William IV. Taylor had been transferred to the 10th Hussars and an extract from the regimental orders explains how this acquaintance with the future monarch had come about. The order read : " Captain Thomas William Taylor is detached on special duty with H.R.H. the Duke of Clarence who is serving in an amateur capacity with the land forces before Antwerp." The royal Admiral of the Fleet, who was no amateur on the quarter-deck, presumably felt himself to be in need of professional military assistance when dabbling in operations ashore, and had applied to the War Department " for a discreet officer of good military repute." The application had been passed to Taylor's friend Palmerston, the Secretary-at-War, who knowing that Taylor had the necessary experience as Military Secretary to Lord Minto, had summoned Taylor to his office and had offered him the appointment. Taylor, who secretly had a partiality for royalty, had jumped at the job and in this easy fashion the appointment had been made.

The first meeting between the Duke of Clarence and Taylor seems to have afforded both parties satisfaction. Taylor was in high spirits and wrote to his wife :

" I formed a very agreeable impression of His Royal Highness the amateur ' Land-lubber,' as he jokingly calls himself, and I flatter myself and hope that he formed the same of me. He looks the picture of a jolly tar, but in himself is not of a very personable appearance, the regal head, if I may say so without disrespect, reminding me of one of our Devonshire pumpkins which the gardener has pared off at the top, but maybe the pumpkin contains many seeds of wisdom, we shall see."

The liquidation of the last elements of French resistance in Belgium provided an interesting object lesson for the royal observer and of relaxation for his professional adviser, who records that His Royal Highness displayed great coolness under fire.

When in April 1814, the Duke of Clarence hoisted his flag in the *Impregnable*, he " requested the pleasure of Captain Taylor's company on a mission of some importance." The *Impregnable* was to act as escort to the yacht *Royal Sovereign* which the Prince Regent had placed at the disposal of Louis XVIII to convey this obese and ungainly representative of the Bourbon family to France. Taylor, despite his reverence for royalty, does not appear to have been impressed by the French monarch and was still less impressed by his entourage. In a letter to his wife describing the farewell gathering on board the *Royal Sovereign* he writes :

" His Majesty when not dozing was very affable and gracious, but to my mind, seems a poor sort of fish and not likely to last long ; as for his suite, you never saw such a crowd of frog-eating sycophants and mountebanks ; each for himself and devil take the hindmost seems to be their motto. H.R.H. does not stomach them very kindly and will, I fancy, be glad to see the last of them."

The comradeship thus established in the field and on the quarter-deck between Taylor and the future King of England laid the seeds of a lasting friendship which in due course developed into the intimacy of the royal bedchamber, but a good deal was to happen before then.

At the end of May, having completed his tour of duty with the Duke of Clarence, Taylor returned to the prosaic duty of regimental routine. The 10th Hussars were stationed at Hounslow, and during the uneasy peace which followed Bonaparte's abdication and his removal to Elba, the regiment pursued the amenities of garrison life and the married officers enjoyed the company of their wives and families. In July H.R.H. the Duke of York, as Commander-in-Chief, carried out an inspection of the regiment and congratulated the Colonel, Lord Robert Manners, on the turn-out of the men. He afterwards dined with the officers and was interested to hear that Taylor had been with his brother in Belgium and had afterwards had a hand in transporting " that miserable lump of Bourbon " across the Channel.

Taylor's peaceful domestic life at Hounslow was brought to an end when the news arrived that Napoleon had escaped from Elba, had landed at Cannes and was proceeding towards Paris. The 10th Hussars, being one of the few cavalry regiments available, was augmented to ten troops ; and six troops under Lord Robert Manners were ordered to proceed at once to Belgium, as the Duke of Wellington rightly assumed that this country would become the battleground. In the beginning of March, the 10th landed at Ostend and the headquarters proceeded to Charleroi. Taylor was very disgruntled at finding himself in command of a squadron which was split up into troop detachments forming part of what the Duke of Wellington was pleased to call " the worst army ever brought together," consisting as it did of a small proportion of British with Hanoverians, Dutch and Belgian troops. The force was strung out in a long line from Charleroi to Antwerp for the purpose of covering Brussels. These detachments seem to have been billeted on the inhabitants and, in spite of Taylor's boredom, it appears to have been a free and easy form of existence. He writes to his wife from Distelbergen, near Ghent, on 20th March 1815 :

" Our squadron was much scattered, some in one place, some in another ; God only knows how I shall collect them in case of attack. I was in a distiller's house and I must say, better quarters or civiller people I never wish to meet with. We dined at Ghent in the Hotel de Cerf and had good ' feed.' Louis XVIII, whom I met when with the Duke of Clarence, was there, living very quietly. A French Dragoon officer who was with him, told me three hundred Cuirassiers had deserted or rather come over to him. Plenty of uniforms of all kinds. Our troops— i.e. infantry—come up in boats from Bruges and Ostend."

When belated news of Bonaparte's rapid advance through France arrived by an express runner, Taylor had all his work cut out to collect his scattered troops. Having been Military Secretary to Lord Minto for five years, he was not impressed by the Staff arrangements in Belgium. He kept a punctilious war diary and on 22nd April writes :

" Hopeless muddle everywhere ; march in hard rain to join the rest of the regiment ; by some wise management, went to headquarters, which have now moved to Ostaire, where there was no sign of them ; then we had to come back here (Distelbergen) where we found they were still dispersed over five or six miles of country. The people themselves seem to dislike the French as much as I should wish. March to-morrow to Oudenarde ; the name is pleasing to an English ear. News we have none ; we hear nothing."

During the Hundred Days, Taylor saw a good deal of that somewhat dilapidated monarch, Louis XVIII, who, Taylor says, " according to his lights, affected an agreeable and affable manner." He was however inclined to be suspicious of the monarch's entourage, for on 5th May he notes :

" In Ghent I came across my cousin Colonel Reynell, who commands the 71st Regiment. We passed by the Church in which poor Louis was at this time attending Mass, and we saw his coach at the door ; several French officers were standing

25

about it, half of whom for anything we know may be sent as spies, and some have actually been arrested on suspicion ; too terrible that Royalty should have come to such a pass."

The process of collecting the scattered detachments of the 10th Hussars seems to have been a long drawn-out engagement ; wine, women and song being contributory causes. No route was laid down and Taylor with one troop meandered along the Scheldt, finding it "as pleasant as the Cam in one of its deep reaches where there is least stream." Fraternization with the inhabitants was rife, and discipline was at a discount. Stragglers of the 10th gradually arrived in twos and threes, in various stages of intoxication, accompanied by female admirers picked up on the way. Taylor's troop, which by now had swelled to nearly two squadrons, at length found itself at Berthem. The people here were very co-operative and the Mayor's deputy was of great help in chasing away the camp houris and finding billets for the men.

The regiment, more or less intact, was eventually concentrated near Oudenarde and to celebrate the occasion was inspected first by the brigade commander, Sir Hussey Vivian, and afterwards by Lord Uxbridge, the cavalry corps commander, both of whom, after some rather scathing remarks about the lack of discipline, expressed themselves as on the whole satisfied with the turn-out. Taylor, thinking the time opportune to take a little leave, applied to Sir Hussey Vivian, who rather scratchily remarked that it was no time to apply for leave but that he might act as his courier and carry his despatches to the Duke of Wellington.

Taylor arrived in Brussels on 7th May, but found hotel accommodation limited—and small wonder, for apparently the whole hotel was occupied by the Prince de Conde, who had fought against the revolutionary force in 1792 and had after-wards joined the British army. He was surrounded by an enormous retinue and had forty horses. However, Taylor finally found very comfortable quarters in the Hotel Duc de

Clarence, and spent a convivial evening with some brother officers. His Colonel, Lord Robert Manners, was there and during the course of conversation he learnt that Howard, the adjutant, was dining with the Duke. Lord Robert remarked that for his part he preferred real enjoyment amongst themselves to make-believe, which was all that Howard would get at a stiff dinner party with the Duke.

Though Taylor apparently agreed with the Colonel, there may have been an element of sour grapes in his acquiescence, for he made frequent and determined efforts to dine with the Duke and eventually, to his great delight, brought it off.

After a week in Brussels, he with the other officers of the 10th reluctantly left the gaieties of the capital behind them and returned to their regiment at Oudenarde, where they continued for the time being their care-free and meandering existence. Taylor had no illusions on the subject, for in a letter to his wife, he says :

" We are on the edge of a catastrophe unless these tyrants get a drubbing ; I hope we shall really move soon and be in the ball. I fancy we shall have no separate movements but that the whole allied army (if we can remain allied) will advance as one body and attempt to penetrate to Paris."

Towards the end of May there was a regular galaxy of field-days and reviews attended by the rank and fashion of Brussels ; ladies on horse-back, in habits, feathered hats and flowing veils, enhanced the beauty of the scene. Taylor, as was natural, says that the cavalry, as always, came in for especial admiration. The Duke apparently was not averse to ladies attending, rather the reverse ; but he did recommend the English families to quit Brussels when the move began, since he thought they might be liable to inroads from the garrisons of frontier towns. What kind of inroads the Duke had in mind, or whether such inroads would come from our troops or those of the enemy, he did not state. Taylor's opinion was that they might come from either.

However much the ladies might enjoy reviews, ceremonial parades were no more popular with those condemned to take part in them than they are to-day. Taylor retailed the news of the day to his wife.

" Generals on the war path again," he writes. " On 24th May the Prince of Orange reviewed Lord Edward Somerset's and General Ponsonby's Brigade of heavy cavalry. Not content with this, on the 26th Lord Uxbridge had out the Hussars and General Vandeleur the Light Dragoon Brigade, in the great meadow near Scanderbeck on the Dender, preparatory to the great review, to see how we should fit. In the evening, hearing the Duke had a ball at Brussels, and thinking it a good time to be introduced, I agreed to ride there with Shakespear. We got off from Voorde about half past eight and reached Brussels at eleven. Tried three times before we could get in—however succeeded at last—dressed and went to the ball—found them at supper—met many I knew, but no chance of an introduction to the Duke. Renewed my acquaintance with Sir Sidney and Lady Smith whom I had met before. They introduced me to Miss Rumbold—talked about their brother in India whom I knew in Lord Minto's time. The Prince of Orange was waltzing with the other Miss Rumbold who is a pretty girl, a case of sweet oranges ! The Duke not visible so that I could not put into practice the scheme of dining there to be introduced. I am very easy about it, but was determined to have a good try. Now I shall let it come of itself, having made three journeys in vain."

The great review by the Duke took place on 29th May, when forty-six squadrons of British cavalry, six troops of Horse Artillery and a mounted rocket corps marched past him, Blücher also being present.

The Duke appeared to be highly pleased with the deportment of his mounted branch. To celebrate this success, the 10th Hussars decided to enjoy a little relaxation the next day. Taylor gives an account of the jollifications as he calls them :

" On the 30th we had the second races in a meadow near Grammont. It was a pretty scene, ladies in abundance as usual dressed in all their finery, but the weather was bad which was a pity. There were some good races though, and afterwards the regiment gave a cold dinner in a stable (meant to have been out of doors). The Prince of Orange was there and seemed well pleased and paid us many compliments which cost him nothing. The boys got lively on champagne and overset my cabriolet into a ditch but no harm done. That night I rode with Howard (the adjutant) to Brussels where we supped and slept. On the 31st we left our horses and went in a cabriolet to Malines ; thence we went to Antwerp where we inspected churches and the docks. The next day we returned to Brussels and so back to Voorde. Things look as if we really should advance soon. Neither side is ready but it is time to begin, I think."

Napoleon was evidently of the same opinion, and was quicker off the mark than we were. His rapid and secret advance across the Belgian frontier, when he occupied Charleroi on 15th June, driving a wedge between the British and Prussian armies and giving Blücher a sound drubbing at Ligny on the 16th, are matters of history. That he caught us napping is equally so, for even on 15th June Taylor, writing to his wife, says :

" As for news, I have none to tell you ; we had a strong report the other day of Buonaparte at Maubeuge, but it seems since he was in Paris at the time. I heard yesterday morning from the barber who cut my hair that the French had carried off some cattle from the neighbourhood of Mons ; that some Belgian troops had advanced and recovered them, killing forty-five of the French ; probably not true. One hears we are to move soon, but we have heard that from the time we marched into Voorde."

The testing time had come, but even so our high command appears to have been sadly in arrear ; for on the very day that Blücher was being so badly mauled at Ligny another field-day was ordered for the 10th Hussars. This, however, was cancelled, but only at the last moment when it was learned that Bonaparte was in possession of Nivelles. The 10th finally marched at 6 a.m. on the 16th. Taylor, with his staff experience behind him, kept an accurate chronicle of events.

"At 6 we marched," he writes, "the whole of the cavalry and much infantry, Buonaparte having advanced and occupied Nivelles. At first we thought we were going to Enghien. When we got there some idiot told us Brain le Vonte and when we reached there some other idiot told us Nivelles. What a confusion of orders ! Soon we heard heavy firing and were told to advance at the trot and at a pretty pace trotted into Nivelles, out again along the Namur road, nearing the firing and meeting wounded. It was growing dusk as we came into the tail of the action, which had been very severe. Poor Grove of the Guards, and the Duke of Brunswick, a very fine fellow, were killed. Our infantry held a wood and we bivouacked behind it in a wheat field with nothing to eat and no water for hours. At two in the morning ' popping ' began again and lasted most of the morning, till the French were so good as to go to dinner at 1 o'clock. The Prussians had lost 10,000 men and much cannon and had to fall back, which meant that we had to do the same. About three, on came a large body of French Lancers. We formed on a hill with some Horse Artillery and gave them some rounds, then retired in line to another hill. We bivouacked in a grove amidst an inferno of cannonading from both sides and a pleasant night it was !"

Thus ended the action of Quatre Bras on the 16th and our withdrawal movement which went on through the 17th. The stage was now set for the final scene. The next day opened auspiciously for Taylor, for he was the means of conveying some welcome information about the approach of the Prussians to the Duke, receiving his thanks which put him in high good humour. He writes :

"On the morning of the 18th I was on outlying picquet in advance. I had just posted vedettes when a Prussian officer with a patrol came to communicate that General Bulow with his corps d'armée was arrived at Saint Lambert and that I must communicate this to the Duke of Wellington instantly, which I did. The Duke exclaimed, ' Damme, sir, you have brought the tidings which I have prayed for ; accept my gratitude.' Soon after my vedettes reported cavalry advancing, and so the ball was opened. We had a lively skirmish with the French Lancers and then I retired through the village of Ohain to join the brigade. Our line was now formed, that is the second line which was all cavalry, the infantry forming the first line. Our line is on the Northern ridge and there is a valley between us and the French on the opposite ridge, also drawn up, in two lines with, I believe, the Imperial Guard in reserve."

Taylor never forgot that he was a cavalryman, and it is as a cavalryman that he tells his story. As the cavalry really only came into the picture after the failure of the French to capture Hougoumont, when Napoleon directed a grand attack to be made on the allied left centre, it is at this juncture that he again takes up the story.

" By 1 o'clock the cannonade had become heavy, and suddenly the French advanced. They get to the brow of our hill ; the Belgian and Dutch brigades run away ; a Hanoverian regiment is the next to give, but the Duke who was in the hottest fire, was as usual too quick for them ; he charged them like a bull with his head down and turned them back himself ; then Picton with Pack's and Kempt's brigades fired a volley, charged and drove the enemy down the hill. Lord Uxbridge with the Life Guards and the Blues charged Kellermann's Cuirassiers in headlong rout down the road ' culbutting ' them like nothing."

So far, so good, but the end was not yet. Taylor, shrewd as usual, notes that the position was very critical since there was as yet no sign of the Prussians, and Bonaparte was making frantic efforts to beat our inferior force before they could join us. He describes the final effort when Napoleon ordered all his cavalry to attack the allied centre and right and the Old Guard to advance.

" At last, about 4 o'clock, we saw the Prussians a-galloping, coming on the French right, and none too soon, for the French were driving in our right. Lord Uxbridge ordered our brigade to charge ; the 10th were leading and we dashed into a medley of Lancers, Cuirassiers, Infantry, Dragoons, guns, etc. Such a scene, I can hardly help laughing at the recollection. They were fairly cowed ; great hulking Cuirassiers galloped as hard as they could—tumbled off to save themselves ; I got separated and one Cuirassier made a good attack on me, which I caught on my sword and gave him a back-hander, on which we parted, as saving your presence, I was running away, being alone amongst a whole lot of them, though they were so anxious about their own bacon that none but he thought of mine. I can laugh now at the style my little horse, Chopin, went over a Lancer officer, horse and all, and the fright he was in."

Taylor was in at the death and helped to complete the discomfiture of the Old Guard. He describes the scene thus :

" I only remember that the French going over the rising ground struck me as the gayest-looking army I ever saw with cuirasses, helmets, fur caps, lances, flags and varieties of uniforms. As they reached the top, they attempted to deploy, but Maitland's Guards showered volleys into them and drove them headlong down the hill. Now it was our turn, and the hurry-skurry we had was the most comical thing. We charged them as they ran and got right in amongst infantry, Imperial Guard, blue with large fur caps, who were throwing down their arms and roaring ' Pardon ' on their knees many of them. I am happy to say the Duke saw all our charges and shouted, ' By Gad, well done, 10th,' though he has always had an anti-cavalry twist. We handed over the pursuit to the Prussians who can be trusted to do the thing properly, and not show too much mercy ; the brutes deserve none after piking the prisoners of the Life Guards in cold blood because they said we used rockets in the pursuit. Our business was finished and it was moonlight by the time we formed up. The moon over the battlefield made no bad picture."

It would seem a fitting climax to leave Taylor on the moonlit battlefield, but he had some pertinent comments to make when the aftermath of battle had subsided, so it is worth while following him on his road to Paris. Writing to his wife on the 22nd June, he says :

" The result of this bloody battle was such that one cannot but hope that it is intended the military pride and ferocious spirit of the French nation are to be humbled, so as to prevent their being any longer a curse to Europe, as they have so long been."

He goes on in lighter vein :

" I have been much amused with Lord Uxbridge going to take Buonaparte with the Life Guards, but being prevented by being wounded. The fact is he received a grape shot above the knee when he was next door to me. To ease him I pulled off his boots. Though I do not admire other parts of his conduct, his bravery and skill in action are conspicuous, and the fortitude with which he bore his wound and the subsequent painful operation does him great credit. He is Marquis of Anglesey by the battle ! The battle has also done me a good turn for the Duke has recommended me for the brevet rank of Lieut.-Colonel and sent me an invitation to dine with him, rather the day after the fair, but better late than never."

The army of occupation advanced in lovely June weather through the French countryside by way of St. Quentin, Laon, Beauvais and Senlis, arriving outside Paris in the early part of July, and on the 5th he writes to his wife :

" The thing is done ; it was announced to the army yesterday that by a convention entered into with the French, Paris and Montmartre are to be given up to-day. The ' Frogs ' are blowing up things in Montmartre and the so-called statesmen are blowing up themselves. Such a parcel of monkeys with a mixture of pride, vanity and meanness, I have seen a more dignified assembly round a banyan tree ; at any rate they talk less nonsense than these jabbered at their late meetings. You will be glad to hear that I am to dine with the Duke in the near future."

Taylor found a lot of old friends in Paris and seems to have had a pleasant time. He and the Colonel of the 10th, Lord Robert Manners, made many expeditions together. The 8th July was a blazing hot day and the Colonel and Taylor had a refreshing bathe in the Seine in the Bois de Boulogne ; afterwards he writes :

" We dined at a restaurateur's with two old friends, Sir Lowry Cole and Lord Athlone, who was a brother officer of mine in the Carabineers when he was Lieut. Ginckell—an odd fish enough. In the evening we rode to St. Cloud which Blücher occupies ; he is an uncouth looking old man and was spitting over a bridge when I saw him. The Prussian soldiers were catching goldfish in the ponds as fast as they could. On the way back, we looked in at the Guards in the Bois de Boulogne. There are two cavalry brigades in Paris, one the dirtiest and worse we have, I rejoice I am not in it."

Paris was very pleasant, but also very expensive, and Taylor, who was of an economical turn of mind, writes :

" I should be sorry to pay the expenses of some of the young men I know at 150 Napoleons each during their stay in Paris ; the fact is Paris must be dreadfully dear to a young man that does not think about it ; a good dinner at a restaurateur's with champagne and burgundy, which every young Englishman thinks he must drink, will seldom be less than 20 francs ; then he must go to the play, the price just as high as English at the good houses, and that with a fiacre 10 francs more, and still more again if he has a delectable companion in the fiacre. I had to cut Beauvillier's after two treats and went to dine at humbler places. I have been buying tea to-day, which is now become pretty good hay by being in paper the last six years. The Frogs can make coffee, though ! "

Taylor, whose financial resources were dwindling, was rather relieved when the 10th were ordered back to Beauvais ; he had also learnt that this was a prelude to his return home. On 1st August he is in high spirits and breaks into verse :

> The Duke commands and we obey,
> Over the Oise and far away :
> All through Beaumont to Beauvais.

The dinner with the Duke came off at last at Calais, in the Hotel Dessin. The Duke had come to see Captain Hill, the Chief Agent for Transports, and the result was a very comfortable little dinner party à trois in the Hotel Dessin. Taylor had seen a good deal of Hill at Ostend during the disembarkation of the expeditionary force, and had made great friends with him. Taylor says of the dinner :

" The Duke in fine fettle, Hill also very pleased with himself as he had just been nominated by the Emperor of Russia to be a ' Chevalier de St. Vladimir ' for his help in embarking a division of Russian troops. Very nice, no doubt, but no pay attached ; I reckon I have done better by being made a brevet Lieut.-Colonel."

Chapter Four

IRISH BLARNEY

TAYLOR was something of an optimist when he imagined he was going to return to England that year. The fact of his having been promoted to be a brevet Lieut.-Colonel, however fortunate in itself, delayed his return for a year and a half, for he was seconded as a colonel on the staff to Lord Hill, the second-in-command of the army of occupation. Lord Hill occupied the Hotel de Montesquieu and frequently had to act as host for the Duke of Wellington, who usually contrived to be absent on state affairs when there was any likelihood of his being called upon to entertain guests. Taylor had frequently to attend functions given in honour of various members of the Government " whom the stirring events had brought to Paris." On one occasion the Foreign Secretary, Lord Castlereagh, and the Duke of York came. His Lordship, exhausted no doubt by the cares of office, usually retired to bed early and Lord Hill and his staff would willingly have followed his example, but His Royal Highness was not so easily disposed of. As titular head of the army, he perfunctorily discussed current events with his service chiefs after dinner, but this soon gave place to the more serious business of hazard or bezique which offered a sporting chance of replenishing the depleted royal purse. This was apt to be a lengthy business from which, however, Taylor says " it was impossible to withdraw oneself with propriety." After a year or so of this sort of thing, Taylor's purse began to feel the strain, and it was with a

36

feeling of relief that he at last obtained his release in March
1818.

On his return from the army of occupation, Taylor shortly
afterwards received an invitation from the Duke of Clarence
to spend a few days at Bushey Park. Here he was introduced to
various members of the numerous family presented to her royal
master by Mrs. Jordan, from whom he had parted seven years
previously. Taylor was rather uncertain what attitude to adopt
towards what he called " the mixed brood." He writes :

" They seemed to be like the sands on the seashore in number,
the sexes were mixed but they were all happy and jolly ; I could
not of course regard them as Royalties in the true sense of the
word, nor did they want me to, so I treated them as playful
puppies from a large litter. The eldest son, Captain Fitzclarence, as A.D.C. to Lord Hastings has distinguished himself
in the Pindaree war and H.R.H. is very proud of him."

H.R.H. was also at the time very pleased with himself ; for
the death of Princess Charlotte in the previous November had
materially altered his prospects and put him in the running for
the Crown of England. Taylor goes on :

" It is now almost an open secret that H.R.H. is going to
enter into the bonds of legitimate matrimony. Princess Adelaide is the favoured lady and she and her mother are coming
to this country. H.R.H. has asked me to be one of the grooms
at the wedding. All rather awkward for the sands on the
seashore ! "

Taylor, in his capacity of groom, duly attended the marriage
of the Duke of Clarence and the re-marriage of the Duke and
Duchess of Kent in July. The Duke and Duchess of Kent had
been married abroad earlier in the year, but it was considered
advisable that the ceremony should also take place according to
the English rites and the double wedding was celebrated in the
old Queen's drawing-room at Kew. The Duke of Clarence

was suffering from spasmodic twinges of gout, perhaps induced by this public token of respectability, and Taylor's duties more resembled those of a valet, resolving themselves into a game of " hunt the slipper." Taylor, describing the event, writes :

" Save for the altar which had been erected it was more like a drawing-room reception than a wedding. The Queen of course was the principal figure and next the Prince Regent who gave both the brides away. The Prince for him was pretty firm on his legs, much more so indeed than my own royal master who could scarce stand for the pain in his big right toe. The Archbishop was overlong in his discourse and H.R.H., who could stand it no longer, whispered loudly to me, ' For the love of God, find me a soft boot.' Thanks be to Providence, his lacquey had brought one mirabile dictu."

The Duke and Duchess of Clarence received a most enthusiastic send-off on their journey to Clarence House and all the customary tributes were paid even to the wedding slipper. Taylor writes :

" Whilst the Queen and Prince Regent wished the Royal couple God-speed, we all stood bowing and scraping and then I helped His Royal Highness into the carriage as he was still very lame. As the carriage drove off it was very comical to see a ' soft boot ' tied on to the rumble ; I suppose by his lacquey."

The Clarences shortly afterwards went abroad and some time was to elapse before Taylor again came in contact with the Duke. But there were chance meetings with his son, Captain Fitz-clarence, at the United Service Club, of which they were both members, and Taylor seems to have been attracted by this curious young man who was his junior by twelve years. Taylor felt a deep sympathy for him in his difficult position. Of his first meeting with George Fitzclarence, Taylor says :

" He did not at first sight attract me in looks or manner ; dark browed and seemingly sulky. His cynicism regarding his Father's wedding and his somewhat coarse allusion to the unattractiveness of the bride at first repelled me, but I decided later that it was to cover his sensitiveness over the peculiar position in which he was placed."

Taylor was on duty with his regiment at the Coronation of George IV on 19th July 1821. In view of the sympathy expressed by a large portion of the population for Queen Caroline, the Government were taking no chances and in order to ensure the preservation of the peace had drafted large forces into the metropolis. Taylor records his disgust at the sight of a Queen of England being harried from door to door when she attempted to gain admission to Westminster Abbey. Almost immediately after the Coronation the regiment proceeded to Dublin, and on 12th August escorted the King from Howth to the Vice-regal lodge in Phoenix Park, where it remained until his departure. Queen Caroline had only died on 7th August, but this did not prevent the King from continuing his liaison with Lady Conyngham who, Taylor writes, was " constantly at Phoenix Park but did not appear much in public."

Taylor, who foresaw his being stationed in Ireland for a considerable time, brought his wife and family to Dublin, where they took a house in Grafton Street. There was considerable friction at this time between the Orangemen and Roman Catholics and rightly or wrongly the Orangemen thought that the new Lord-Lieutenant was biased in favour of the Catholics, and decided to mob him at the Theatre Royal. It so happened that Taylor took his wife to the theatre on 14th December 1822 and on the arrival of Lord Wellesley the crowd broke into cheering. During the playing of the National Anthem, however, a chorus of hisses started, and a bottle supposed to be aimed at the Lord-Lieutenant was thrown from the gallery and fell near the Vice-regal box. The noise became so appalling that Taylor, not wishing to be involved in a vulgar fracas, took his wife out. He apologised to his wife for the misbehaviour of " these pestilential Irishmen " but thought that Lord Wellesley was not the man to govern them, wherein he showed a certain shrewdness.

Whilst in Dublin, the time passed pleasantly enough. Mrs. Taylor had her full share of balls at the Castle, race meetings and the usual amusements which appeal to the feminine mind. In 1825, the regiment was moved to Ballinrobe, Athlone and Loughrea, and the lotus-eating life of Dublin was replaced by continual calls in aid of the civil power. The Catholic Association founded by Daniel O'Connell in 1823 was the root of the trouble and O'Connell was busy making trouble between the landlords and tenants. In July there was a nasty riot in Galway, and a detachment of the 10th Hussars, headed by Taylor, had to make a charge at Oranmore against a mob armed with scythes and a few ancient firearms. At the end of 1826, the regiment embarked for England and marched to Exeter, thus bringing Taylor to his native soil. In January 1827, Taylor with a detachment was on duty for the funeral of the late Commander-in-Chief, the Duke of York. He then took the opportunity of going to Ogwell for some leave.

It was not until May of that year that Taylor paid another visit to Bushey Park after the return of the Duke and Duchess of Clarence from the Continent. By the death of the Duke of York, the Duke of Clarence had become heir-apparent to the throne. He did not feel called upon to display any excessive grief over the death of his brother, for whom he had never felt any particular affection. He confided to Taylor that in his opinion he himself was a better sailor than ever his brother had been as a soldier and that perhaps he would make no worse a King. Taylor, whilst not forgetting the faults of the Duke of York as a soldier in the field yet gave him his due for his merits as a commander-in-chief, did not feel called upon to argue about the rivalry of the royal brothers, but reserved judgment as to the Kingship.

Meanwhile the Duke's appointment as Lord High Admiral had afforded him intense gratification. As Taylor put it :

" H.R.H. is delighted at coming back to the Navy and has great schemes afoot ; he looks and is more the jolly tar than ever." The " Rake's Progress," as Taylor flippantly described the new Lord High Admiral's progress by land and sea in order to inspect the ports and arsenals of the kingdom, was no inept designation. The operation, which took place in 1827, was conducted on a princely scale as was perhaps natural and " made a great impression on the common people." It also produced a similar effect on the common purse which Mr. Canning and Lord Goderich were content to overlook. When however the Duke of Wellington assumed office in the next year, it became apparent that the former Commander-in-Chief and the Lord High Admiral did not see eye to eye on matters of finance. The Duke determined that, Prince or no Prince, he should not play ducks and drakes with public money. The military martinet's uncompromising attitude defeated the easy-going sailor, who wisely enough gave up the unequal contest and resigned the office it had given him so much pleasure to hold. Writing to Taylor after his resignation, the Duke of Clarence said : " You will have learnt from the newspapers that I have let go my sheet anchor to appease that hook-nosed pillar of respectability."

For the next two years, Taylor was Commandant of the Riding Establishment in St. John's Wood where his time was mostly taken up, as he says, " with teaching oafs with no horse-sense and precious little other, to ' make much of their horses,' with little enthusiasm on the part of man or beast." Among his pupils were " a dozen or so men whom Mr. Peel wished to be trained as horse constables for his new police." This appointment terminated just before the death of George IV in June 1830.

During the latter part of 1830 and the whole of 1831, Taylor was seconded as Inspector of Yeomanry. It was in the summer of the latter year that he was detailed to accompany Captain Hill, who had been appointed Commissioner to supervise the relief of the distressed areas in Ireland. The last time Taylor had met Hill had been in 1815 when he was Chief Agent for Transports, and the two had dined with the Duke of Wellington at Calais. In Ireland, the failure of the potato crop on which the peasants mainly relied for food had caused severe distress along the western coast. This failure, coupled with the rack-rents extorted by middlemen, provided fruitful material for agitators in disquieting the minds of the peasantry. Added to this, O'Connell was making mischief by starting a repeal campaign and feelings between Protestants and Roman Catholics were highly inflamed. The whole situation afforded little satisfaction to the Ministers of the Crown, part of it requiring spiritual recognition whilst another part sought more material assistance in the shape of meal and potatoes. The material needs of Ireland and incidentally those of Lord Grey's administration prevailed, hence the appointment of a civil Commissioner.

Hill's warrant from the Government actually was not worth the paper on which it was written ; for it placed all the onus of responsibility on the Commissioner without any corresponding guarantee from the Government. The First Lord of the Admiralty, Sir James Graham, under whose jurisdiction Hill as Comptroller of the Victualling Yards came, said in a letter to Hill on 6th June :

" I entrust this important and confidential mission to you in the full belief that you will execute it with integrity, zeal and despatch, *without* expense or embarrassment to the Government, relying as far as possible on the generosity of private individuals, and I feel assured you will not disappoint my expectations."

Taylor met Hill on the quay at Holyhead on 7th June. Hill informed Taylor that they would get no thanks from the Government and still less from " these pestilential Irishmen " whatever the result of their labours might be. Taylor replied that he had orders from Lord Goderich to inspect the Constabulary and that he could call on them for assistance if necessary. Hill and Taylor arrived in Dublin on 9th June ; they lost no time in reporting to the Marquis of Anglesey, the Lord-Lieutenant, and the Chief

Secretary, who had been instructed by the home Government to render every assistance. The Marquis at once recognized Taylor and greeted him with effusion. He recalled the occasion when he was wounded at Waterloo and reminded Taylor of his debt to him for his presence of mind in pulling off his boots. Taylor, who fancied his colleague was being left out in the cold, introduced Hill as the Commissioner appointed to supervise the relief of the distressed areas. The Lord-Lieutenant shook his head with distaste and recommended Hill to see Stanley, the Chief Secretary, who would be more likely to help. He concluded by asking Taylor and Hill to return and dine with him.

Hill had decided to make Westport his headquarters and they left Dublin for that place next day. He had arranged for large consignments of oatmeal and potatoes to be sent there from Deptford victualling yard, and as a precautionary measure had asked Taylor to arrange for an armed guard of yeomanry and constabulary to be mounted. It was as well he did so, for Taylor writes : " On Saturday at noon a mob attacked the police and military, when the latter fired, killing one man and two women. The man confessed before he died that he was in fault and not in want, and it was found he had stolen £50 worth of meal." The dead man's mentality was symptomatic of that of some of his kind, and the home Government may have been wise in their generation when they disclaimed responsibility for any excess of generosity on the part of their Commissioner.

Hill's co-ordination of a transport system of his own making, comprising coastguard cutters by sea, ox-carts and any others that came to hand by land, made possible the establishment of various food depots in Galway, Mayo and Sligo, the main centres of famine. Supervision was not easy, and entailed endless journeys in incredible discomfort. Hill had to compete not only with the stealing and grabbing habits of the population, but with what was even more trying, their non-stop blarney.

A sample of a day's proceedings is given in Taylor's journal, which he kept for Hill, who had no time for writing.

" *16th June :* Started for Castlebar in a car and got there at
5.30 a.m. ; got into mail-coach at 6 and arrived at Ballina
10 a.m.   Left at 11 in post-chaise for Belmullet ; Hill called on
the Rev. Mr. Stalker, who was confined to his bed, having been
thrown out of his gig.   He received a deputation who complained of great distress, but all the men looked as though they
had too much to eat and not too little.   Called on the village
surgeon to examine his sick-list, but we found him drunk ; had
a mutton chop and some whiskey at a dirty inn and slept there
in dirtier beds.   Lord G. Paulett of the sloop *Nautilus* joined us.
Next day I felt so unwell had to take medicine (not from the
drunken surgeon).   The day after saw the market at Castlebar,
potatoes 3½*d.* a stone, mutton 3*d.* a pound, beef 4*d.*   No sign
of distress here.   Whiskey or poteen seemed to abound, judging
by the men's faces and the odour they exuded.   Jack Joyce, a
large landowner, had taken too much and no doubt said more
than he meant to ; he told Hill his men were well off ; one of
them had ten cows and forty sheep, but as charity meal was
going about they had some."

Market day was scarcely the best one for the Commissioner to
hold an evening meeting, but it had been so arranged and Taylor
goes on :

" Went to the Central Committee which was the most stormy
and abusive we ever saw.   Sir R. O'Donnell and Hughes, a
priest of Newport, attempted to incite the people against us.
Sir R. Blosse, in the chair, made a feeble attempt to intervene,
and he and the chair were upset.   After being there five hours,
Hill agreed to grant relief to 216,643 at 7*d.* per head, per week."

Such munificence on the part of the Commissioner brought a
query from Sir James Graham as to whether 3½*d.* per head would
not have sufficed.   The rowdyism accompanying the gift had
also made Sir James rather nervous and in a private letter to
Hill, he writes :

" In consequence of your report and a report made to me by
Lord Sligo, that vessels arriving in Westport laden with pro-

visions would be exposed to violence and plunder amidst the excitement prevailing in a population reduced almost to the extremity of famine, you may, if you wish, ask Colonel Taylor to arrange for reinforcements of police or yeomanry, but the responsibility for any action must rest with him. I shall be anxious to hear of your safety after your arrival at Newport."

Commissioner Hill thought it well however to allay Sir James's anxieties and to inform him that he had the position well in hand. This brought another effusion from the First Lord : " Your message is highly satisfactory. Keep as much power as you can in your own hands and trust as little as possible to others, even the Irish Government." The reference to the Irish Government was a little unkind, but Sir James was not always tactful.

Hill had frequently to call on Taylor in his military capacity for assistance and the latter cites an instance :

" *23rd July.* Having received reports that a mob was lying hid near Ballintulbers to attack meal carts, I directed Lieut. Colt with a troop of the Sligo Yeomanry to go there with an escort to protect them. Lieut. Colt behaved very well, and used the utmost forbearance, but was compelled to fire in his own defence, killing three men. Hill reported this to Sir James Graham, which no doubt made him uncomfortable, it is to be hoped so."

Open violence could be dealt with promptly but " hidden malice," as Hill described it, took longer. This undesirable trait was usually made manifest in a deputation of priests and clergy of rival denominations. One such meeting at Castlebar is typical. Taylor writes :

" *25th July.* We met the Central Committee who talked a great deal ; the clergy were the greater nuisance though, and whilst the Central Committee said what they thought to be the truth, the priests said what they knew to be lies. Priest M'Hale, who complained that the Indian meal made his people ill, was found to have taken it himself. Priest Lyons of Belmullet accused Hill of only giving Protestants meal and was extremely violent, but we set him to rights and kept him in good order. Curate Walsh of Castlebar asked why whiskey could not be included in medical comforts, but as he had taken overmuch himself we did not listen to him. None of these persons' statements can be relied on. There was one priest, however, who we had friendly recollections of who called on us at Connell's Hotel in Galway, a very dirty house, and the landlord gone to bed drunk. Priest Gallagher, who was drinking tea with us, said the magistrates in Galway were no good—the landlord of this house was one ; he also said that they were all common shop-keepers who were afraid to act and gentlemen would not act with them. A very civil man."

Commissioner Hill had orders to report on certain landlords who were suspected of being the cause of a good deal of the disaffection. He cites a particularly bad specimen, Sir Samuel O'Malley, who was the sole owner of Clare Island. This man, writes Taylor,

" is a perfect tyrant and worse ; he gets over £700 per annum rents from the poor inhabitants who are starving, and does not give one farthing to their relief. The poultry and crops are destroyed by wild-fowl, but no one is allowed to carry a gun except his driver M'Que, a very villainous sort of ruffian. He drives for the rents with his gun and threatens all who oppose him. Sir S. O'Malley was impudent enough to ask our aid in making a new harbour. Hill told him the island required a new master more than a new harbour."

By the beginning of August, the Commissioner's measures for relief had achieved their object and the Lord-Lieutenant wrote : " In consequence of your report, I have ordered the additional troops to be withdrawn. I must congratulate you on your judicious exertions in the arduous task you have had to perform. I hope to see you on your return to Dublin."

On a final tour of inspection, Taylor notes : " Hill received no complaints except one from the contractor who makes coffins for the poor of Westport and surrounding parishes ; he

said he generally makes about forty coffins per month, but in the
last two months he has only made ten."

Hill and Taylor arrived in Dublin on 6th August and were
pleased with their reception. The latter says in his journal :

" An escort of cavalry attended our carriage to Black Rock
where we were received by Lord Anglesey who was vastly civil
and invited us to dinner at six. Returned to Dublin and passed
Sir S. O'Malley in the street, who shook his fist at us. Dined
with His Excellency. Captain Henry sat at the head of the
table and Sir William de Baire at the foot. Sir Hussey Vivian
and Lord Fitzroy there, altogether about sixteen persons. No
ladies at dinner which was as well as the wine was free and
conversation lively. When we retired Lady Anglesey and some
other ladies were in the drawing-room. Lady Anglesey had
plenty to say, but the rest were prim. Got on board the Post
Office packet at 10 p.m. and arrived at Holyhead in seven hours."

The final episode was their meeting with the Sailor-King
when Hill received the order of knighthood. The occasion was
informal as between one sailor and another. His Majesty's
" Sink Mr. Commissioner and rise Sir John," when conferring
the accolade, was more reminiscent of the wardroom than the
audience chamber, which was all the new knight could have
desired.

Chapter Five

SAILOR-KING AND SOLDIER-GROOM

TAYLOR returned from Ireland in time for the Coronation of William IV on 8th September 1831.

"It was a very stately affair," he writes, " the Royal coach containing the King and Queen was drawn by eight horses, of which two were jibbers ; the crowd cheered tremendously when the King put his hand out of the carriage window and shouted to the grooms in charge, larboard or starboard. Westminster Abbey was full to overflowing and there was a wonderful array of colour. Nearly all the members of the House of Commons were dressed in some kind of uniform which I suspect they had no right to wear ; some had even decked themselves out in highland costumes. Uneasy lies the head that wears a crown ! I was sorry for the poor old King who looked ready to give out his last gasp with that great heavy crown on his head, which it did not fit and came down over his eyebrows."

But though the citizens of London were willing enough to cheer the colourful Coronation procession of William IV, the country as a whole was in a highly explosive state over the Reform Bill.

The question of Parliamentary reform had been a major subject of controversy for nearly fifty years, ever since Pitt had brought forward a motion in 1785 to disenfranchise rotten boroughs returning two members apiece, and to give the seats to the counties and London. His motion was defeated, but the

GENERAL T. W. TAYLOR, C.B.
From a portrait by A. R. Venables

demand for reform grew ever more insistent and came to a head in 1830, after the revolution in France which drove Charles X from his throne.

The Duke of Wellington, though willing to introduce a Bill admitting Roman Catholics to Parliament, was strenuously opposed to Parliamentary reform, and his Government fell. Lord Grey, who succeeded him, immediately introduced a Bill which took away the right of representation from fifty-six rotten boroughs, gave the hundred and forty-three seats thus gained to the counties and the large industrial towns and established a £10 householder's qualification for the franchise. The Bill passed the Commons but was defeated in the Lords. Grey resigned, and the King called on the Duke of Wellington to form a Government, but he failed and appeal was made to the country.

Feelings ran high and there were demonstrations and disturbances all over the country.

Taylor was a witness of the famous Bristol riots, which were among the most violent.

He writes of them as follows :

" It was through no desire of mine that I was drawn into the lamentable proceedings which started at Bristol on 29th October. The King had released me from Household duties since the country was in a disturbed state, and he realized my responsibilities towards the yeomanry. The disturbances at Bristol were the fault of one man and one man only, an insensate popinjay called Sir Charles Wetherell, the Recorder of Bristol. Not content with inflaming the public by declaiming against the so-called Reform measures, he insisted on making a pompous entry into the city, with a cavalcade of Magistrates and Tory gentry. It was the signal for all the ragamuffins, armed with scythes and stones, to attack the procession. Sir Charles Wetherell, though he did not deserve it, was rescued, and escaped through a back door. Meanwhile the mob had got completely out of hand ; never was there such a display of pusillanimity on the part of the Mayor and the Magistrates.

His Worship, shaking like an aspen leaf, came up to me and said : 'I am out of my depth, Colonel, pray help me.' 'God helps those who help themselves,' I replied. 'I will help you this far though, be a man instead of a dolt and read the riot act.' The Magistrates, however, when the riot act was read, would not allow the military to take any part. It was not until the 31st that some of the Magistrates, I suppose, having recovered from some of their stupor, called for military aid, and this only when the Constables, half of whom were drunk, had been overpowered. The Yeomanry were standing by outside the city ; two squadrons of the 14th Dragoons, who were awaiting orders inside, were ordered to charge the crowd, and they did so in earnest with the result that quiet was restored, but over 100 people were killed or wounded. I found myself detailed for a most distasteful task, being appointed a member of the Court Martial which was to try Colonel Brereton, the unfortunate military commander ; the trial did not take place, however, as the poor man shot himself on the morning of the trial."

In the spring of 1832 all tempers had become frayed, including that of the King, who had not only had to deal with a succession of ministers but had been freely insulted by his subjects.

At the beginning of May, he sent a summons to Taylor :

"Pray return at the earliest possible moment," he wrote ; "I need a Master-at-Arms to lay a rattan across the shoulders of a few of my ship's company who have got out of hand."

Taylor did return to his duties at Court, and that the King had not exaggerated the unpleasantness of the situation is clear from Taylor's record of the incident of 12th May. He writes :

"The masses are in an ugly mood, incited no doubt by evilly-disposed agitators for their own ends. On 12th May the Royal party were subjected to a most disagreeable experience whilst driving from Windsor to London. All went well until we reached Brentford when Bedlam was let loose. Groans and hisses greeted their Majesties and their carriage was pelted with mud and filth of every description ; a dead cat landed on my horse, which made him kick out furiously, knocking down two men like ninepins, which caused me little regret. Captain Lambton of the Life Guards, in command of the escort, behaved splendidly and closed up his men against the carriage windows ; thanks to his presence of mind, their Majesties escaped harm. The Queen was much shaken, but remained calm, and soothed the lady-in-waiting who was squealing like a frightened rabbit. I had no rattan handy, but the escorts used the flats of their swords to good effect. The King's face was purple with anger and I feared he was going to have an apoplexy. ' Let the damned lubbers have it, Taylor,' he shouted out of the window. ' By God, if I were aboard ship, I would teach 'em manners.' This sort of thing continued all along the road and when we entered the Park, howls of execration went up amongst the mob and continued all the way to the Palace. Shortly after our arrival, the Duke of Wellington had a short audience of His Majesty on the question of forming a new administration. His chances do not seem to be very hopeful. His Grace met with a very hostile reception when I escorted him out. Things are in a terrible mess over this parrot cry of Reform. The very Throne itself is threatened ; pray Heaven Lord Grey will see reason."

The King according to Taylor " was unable to digest the Duke of Wellington's medicine, and so swallowed Reform like a dose of calomel, unpleasant but in the circumstances necessary." The situation eased after the passing of the Reform Bill on 7th June, and the Court adjourned to Windsor for relaxation.

"The Queen and I need a rest from the importunities of vexatious persons," the King told Taylor, and added, " Pray see that all is ship-shape at the Castle, particularly the arrangements for the closet."

Taylor was puzzled for the moment.

"Does your Majesty mean the audience chamber ? " he said.

" No, you soft-head," the King replied, " I have in mind the new contraption being fixed, in which water takes the place of words."

A pleasantly informal atmosphere seems to have pervaded the royal house-party at Windsor in the June of 1832 ; ministers were conspicuous by their absence and the guests were of their Majesties' own choice. The Chancellor of the Exchequer, Lord Althorp, made a bid to be present, presumably to keep an eye on the royal expenditure, but the King would have none of it.

"I want no prying Pursers aboard," he told Taylor; "they can look for prize-money elsewhere."

Taylor, in a letter to his wife, writes:

"The King is determined to put the annoyances of State behind him for the time; the Queen, poor soul, who has many cares of a different nature, supports him nobly. Her conduct and devotion under the most trying circumstances, are worthy of the highest praise."

In paying this tribute to the Queen, Taylor was referring to her unremitting kindness to the sons and daughters of her husband by Mrs. Jordan, two of whom, Captain George Fitzclarence, now the Earl of Munster, and his sister, Lady de Lisle, were among the party on this occasion. Other guests were the

"Duke and Duchess of Buccleuch, the Duke being a very gentlemanly sort of man with whom I had many interesting confabs; Lord and Lady Winchester with their charming young daughter, Lady Cecilia Paulet, who was much in favour with the K. Lord Albemarle (in waiting) Sir Henry and Lady Wheatly, Sir Herbert and Lady Taylor, who was Military Secretary to the Duke of York, and last but not least dear old 'Daddy Hill' whom I had not seen since Waterloo and the Army of Occupation days. The King found a word for everyone, but was mostly taken up with Princess Augusta. A most pleasant company."

On 19th June the royal party attended the race meeting at Ascot, which seems to have attracted all the rank and fashion. It was a perfect day, marred only by an ugly incident when a disgruntled pensioner made a vicious and unprovoked assault on the King. Taylor was in high spirits, for he was to meet his two daughters, Ann and Harriet, who were in Lord and Lady Minto's party. The two girls were noted beauties, Ann with a mass of fair hair and a peach-blossom complexion, and Harriet a striking brunette. They were popularly known as the Rose and the Lily of Devon, and on this occasion each wore the flower after which she was named. Taylor describes the day's events :

" We drove in six carriages in state to the race-course. To my delight, almost the first people I met were Lord and Lady Minto, Lord Melgund, Lady Fanny Elliot and Ann and Harriet. Great excitement as Lord Minto has a horse running in one of the races. Lady Minto was looking particularly handsome and well-dressed, that is to say as well as the present fashion for ladies will allow ; what I believe is known as the long pointed stomacher does not, to my mind, enhance feminine charms. Lady Fanny is becoming quite a beauty, but I am told that Ann and Harriet hold the field. The King who even now seldom misses anything in the way of beauty in females and had heard of ' your lovely daughters,' ordered me to present them. He paid them such glowing compliments that I fear their heads will be turned. H.M. was in fine fettle, joking with his old ship-mates, many of whom were present. He talked a lot with Admiral Beresford (brother of the Marshal). I met the Admiral last when he was in command of the *Royal Sovereign* yacht which took Louis XVIII across the Channel. Like everyone else, he was thankful to see the back of that Monarch. The King as usual mixed freely with the crowd, and it was this misplaced con-fidence which nearly proved to be his undoing. By the mercy of Providence, what might have proved tragedy had something of the comical in it. Their Majesties were passing the saddling ring when there was a sudden commotion amongst the crowd. Someone shouted, ' Murder ! Hold him ! ' and something which sounded like a musket ball sang past our ears and burst with a noise like a cannon shot. A dastardly fellow in the crowd had hurled a large stone at the King. The missile fortunately missed its mark and crashed into the glazed hat of a Peeler, taking it off in fine style. The Queen was much alarmed, not for herself but for the King, who was merely in one of his furies. 'You lop-eared lubber,' he shouted at the Peeler, 'give over chasing your damned hat and go catch the ruffian.' The villain, I am thankful to say, was soon afterwards secured."

Lord Hill, the Commander-in-Chief, before leaving took Taylor aside and told him that the King desired he should be released from his military duties and officially appointed Groom of the Bedchamber. The Commander-in-Chief had therefore arranged that Taylor's appointment as such should be gazetted as from 14th February 1833. He wrote in great jubilation to his wife :

" Daddy Hill has given me some good news and I now know where I am ; I am vastly pleased that I have been appointed Groom of the Bedchamber, which I think is a very high honour. Hitherto I have merely regarded myself as a soldier groom ; I am now, as it were, promoted from the stables to the Court. I trust that I shall rise to the occasion."

His wife wrote back pithily : " I rejoice that you are pleased, but for myself, I would as soon clean out horses as a bedchamber."

Taylor's duties, though not unduly arduous, varied according to the King's whims and fancies, which were quite unpredictable. In another letter to his wife, he writes :

" You do not seem to understand that my post as Groom of the Bedchamber puts me on a much more intimate footing in the Household. The K., as you know, has his peculiarities, and I am anything from apothecary to riding-master. I am, if you please, not master of the King's purse but of his calomel which his lacquey frequently forgets and which, as the King says, his liver demands after a Knights of the Garter dinner, or an interview with Lord Brougham. H.M. is no horseman himself, but the Queen is very fond of riding ; having been Dragoon, Hussar and Lancer, I am in charge of the equestrian arrangements.

This gives me great pleasure as I am thus able to improve my acquaintance with the Q. whom I greatly admire."

He adds as a sop to Cerberus :

" Pray now, do not be jealous, as I refer to her character and not to her outward attractions, which saving her presence, are not very pronounced. This afternoon (10th April) we had a delightful gallop in Windsor Park, starting from His Majesty's Cottage, where we let out a pet antelope which gambolled with us all the way. The party consisted of the Queen, Miss Bagot, a pretty maid of honour, Lord Falkland and myself. The Q. and I had a very pleasant confab. whilst Lord Falkland entertained Miss Bagot, who is too young for yours truly."

Taylor, with a touch of naiveté but scarcely of courtierism, adds : " The Queen when riding wears a veil, which much improves her appearance ; so also does Miss Bagot, who really has no need of one."

When the royal family returned to London Taylor appears to have had nostalgic recollections of the rural rides at Windsor and of the general homely atmosphere which the place engendered as opposed to what he calls " the unfriendly pavements of St. James and the garish splendour of the Brighton Pavilion." He was an excellent domestic correspondent, and writing to his wife from St. James's Palace, he says :

" I miss the glades of Windsor and Virginia Water, as Bishop Heber says, ' where every prospect pleases, and only man is vile.' The change is reflected in the King who at Windsor rattles off his quarter-deck jokes, but here seems moody and irritable. Ministers drive him mad with their continual bickering over matters that he knows little about and about which he cares less. At present it is the slave question which Mr. Stanley has taken up in the House of Commons and which Lord Grey and Lord Brougham are squabbling about with the Duke of Wellington, and Lord Ellenborough in the House of Lords."

The result of this "squabble," in which Lord Grey and his supporters won, had rather more far-reaching results than the King "knew of or cared about," since on 28th August 1833, he was forced to give his assent to the Emancipation Act which virtually freed all slaves throughout the British colonies. The King apparently acted on the motto "live and let live," for in his younger days he had, like other members of his family, except the Duke of Gloucester, been opposed to the abolition of the slave trade.

"Much good may it do 'em," was his only comment on the transaction he made to his Groom of the Bedchamber, but whether the remark applied to Lord Grey, Mr. Stanley, the emancipated negroes or all of them together, is not recorded.

As Taylor became more intimately acquainted with the inner workings of the royal household, he could not fail to notice the domestic upheavals which frequently occurred in the royal family. The chief disturber of the peace, so far as the King was concerned, was his sister-in-law, the Duchess of Kent, of whom Taylor writes :

"She strikes even myself, who knew her but little, as a most enraging person, flaunting her position as mother of the heiress to the throne ; as for the King, the mention of her name brings a rush of blood to his head, though he will do anything for his niece, the little Princess Victoria."

Another bone of contention in the family circle was Taylor's old acquaintance, the Earl of Munster, who visited his father when the mood took him. Taylor, writing to his wife in July 1834, says :

"I see a good deal of George Fitzclarence, one way and another, generally at the United Service Club, and sometimes at St. James's Palace or Windsor. I must say that I think his behaviour to the King and Q. leaves much to be desired. He pays little attention to the Queen ; he tells me he comes as a matter of duty to receive the paternal blessing. I suspect myself that he comes as a matter of necessity to receive the paternal largesse, but I rather fancy that he as oft as not goes away without either."

On 16th October the buildings of both Houses of Parliament went up in flames and were totally destroyed. A month later, the Melbourne Ministry metaphorically went the same way. Taylor, who was then with the King at Brighton, describes their passing in his journal :

"I mislike this place, haunted as it is by unpleasant ghosts, but the smell of the sea puts new life into H.M. On 14th November Lord Melbourne came to see him and suggested that Lord John Russell should take Lord Althorp's place as leader of the House of Commons and, as the King told me afterwards, wanted to make hay with the Cabinet. The King made hay of Lord Melbourne instead. 'Damme, sir, I want none of your Russells or Spring Rices, since you cannot oblige me, I will ask the Duke of Wellington what he can do about it.' Lord Melbourne returned to town with a flea in his ear. This was not the end of the story. A very insulting article has appeared in the Times newspaper which accuses the Queen of meddling in state affairs. This was too much for the King, and we really felt he might have an apoplexy. 'This is the doing of that spiteful feller, Brougham,' he spluttered. 'He and the rest of the pack shall go.' He was as good as his word and dismissed all the Ministers before any others were appointed."

When Peel's Ministry came to grief over the Church of Ireland question, and was succeeded by the second Melbourne administration in April 1835, the King said to Taylor : "The same miserable crowd of barnacles aboard, save Brougham, who I pushed through the lubber's hole."

The King, it is true, excepted from his contemptuous condemnation Palmerston, the Foreign Secretary, with whom he got on very well. He was also on the best of terms with Lord Minto, who succeeded Lord Auckland as First Lord of the Admiralty in September. This was most satisfactory for Taylor, since Lord Palmerston and Lord Minto were two of his greatest friends and the result was the formation of what Taylor calls "a delightful *partie carée* of all the talents."

With the dismissal of Lord Melbourne in favour of Sir Robert Peel, the King ceased to interfere to any extent in politics.

"I shall now, please God," he said, "rest on my oars."

The process was not particularly restful to anyone in the royal household, for it developed into a succession of violent quarrels with the Duchess of Kent. Taylor, as a dutiful husband, kept his wife in touch with affairs. Writing from St. James's Palace in December 1835, he says :

"Affairs have been rather uncomfortable here of late. The K., I can see, is not himself and the cause is his irritation at the behaviour of 'that woman at Kensington Palace,' as he calls her ; the root of the trouble is, I believe, that she keeps Princess Victoria from appearing at his drawing-rooms ; he is, as I have told you, very touchy where his dignity is concerned."

Writing a little later in May, he says :

"Ann and Harriet will have told you that they arrived safely at the Mintos. Wonders will never cease. On the 17th there was a Royal night at the opera house ; the opera was 'Lucrezia Borgia.' Those invited were the Duchess of Kent and the young Princess (*entre nous*, the K. did this to assert his authority) and the Mintos with Ann and Harriet, and Ann's beau, Walter Carew, in train. He is very well as a country gentleman, but is to my mind something of an oaf, and I should have thought Ann could have done better for herself. The K. and Q. and her sister, the Duchess of Saxe Weimar, were in the Royal Box with Lord Wiltshire and myself in attendance. The Duchess of Kent and the Princess were in a box opposite. The K., when he saw them, said in a loud voice, 'Begad, one more for the muster book,' then, having got this off his chest, which no one understood, least of all the Duchess of Kent, he settled himself down and slept through the whole performance."

As 1836 wore on the King appeared to be slowly but surely going downhill, both mentally and physically—or so it seemed to Taylor who was in constant attendance on him.

" The King in a very tiresome humour to-day," he notes in his journal of 15th May, " his liver torpid despite a large dose of calomel and his brain still more so. He slept most of the day ; when he did wake, was very fretful and kept harking back to the abandonment of criminal proceedings against the Duke of Cumberland and the Orangemen. ' By God,' he said to no one in particular, ' I would like to see Ernest axed and the rest hung and quartered.' Then he would come back to the Duchess of Kent and ' her devilish goings-on ' ; it all becomes very wearisome and I doubt much how it will end."

With the approach of summer, the King seemed to improve in health, and in August prorogued Parliament in person for the autumn recess. The birthdays of the King and Queen fell within a few days of each other and a banquet had been arranged at Windsor to celebrate the joint events on 21st August. It was one of the last occasions on which Taylor was in attendance on the King and he says : " It was a mighty harassing affair." The King could hardly do less than invite the heiress to the throne, who was of course accompanied by her Mother. Taylor, describing what happened, writes :

" When the K. came into dinner, I saw that he was vexed about something ; his face was very red and there was a pulsing movement in his temple which was a sure danger-signal. There were about a hundred guests to dinner and the Duchess of Kent sat on the right of the K. When dinner was over and after his health was drunk, the King stood up to reply. The lacqueys had fortunately left the room and I wish now that I had followed suit, for the scene affected me very painfully. Whether the Duchess of Kent knew what was coming, I know not ; at all events the K. launched a shattering broadside against her in which his pent-up feelings of months exploded. He rated her as he would have any scullion for her studied disrespect to him in keeping the young Princess away from Court. 'I'd have you know, Madam,' he ended up, 'that I am the King and also the Uncle of the Princess, and that I intend to have my orders obeyed ; you will please to see that the Princess attends my Court in the future.' I could not but feel sorry for the Duchess, though no doubt she has been to blame, but methinks the K. should have behaved more gently to a woman in public. The whole company was aghast and there was a horrible silence. The Duchess became very white, the Q. pink, and the King redder than ever. The young Princess sought refuge in tears. The Duchess left next day in high dudgeon and returned with the Princess to Kensington."

In February 1837, Taylor had a letter from Lord Hill, telling him he had been gazetted to the colonelcy of the 17th Lancers and at the same time offering him, subject to the King's approval, the appointment of Lieut.-Governor of the Royal Military College at Sandhurst. The King, who was not at all anxious to lose his Groom of the Bedchamber, was however averse to placing any obstacle in the way of his promotion. "I have given my consent for your appointment to Lord Hill," he said and, perhaps realizing that his sands were running out, added with a touch of pathos combined with humour : "Maybe you will be of more service to a Queen as a soldier than as a Groom of the Bedchamber."

Part Two

THE BARONET

Chapter Six

CORONATION MAD

COLONEL TAYLOR, in his light-hearted chatter to his wife, had described Sir Walter Carew as being very well as a country gentleman but something of an oaf. He had no doubt overlooked the fact that Sir Walter was one of the largest landowners in Devonshire and, apart from well-chosen and safe investments, derived a net income from his property not far short of £30,000 a year. His daughter Ann at all events, who was a quick-witted young lady and had been brought up in the hard school of comparative poverty, was not slow to perceive that her suitor had certain definite advantages to recommend him. She had known Sir Walter off and on for several years, but had finally become engaged to him at a croquet match at Denbury Manor in 1836. The circumstances leading up to the engagement were curious rather than romantic. Ann was partnering Sir Walter in the game, which he did not understand and which quite frankly bored him to distraction. One of their opponents, a flighty young woman, apparently with more muscle than sense, let fly with a mighty smite and the ball caught Sir Walter in his midriff, knocking the wind clean out of him. He lay on the ground and Ann, with great presence of mind, ran indoors and fetched a glass of brandy, which Sir Walter gulped down with relish. Sir Walter, who had always been very much taken up with Ann's looks, is said to have observed : " Beauty combined with usefulness, what more could a man want ? " The courtship was settled as easily as that.

The wedding took place at Ogwell in January 1837 and was the social event of the year in county circles. Many notabilities attended, including Colonel Taylor's old friends, Lord Palmerston, the Foreign Secretary, the Commander-in-Chief, Lord Hill, and Sir Herbert Taylor who, in his capacity as Private Secretary to the King, presented to the bride on behalf of His Majesty a superb rose emblem set in emeralds, with a card bearing the inscription : "To the Rose of Devon. William R." It will be recollected that the Rose and Lily of Devon had been presented to the Sailor-King at Ascot in 1832 and had found favour in his eyes. Colonel Taylor was shortly to dispose of Ann's sister Harriet to another wealthy suitor, Mr. William Fortescue of Fallapit who, like Sir Walter, kept his own pack of hounds and was a prosperous country gentleman. On thinking things over, he probably decided that he might have done worse.

In the first flush of marriage the gratification of having gained the two most beautiful brides of the year proved to be all-sufficing for Sir Walter Carew and Mr. Fortescue, who were both assiduous in dancing attendance on their wives. In the late autumn of 1837, however, the hunting season was in full swing and the two bridegrooms as masters of hounds had extraneous interests with which to occupy themselves.

It was Harriet Fortescue who, being completely uninterested in hunting or sporting topics, proposed herself to stay with her sister, and her husband had thankfully agreed. The chattering of the girls on one theme—the Coronation to be held the following June—drove Sir Walter crazy, especially after a day's hunting when he wished to relax, fortified by a succession of hot toddies of which Archman, the butler, had brought the mixing to a fine art.

The situation was relieved to some extent by the appearance of Fitzwilliam Taylor, the brother of the two girls, who had just completed his time at Christ Church, Oxford. Sir Walter, who was inclined at first to think him something of a nincompoop as he did not care about hunting or shooting, considered that at all events he would act as a buffer between himself and the girls.

SIR WALTER CAREW, BARONET

Fitzwilliam Taylor was destined for the Church and Sir Walter had promised his father that he should be presented with the coveted living of Haccombe which carried with it the title of Archpriest and the not inconsiderable stipend of £1,500 a year, and whose incumbent was responsible only to the Archbishop of Canterbury, by-passing all intermediary Church dignitaries.

The experiment from Sir Walter's point of view worked exceedingly well and although Fitzwilliam was younger than his sisters they had a great deal in common. He had a fund of small talk and related how he had been summoned before the Duke of Wellington, the Chancellor of the University. The Duke, whose opinion on Catholicism was well known, had heard from Colonel Taylor that his son was in all probability going to become an Archpriest, and being suspicious of anything relating to the Roman priesthood asked Fitzwilliam what kind of Archpopery that might be. This amused the girls intensely and Fitzwilliam continued the story. He told the Duke that so far from being anything to do with Popery, the title of Archpriest at Haccombe was an honourable and ancient order of the Church of England. The Duke was still curious and asked Fitzwilliam what the job was worth to him. When Fitzwilliam told him, the Duke, with his well-known disposition to economy, was astounded and said that he must get Lord Melbourne to look into it. Fitzwilliam told the girls that he very much hoped the Duke would forget all about it as Sir Walter would be very much put out and so incidentally would he himself.

The next day at dinner, fortified by the presence of her brother, Ann tackled her husband on the subject of attending the Coronation, a subject she well knew was taboo. She asked Sir Walter if he had forgotten the portrait of herself and Harriet which was painted by Mr. Hayter, who had related that when he showed the portrait to the Queen she had expressed a hope that she would see " those young ladies at Court." Ann then asked Sir Walter if he did not think it would be appropriate if he conducted them there.

Sir Walter was not impressed by this suggestion and put forward a counter-proposal, which was in fact an order and intended to be taken as such. He proposed that Fitzwilliam and his sisters should go to their father who, he said, was accustomed to Queens and Courts and would possibly have patience with them, which he certainly had not. He ended up by saying sarcastically that perhaps their father would make the two girls maids of the bedchamber.

General Taylor, as he had now become, was at this time Lieut.-Governor of Sandhurst and was fully occupied with the two hundred or so gentlemen-cadets under his charge ; he therefore looked on Sir Walter's proposal with mixed feelings. He had a family of nine, and since he had disposed of two daughters to the best possible advantage, he felt that he was hardly getting a square deal. What were husbands intended for but to look after their wives ? Two idle good-for-nothings, he thought, with too much money and too little sense. Mrs. Taylor, who had less to occupy her mind, was pleased at the prospect of seeing her children again. Sir Walter Carew, with an eye to expense, had suggested that the party should travel to London by accommodation coach, and post on to Sandhurst from there. Lady Carew, however, firmly put her foot down and insisted that they should post the whole way. Fitzwilliam backed her up, saying that " they would smell of the coach for a week afterwards." After much demur Sir Walter, seeing that he was in a minority, gave way ; and the party, consisting of Fitzwilliam Taylor, the two girls and Lady Carew's maid, Ellen, left Haccombe in a postchaise on March the 15th. Fitzwilliam was inclined to be of an indolent disposition and it suited him very well to loll in a chaise with his good-looking sisters. He wished, however, when they stopped for refreshments that more of them was visible to the public eye ; the shapeless garments of 1838, shrouded in shawls and surmounted with poke bonnets and lace veils to protect the complexion, precluded the exhibition of their charms. However, they could not but help raise their veils when they stopped at the George Inn at Amesbury for dinner, and Fitzwilliam was pleased to see glances of admiration for his sisters from other occupants of the coffee room. Ellen, of course, had perforce to travel inside the chaise, but she could not be permitted to eat with the quality and she and the post-boy were having their dinner somewhere in the back regions.

The only unpleasant incident of the journey occurred on the last stage when they were crossing the Harford Bridge flats. Dusk had just fallen and the horses had slowed up while climbing a slight incline. The inmates of the chaise were all apparently dozing, or in a state of suspended animation, for they were completely taken unawares. Fitzwilliam Taylor, describing the occurrence, writes :

" I was in a comfortable doze when I was awakened by a tapping at the window. I lowered it to find the post-boy outside, who said two gentlemen wished to speak with me. Footpads, I thought, and fumbled on the seat for the horse-pistol Walter had given to me. I found it and pointed it through the window, when the infernal thing went off. Ann and Harriet who had woken up were quite calm, but Ellen let out a squawk like a frightened hen. I jumped out of the chaise and heard the sound of horses galloping away. Our horses were unhitched and were grazing by the side of the road. I saw the post-boy come slinking back, who gasped out. ' They was highwaymen, your honour, but they've runned now.' ' Get your horses in, you miserable craven,' I said, ' or this pistol may go off again.' I felt wondrous brave as I climbed back into the chaise, and the girls looked on me as a hero. I kept the pistol ready for the rest of the way, though I was very uncertain as to how the thing worked."

There was considerable excitement in the withdrawing room of the Lieut.-Governor's house when Fitzwilliam followed the girls in still holding the horse-pistol. General Taylor was extremely annoyed at the unceremonious entry and, asking Fitzwilliam what he meant by playing the highwayman, ordered him to explain himself and to hand over "that blunderbus." Ann Carew repeated the whole story and described how Fitzwilliam had risen to the occasion, scaring the would-be thieves away by the pistol-shot. The General calmed down after hearing this explanation and complimented Fitzwilliam on his presence of mind ; he thought it a pity, however, that Walter Carew had not the sense to teach him how to handle a pistol. Lord Hill, who was staying there, was much amused and thought that Fitzwilliam had missed his vocation by not becoming a soldier.

Lord Hill was combining business with pleasure. He was a very old friend of General Taylor and it was he who had nominated the latter as Lieut.-Governor of Sandhurst. He had come down ostensibly to inspect the gentlemen-cadets on the passing-out parade which was to take place on 30th March. He thought it quite unnecessary however for the Secretary-at-War to be present, which Lord Howick had announced his intention of doing. He complained to the General that politicians drove him mad and grumbled that they seemed incapable of leaving soldiers to do their job. General Taylor cordially agreed but thought it politic not to air his opinions on the matter even to "Daddy Hill."

There was a large and fashionable gathering for the parade on 30th March. The Marquis of Anglesey was there to see how his son, Lord George Paget, the senior gentleman-cadet, comported himself. Lord and Lady Palmerston, the Home Secretary and Lady John Russell, and finally "the richest woman in all England," Angela Burdett-Coutts, with her father, Sir Francis Burdett, were also of the party. The gentlemen-cadets made a brave showing in their scarlet tunics and high leather stocks, and marched past to the tune "Heart of Oak." Ann Carew and her sister had a private wager as to who was the best-looking cadet, which was a strange pastime for newly-married wives, but as Ann said, "Like as not Walter and William are choosing the best-looking hound." Ann's choice fell on Lord George Paget, but Harriet preferred Lewis Nolan as her beau-ideal of a dashing soldier. Lord Howick, as Secretary-at-War, took the salute and afterwards voiced the usual platitudes in a speech to the cadets which Ann said reminded her of a dissenting minister. The party later adjourned for dinner to a large marquee, overlooking the lake. The entertainment lasted for three hours ; it was apparently a painful proceeding for Ann Carew, for she writes : " I was seized of a troublesome colic, due to the richness and quantity of the viands ; the ladies could not retire so we perforce had to stay and watch some of the gentlemen getting rather tipsy, which did not amuse us."

Angela Burdett-Coutts, who was about the same age as Ann and Harriet, had made great friends with them and had asked them to stay with her at her house in Stratton Street for the Coronation festivities. She was a serious-minded young person and was much taken up with good works, but she was able to gratify her charitable tastes for she had inherited a large fortune from her grandfather, Thomas Coutts, together with a share in the banking business in which she took an active interest. She had met most of the leading lights of the day at her father's house in St. James's Street, and was, incidentally, a friend of the Queen. This fact alone was sufficient for Ann and Harriet to accept her invitation gladly. General Taylor, meanwhile, had read the Riot Act to his two sons-in-law and had peremptorily ordered them to come to London and look after their wives. Sir Walter and William Fortescue never put pen to paper unless they could help it. They both, however, had a wholesome respect for the General, and he received an ill-written and worse spelt letter from Sir Walter : " Since you encist," the letter ran, " in carting us from our homes, and since as the *Morning Chronicle* ses you have all gone 'Coronation Mad,' William and self will take the coach to London in June. Tell Ann and Harriet that we will not loge with her monnaid female, but we will put up at the Golden Cross Inn at Chairing Cross." This was the most that could be expected, but having gained his point, the General was content to let the matter rest.

The Quicksilver coach from Exeter to London was due to arrive at Charing Cross at 6 o'clock in the evening of the 10th June. Ann Carew and Harriet Fortescue in summery muslin dresses were seated in Miss Burdett-Coutts's barouche when the coach with a jingling of bits drove up to the Golden Cross Inn. The only outside passengers were Sir Walter Carew and William Fortescue. The two girls each wore their favourite flower in order to make identification easier for their husbands in the crowd. It might have been imagined that after a parting of some months there would have been some semblance of affection on the part of the husbands on meeting their wives. That was not the Carew or Fortescue way. Sir Walter and William Fortescue spotted the rose and the lily when they descended from the coach and they each grunted "Hullo!" They then returned to abusing the guard who was struggling with their baggage.

The two gentlemen were obviously tired after the dusty journey and thoroughly disgruntled at being forced to come to London; having finished with the guard, they proceeded to vent their spleen on each other. Ann Carew, seeing that no sense could be got out of them, suggested to Harriet that they should leave them to quench their thirst and recover their tempers as Angela Burdett-Coutts would be waiting for them.

On 12th June William Fortescue was detailed by Sir Walter to "keep the girls quiet" and called for them in Stratton Street to take them to the Zoological Gardens in Regent's Park. Sir Walter had other fish to fry; he saw an opportunity of having a go at Dr. Phillpotts, the Bishop of Exeter, with whom he had several scores to pay off, and he attended the Archbishop of Canterbury's public dinner at Lambeth Palace. The host, Dr. Howley, was a very meek and quiet man, not dignified but very civil and attentive. At the end of dinner, as was his custom, he invited observations from diocesan representatives. Sir Walter, as patron of a peculiar living, was on his feet in a moment. Pointing to Dr. Phillpotts, he requested the Archbishop to order the Bishop of Exeter to keep his Rural Deans in order and to forbid them to trespass on his preserves. He ended up by informing Dr. Howley that on several occasions he had had to see them off the premises.

There was an uneasy silence, Dr. Phillpotts looking down his nose and the Archbishop peering mildly through his spectacles in perplexity. Dr. Howley finally consulted his chaplain-in-ordinary and suggested that " the worthy Baronet would indite a letter setting forth his complaint." Sir Walter, having voiced his complaint in public thereby making Dr. Phillpotts decidedly uncomfortable, had no intention of pursuing the matter further.

Sir Walter and Mr. Fortescue made the occasion of Ascot races an opportunity for doing their duty to their wives and for the four days of the races, in which they themselves were interested, behaved punctiliously. Miss Burdett-Coutts had offered the girls the use of the barouche, but Sir Walter would have none of it. He chartered a coach and four which he drove himself. He bundled the girls inside on the pretence that their " racing finery would be flummoxed a' top the coach," but in reality to carry on a lively conversation with the Rev. John Russell, a sporting crony from North Devon, whom he had persuaded to join the party. Ann Carew notes in her diary :

" *16th June*. A great concourse of people to-day. The Queen, attended by the Duchess of Sutherland and Lady Lansdowne, was only received tolerably well ; some shouting, not a great deal, and few of the gentlemen took off their hats. This mark of respect seems to have gone quite out of use, and neither her station nor her sex procures it. All the world went on to the Royal Stand. There we met Lord Palmerston who introduced us to Lord Melbourne, who seemed never to leave the Queen's side. We were presented quite informally to the Queen by Lord Melbourne, and she remembered Harriet and myself from Mr. Hayter's portrait. She was most gracious and we felt very pleased with ourselves. The gentlemen would not come on to the Royal Stand, but went instead to the Jockey Club where they found a common sort of man to make bets with. I was very surprised at Mr. Russell doing this as he is a clergyman. Harriet and I went back inside the coach as usual. When we got back Angela met us with the most wonderful news. The Duke of Wellington has asked her to join his party and to bring ' the two young ladies staying with you ' to go to the Queen's Ball at Buckingham Palace on 18th June (Waterloo Day). He told her that he was afraid the French coming for the Coronation might be offended at the ball being held on that day, but that was none of his business, it was accidental anyway and not meant as a celebration. Harriet and I will be very busy to-morrow and next day getting our dresses ready."

Sir Walter and Mr. Fortescue held as it were a watching brief for their wives, which was a convenient method of letting them go their own way. On the day of the ball they decided that as the girls were well catered for, they would enjoy a whitebait dinner at Greenwich. They accordingly embarked on Mr. Wimhurst's new screw steamer *Archimedes* which was making a trial run. The trial was not very satisfactory, as when the *Archimedes* was getting up steam to leave the Greenwich pier, the boiler blew up, and whilst the girls were whirling round the ballroom, Sir Walter and Mr. Fortescue spent an uncomfortable night in a riverside inn at Greenwich.

The ball, which was more or less an informal affair, and was a prelude to the more serious Coronation celebrations, was thoroughly enjoyed by Ann Carew and her sister; Ann gives a detailed account of it in her diary :

" We arrived at the Palace about 10 o'clock, and had to submit to being stared at by the crowd, some of whom pressed their faces against the windows of the carriage. At last the Peelers cleared a way for us and we entered the Palace. In the vestibules we came across the Duke and Lord Anglesey, with several old red-faced men who, we were told, had been to the Waterloo dinner. I remembered the Duke in 1832, and noticed how old he had got. He is no longer so straight and upright. The Queen looked very happy and amiable ; I only saw her dance with

Lord Fitzalan. Before supper she sat on a sofa in the with-drawing room looking at the waltzing. Her mother sat on one side of her and the Princess Augusta on the other. I danced twice with Lord Melgund, and once with Louis Napoleon (a nephew of the great Napoleon) who has just arrived in England. Harriet danced a good deal and was introduced to a funny Jewish looking man, a Mr. Disraeli, who is member for Maid-stone. Angela knows everybody, but she was so busy talking that she did not dance. Mr. Strauss and his musicians played divinely ; we got home at 3 o'clock tired out but very happy."

The next day General Taylor arrived in London ; he had been invited by the Duke of Wellington, as an old Waterloo officer, to join his party in welcoming Marshal Soult who was due to arrive in London on 20th June as Ambassador Extraordinary of the King of the French. This fitted in very well with the General's own plans as from reports received he was not satisfied at the way in which his two sons-in-law were performing their duties, and wanted to keep an eye on them. He was furious when he heard of their escapade in Greenwich and still more so when on calling at the Golden Cross Inn a day or two later he found that they had gone to a cock-fight in the cock-pit in St. James's Park.

"Cannot you," he wrote to Sir Walter, " have some notion of the proprieties ? It would be well if you left your sporting instincts in Devonshire and attended to the girls. I am putting up at the Hanover Square Hotel and invite you to join me."

This curt epistle apparently had the desired effect and brought the recalcitrants to heel, for Ann Carew writes : " Papa has had a wonderful effect on Walter and William ; they have been very attentive to us since he has been in London."

Fitzwilliam Taylor, who had been attending Dr. Hampden's Hampton lectures as a short cut to entering Holy Orders, joined the party at the Hanover Square Hotel on 26th June, for the Coronation. He took over the role of diarist for the Coronation from Ann Carew, as being the last from school, and his account makes interesting reading.

" *27th June, 1838.* The state of the town has to be seen to be believed. The crowd, and the noise, are indescribable. The park is one large encampment with flags floating from the tops of tents. Horsemen and carriages jammed ; the pavements choked with timbers ; a continual hammering and falling pieces of timber threatening the head. A thronging mob of people, gaping at everything and nothing. From the top of Piccadilly to Westminster Abbey there is a never-ending line of scaffolding. Five hundred thousand people are believed to have flocked into London, and Miss Burdett-Coutts said that she had heard from Mr. Spring-Rice that £200,000 had been paid for seats alone. Walter and William bear up pretty well, but Walter says he will be thankful when all the nonsense is over. Incidentally it was very nearly over with Walter this morning. We were walking down Piccadilly when someone up above shouted, ' Look up, guvnor.' Walter looked up and at that moment a hod of bricks hurtled down, and the draught took off his silk hat, just missing his head. Walter was not hurt but he was vastly angry and scattered the crowd by his explosive tongue."

There was no balloting for seats even for commoners in 1838, providing there was sufficient influence at work, and this was provided by Miss Burdett-Coutts who was acquainted with all the notabilities of the day. Those fortunate enough to be attached to her party had no difficulty in finding accommodation in Westminster Abbey. Fitzwilliam Taylor takes up his pen again :

" *28th June.* The day was most beautiful and the crowds which thronged the streets were on the whole well behaved. The inside of the Abbey looked very fine and the Peeresses, who were blazing with diamonds, added to the beauty of the scene."

We were on good terms with France, and the diarist continues :

" There was quite a sensation when Marshal Soult entered the Abbey and our old enemy was treated with great deference.

Soon after twelve o'clock the procession began to enter the choir : the Queen looked a tiny little figure, but held herself with great dignity. When the crown was placed on her head, the dukes and other peers did their homage. A shiver went through us as old Lord Rolle, who comes from Devon and whom we knew well, stumbled and fell on the steps. The Queen at once stepped forward and held out her hand to help him ; this gracious act made a great sensation. We heard she sent in the evening to enquire after him. It seemed to me that there was a good deal of fumbling, particularly by the Archbishop who did not seem to know his part. He put her ring on the wrong finger, and it had to be forced on which must have hurt her a good deal. Dr. Blomfield, the Bishop of London, preached a good sermon though he talked too long, and Walter went to sleep. He was woken up by the noise when the Treasurer of the Household, Lord Surrey, threw about medals which were scrambled for by everyone, including the Maids of Honour. At half past four in the afternoon, the Queen, wearing her crown, entered her carriage and was driven away midst the cheers of the crowd."

There was a great display of fireworks in the evening in the Green Park which the Queen watched from the roof of the palace. The Duke of Wellington gave a banquet at Apsley House to which General Taylor went, and taking advantage of his absence, Sir Walter and William Fortescue, who were bored by the day's proceedings, left the girls in the charge of Fitzwilliam Taylor and retired to the Hanover Square Hotel where, as Sir Walter put it, " there is a tolerable cellar and a plausible rogue who ministered to our needs." Ann Carew and Harriet Fortescue expressed themselves as extremely satisfied with their trip to London. Lord Palmerston, who considered that a visit to his constituency was long overdue, and was posting down, had offered to take the girls and their husbands. Sir Walter and William Fortescue, however, preferring the open air and their own company, decided to take the mail coach to Exeter.

Chapter Seven

JOURNEY TO RIVIERA

IN November 1838 General Taylor, who had accumulated
over six months' leave, was staying at Haccombe with Sir
Walter and Lady Carew. Sir Walter, having survived the
boredom of the Coronation, and having got through the summer
" one way and another," was in his element again. He usually
hunted three days a week and shot two ; it was no inconvenience
to him to return home soaked to the skin each evening. It was
an exceptionally wet month with unceasing rain and General
Taylor and his daughter, who were of a less amphibious nature,
were left a good deal to their own resources. On 6th November Sir Walter had left early to go to a distant meet and General
Taylor and Lady Carew were having breakfast alone. Archman brought in the letters which had just arrived, handing one
to the General which he noticed was franked by Sir Herbert
Taylor and bore a postal mark of the Papal States. It was Sir
Herbert Taylor, who had been Military Secretary to the Duke
of York and afterwards Private Secretary to William IV, who
had appeared at Sir Walter's wedding as an emissary from his
Sovereign with a royal gift for Lady Carew. The General
knew that Sir Herbert Taylor had had a trying time during the
illness of King William IV and that after the King's death, as
executor of his will, he had found his time to be fully occupied.
On her accession, Queen Victoria had begged him to retain the
appointment of First and Principal A.D.C. to the Sovereign, but
as neither his own nor Lady Taylor's health was good, he had

received the Queen's permission to recuperate abroad. The General could not imagine what the letter could be about and opened it with some trepidation, thinking his old friend might be worse. He was agreeably surprised to find that it contained an invitation to visit them at the furnished house they had taken in Cannes. The letter of invitation written in Rome was most cordial.

"We have found," Sir Herbert wrote, "a most exquisite little spot on the shores of the Mediterranean Sea, bathed in sunshine, strongly recommended to me by Lord Brougham three years ago. His Lordship, as you know, is apt to be fanciful in his likes and dislikes, and on the fall of the Melbourne Ministry in 1834, he formed an increasing dislike of his colleagues, which I must say was by no means all on his side, and he decided to seek more congenial company abroad. At any rate when he lighted on Cannes in 1835, he was enchanted with the place and its climate. Now I want to ask you to come and pay us a visit, and I only hope that I shall be well enough to return to Cannes shortly as I have again taken the furnished house which I had last winter when my daughter ' Chaddy ' laid the foundation stone of what I hope is to be our future home. Chaddy and her aunt are now at Cannes and will welcome you and Sir Walter Carew and his amiable lady ; it will be fitting for ' the rose of Devon ' to blossom in that sunny clime. I count on your acceptance and D.V. shall hope to see you there, so pray do not delay your departure. You will, of course, engage a courier who is master of the French language ; he will arrange for your carriage and relays of horses on your arrival in France and will decide on the best route. Sir Walter Carew being a judge of horse-flesh will probably not approve of the French animals which are ill-favoured beasts enough, but usually manage to do what is required of them."

Lady Carew was enchanted with the idea but was very doubtful as to Sir Walter's reaction on the subject. The General made light of any objections Sir Walter might make. He reminded her that she had got her way over the Coronation and there was no reason why she should not do so again, more especially as he was there to support her.

Sir Walter Carew, in whom the insular country gentleman's aversion to foreigners and their ways was developed to quite a remarkable degree and who regarded even a journey from Devon to Bath (especially in the hunting season) as an expedition not to be lightly undertaken, at first threw cold water on the scheme, as was to be expected. Lady Carew, fortified by the presence of her father, was insistent and artfully reminded her husband that they had as yet had no honeymoon. Supported whole-heartedly by her father, Lady Carew at length overcame Sir Walter's objections.

General Taylor was fortunate in securing the services of a young Frenchman, the Vicomte de Chesnay, who had lately completed a year's training as a gentleman-cadet at Sandhurst and was delighted to conduct the Lieut.-Governor and his party to the South of France, his own home being near Grasse. Henry, the third footman, who was to act as valet to Sir Walter, and Lady Carew's maid, Ellen, a very attractive Devonshire girl, completed the party. Sir Walter, once his mind was made up to the inevitable, had visions of driving through France in his own carriage, taking the reins himself when the fancy seized him. He was, however, speedily disillusioned by Monsieur de Chesnay, who said he was quite unable to undertake the supervision of an English coachman or even Sir Walter himself, driving on the French roads.

Sir Walter blustered a good deal, but finally gave in, and on arrival at Newhaven the Haccombe carriage and coachmen were sent back to Devonshire.

The party reached Dieppe on 15th November, where an untoward incident occurred in connection with the customs examination. Sir Walter, who looked on luggage as impedimenta to be dealt with by his valet, was walking on ahead with Lady Carew when he found his way blocked by a barrier in charge of a diminutive douanier who ordered him to halt. Sir

Walter, who spoke no language but his own and prided himself on the fact, presumably did not understand the order. He was unaccustomed to opposition from subordinates, least of all from an insignificant "frog-eater." Perhaps unaware of his strength —he was a man of vast bulk—he swept the protesting official off his legs and, followed by Lady Carew, passed through the barrier. Confusion became worse confounded. In a moment Sir Walter and Lady Carew were surrounded by a swarm of gendarmes, like bees from a hive, and street urchins shouting delightedly, "A bas les Anglais."

The situation was only restored by a distribution of largesse among the gendarmes by the Vicomte, and substantial compensation to the douanier whom Sir Walter had manhandled.

The Vicomte had engaged a roomy travelling carriage with a rumble for the servants, and four horses and postillions. The horses were a weedy lot and in Sir Walter's opinion, "only fit for the knacker's yard." But they made a better show when harnessed up to the carriage, and with a prodigious cracking of whips by the postillions, the party left the Relais du Grand Cerf in great style on the first stage of their journey. General Taylor was anxious to travel by way of Paris, for he wished to obtain an audience of the King, Louis Philippe, whom he had met several times in England when he was living at Twickenham, and to whom he had a recommendation from Lord Palmerston. Since, however, they were pressed for time, Monsieur de Chesnay had drawn up an itinerary which followed the direct road to the south through Chartres, Lyons and Avignon. To Sir Walter the route was quite immaterial provided that, as he impressed on the Vicomte, he could find "decent inns with food which would not poison an Englishman's stomach."

The weather, as far as Orleans, was reasonably fine, but after they left that place, where Lady Carew with Ellen in attendance spent a day seeing the sights, including a visit to the house of the Maid of Orleans, it rained continuously for several days. Lady Carew, ahead of her time in her solicitude for servants, particularly of her own sex, asked Sir Walter if Ellen might be allowed to travel inside the carriage until the weather moderated. Sir Walter, who regarded the position of servants from a different angle, was not in favour of the suggestion. General Taylor supported his daughter and Monsieur de Chesnay, who was young and ardent and not at all averse to the companionship of another pretty girl in the close confines of a carriage, agreed with his former chief. Sir Walter, finding the odds against him, grumpily consented, but succeeded in making everyone else uncomfortable. Like the Facey Romford of a later day, he abhorred the impurities of a " shut cab " which, he said, " was well enough for females." He was in no mind to breathe the atmosphere further contaminated by the presence of a servant, and since Lady Carew insisted on both windows being closed, he determined to travel outside. Much to the chagrin of the Vicomte he arranged that that young gentleman should ride in the rumble with Henry, whilst he and the General took their places on the coachman's seat from which they " could keep an eye on the post-boys."

Sir Walter, essentially a man of action, would have much preferred to dispense with the postillions and drive the four-in-hand himself. This, according to the Vicomte, being out of the question, he had to content himself with his fowling piece, an intricate contraption worked by percussion caps. With this weapon he took pot-shots at the red-legged partridges which were occasionally to be seen along the road. The noise upset the horses, provoked irascible ejaculations from the postillions and muffled screams from the women inside the carriage. Henry, seated in the rumble, held Sir Walter's second gun, and presented the appearance of a guard on a stage coach. The general aspect of the equipage must have been curious to the passers-by.

On arrival at Avignon Monsieur de Chesnay, as a good Catholic, recommended a visit to the Palais des Papes. Lady Carew and General Taylor, who were staunch Protestants but took an interest in historical buildings, accompanied him there.

Sir Walter declined, saying that he " had no liking for palaces, least of all Papist ones," a remark scarcely complimentary to the Vicomte. The party eventually arrived at Brignolles, and put up for the night at a wretched hostelry, the Auberge de Provence. Here General Taylor, to his surprise, came upon an old acquaintance in the person of George Fitzclarence, Earl of Munster, who, finding himself at a loose end, had taken up the study of history. He was, he said, collecting material for an account of Napoleon's operations from the time he escaped from Elba and landed in the Gulf of Juan until his final debacle at Waterloo. The Earl, who had mellowed considerably with the passage of years, was delighted to meet the General again and was very interested to hear of his visit to Sir Herbert Taylor.

" That is the man," he said, " who holds my destiny in his hands, since he is the executor of my father's will. Can you find out how I stand ? "

General Taylor replied, " My dear fellow, I am vastly sorry but I cannot interfere in so delicate a matter."

That evening Lord Munster dined with Sir Walter and his party and made himself extremely agreeable to Lady Carew, reminding her of their meeting at Ascot in 1832. Sir Walter, who hated any encroachment on his private preserves and did not approve of the Earl's attention to his wife, afterwards hinted to his father-in-law that the son of a " besmirched play-actress " was not a suitable companion for a young girl. The General, who hated to hear any disparagement of his late master, said huffily : that he would have Sir Walter remember that Lord Munster was also the son of a former sovereign and should be treated as such. Sir Walter, who usually had the last word, retorted a little irrelevantly that a good penny was better than a bad sovereign and he added that a good dinner would be far preferable to the wretched fare the innkeeper had seen fit to throw at them.

From Brignolles the party drove by easy stages to Fréjus, thence over the Esterel mountains to Napoule, and so on to

Cannes, arriving there on 10th December. A slight contretemps occurred at the gendarmerie post of Chateau d'Esterel, where Sir Walter, presumably mistaking a red-trousered gendarme in the bush for a red-legged partridge, let fly with his fowling piece and sprayed the shrub with bullets. Fortunately the gendarme escaped unscathed, but the main guard turned out with muskets at the present and halted the equipage. Sir Walter, as usual, considered himself to be the aggrieved party, and rated the brigadier of gendarmes as though he were one of his footmen. This tirade was luckily quite incomprehensible to the brigadier, and after copious apologies and substantial reparation from Monsieur de Chesnay, the party was allowed to proceed. Lady Carew, who was very much alarmed, lowered a window and begged her husband to come inside out of harm's way. Sir Walter, in deference to his wife's request, went to the door of the carriage, but finding it quite impossible to bear the hot-house atmosphere inside, returned to the purer air on the box-seat.

The Vicomte hopefully asked Sir Walter if he might be allowed to travel inside, as after the recent encounter with the gendarmes, he thought he could be of some comfort to " the females." Sir Walter very quickly put the Vicomte in his place by telling him curtly that he had been brought not to comfort females but to guide the party on the way. After this episode, the travellers proceeded without further incident to their destination.

Chapter Eight

_____

CONTINENTAL HONEYMOON

THE Villa Desmarêts which Sir Herbert Taylor had rented was situated on rising ground facing the sea a short distance from Cannes, off the road to Antibes. The travellers were greeted by Sir Herbert's daughter, Chaddy, and by her aunt, Miss Disbrowe, with the sad news that Sir Herbert was seriously ill in Rome and that neither he nor Lady Taylor would be able to come to Cannes. This was a great blow to General Taylor, who had looked forward, while the young couple made their own amusements, to a quiet and restful time with Sir Herbert, whom he had not seen for any length of time since leaving the Court of William IV. The French servants, to make up for the absence of Sir Herbert and Lady Taylor, had, on their own initiative, paid a pretty compliment to Lady Carew by erecting an arch of artificial roses on which was inscribed : "Bon accueil à la Rose Anglaise." Monsieur de Chesnay was charmed by this graceful homage and translated the wording to Sir Walter, who ungraciously described it as "damned French flummery." Sir Walter had become a little weary of what he was pleased to call "the airs and graces and the making sheep's eyes at females whether mistress or maid," on the part of the Vicomte, and was not sorry to see the last of him when he left for his home near Grasse, his mission completed.

Miss Disbrowe and Chaddy proved to be charming hostesses and did everything possible to make up for the absence of Sir

Herbert and Lady Taylor. Lady Carew revelled in the warmth and sunshine of Cannes and " could not have believed that such weather was possible in mid-winter." She and Chaddy became great friends.

"Chaddy," she writes, "persuaded me to go driving with her in an open carriage, which I had never done before at this time of year."

The novelty of driving with Chaddy as a companion along the Route Royale seems to have adequately compensated Lady Carew, who was a person of simple tastes, for the lack of any other company. There were few shops and fewer people to be seen. Between the Route Royale and the sea lay the dreary waste of marshy land which many years later was to blossom into the glories of the Croisette with its palatial hotels and dazzling shops. Sir Walter Carew, though fond enough of his wife, did not feel himself obliged to conform to the custom of the conventional honeymoon by accompanying her on dreary drives and found his pleasures elsewhere.

" Walter, I am afraid," she rather dolefully records, " does not derive the pleasure that I do in this place, and is always looking for something to shoot or is out with fishermen. Papa is quite happy passing the time with Miss Disbrowe. Sometimes Ellen accompanies me when alone, sitting, of course, with her back to the horses."

It will be noted that, true to the spirit of the age, Ellen was only permitted to share the back seat with her mistress in the privacy of a closed carriage.

Towards the middle of January Chaddy received a bad account of her father, so she and Miss Disbrowe decided that they must go to Rome at once. Sir Walter, who by now was thoroughly bored with his continental holiday, looked on their departure as a heaven-sent opportunity to return home himself. Chaddy and Miss Disbrowe were, however, insistent that their guests should remain at least another month, for the lease of the house did not expire until April. Lady Carew, who was much enjoying her stay in the South of France, gratefully accepted the invitation, and as was usual in her dealings with Sir Walter, had her own way. General Taylor also had a reason for staying on, and Sir Walter, who had a wholesome respect for his father-in-law, did not attempt to cross him. When Lord Brougham ceased to be Chancellor in 1834 and visited Cannes for the first time in the following year the leading inhabitants had requested him to use his supposed influence with the French Government to impress on it the necessity for the construction of a port. Lord Brougham, who had lost what little influence he possessed with his own Government, was presumably flattered by the French request and promised to do his best. At all events he received credit for his efforts ; for shortly afterwards authority for the work was given. For some time past rumours had circulated that King Louis Philippe was to visit Cannes in February for the purpose of inspecting the works, and it was now confirmed that he would do so. General Taylor, who was of an inquisitive turn of mind, had gathered from conversations with various Frenchmen in Cannes that Louis Philippe was unpopular in Paris, but that his stock stood higher in the provinces, perhaps because he was rarely seen there. General Taylor, who was something of a psychologist, was anxious to see how the man who had formerly repudiated his titles and fought as a Colonel of Dragoons in the Revolutionary Army comported himself as King of the French.

The King arrived at Cannes on 19th February and stayed two nights at Pinchinat's Hotel, which Sir Herbert described as " the worst and least accommodating it would be possible to find." It was, however, the only hotel in Cannes and the King had to make the best of it ; it may even have suited his democratic tendencies. General Taylor found that Lord Palmerston's recommendation quickly secured him an audience, and he spent an hour with the King. Louis Philippe was very interested to hear that the General was Lieut.-Governor of Sandhurst and told him that from what he heard, the system of instruction there compared favourably with that of the military college of St. Cyr. The King complained of the class of officer in the French service.

"Our young officers," he said, "are mostly of the bourgeoisie, they have little education, less manners and less esprit de corps. What then can you expect?"

General Taylor thought that this was an odd statement to come from a Citizen King, the "chosen of the people," but he refrained from saying so. He concluded that one of his informants had summed up the position correctly when he told him that Louis Philippe was constantly in the position "de devoir faire bonne mine à mauvais jeu."

Chaddy had recommended that Sir Walter and Lady Carew should pay a visit to the island of Ste. Marguerite, a short distance off Cannes. She had given Lady Carew an introduction to Captain Vidal, the military commandant, and explained that he would show them over the old state prison, which owes its celebrity to the legendary "man in the iron mask." Lady Carew invited Ellen to accompany the party. A fishing smack was chartered and on the voyage over all went well. But on the return journey there was a choppy sea, and it proved too much for Ellen who was violently sea-sick. She received little sympathy from Sir Walter, who considered "that it was only to be expected of a servant when taken out of her proper place." According to his way of thinking such an occurrence could not happen in polite society.

Sir Walter's outlook on Cannes, of which he had hitherto taken a poor view, became more cheerful when, with the assistance of M. de l'Arras, Sir Herbert Taylor's architect, he hired a pair of post-horses and a phaeton together with a man who called himself a "valet d'ecurie." The groom does not, however, appear to have been very proficient. Sir Walter had arranged to drive his wife to the site of Sir Herbert Taylor's house to see how the building was progressing, and had given

orders for the horses to be harnessed. The operation was protracted, and on Sir Walter entering the stable he found the new
groom engaged in putting the cruppers on the heads of the
horses. Sir Walter, who did not suffer fools gladly in the stable,
wasted no words but, as he told his father-in-law afterwards :
" I applied my boot to that part of the groom where the crupper
belongs on a horse and catapulted him out of the door." The
duty of looking after the horses devolved on Henry, the valet,
who thought it a little hard that he should be turned into a
stableman when his time was fully occupied in attendance on
his master.

M. de l'Arras, the architect, who had been recommended to
Sir Herbert Taylor by Lord Brougham, met Sir Walter and
Lady Carew on the site and explained the plans in detail. Sir
Herbert had apparently stipulated that the price of the house
should not exceed £1,600, and since it was of an elaborate
design, this does not seem to have been excessive.

M. de l'Arras was very pleased with himself at having been
selected by two illustrious Englishmen to supervise the erection
of their houses, which would, he said, have the effect of trans-
forming a fishing village into a resort of fashion. He bewailed
the fact, however, that Lord Brougham had not seen fit to
allow him sufficient money to complete the work.

Sir Walter, to whom plans and elevations conveyed less than
nothing, thought the price reasonable enough, but, having large
ideas in conformity with his income, considered the house was
too small for a person of quality. Doubtless he had Haccombe
in mind with its fifty bedrooms. Lady Carew enjoyed her
drives with her husband, and was enabled to practise her gram-
matical schoolroom French on unsuspecting natives. Since they
only spoke the Provençal dialect, however, little progress was
made on either side.

Père Pascal, the Curé, an old man of eighty-four, who had
officiated at Cannes for sixty years and was a friend of Sir Herbert
and Lady Taylor, often paid a visit to the Villa Desmarêts, and

entertained General Taylor with reminiscences of the Napoleonic era. He related how "that double traitor, Murat, formerly King of Naples, escaped to Cannes in 1815, after being defeated by the Austrians. Here he would fraternize with the inhabitants when they assembled in the evening to dance. He would lie on the grass, looking on and smoking and occasionally singing barcarolles." Père Pascal remembered Murat setting out from Cannes to organize an expedition against the reinstated Bourbons with the object of recovering his throne. "He died as he deserved," Père Pascal added, for he was captured in Calabria, tried by court martial, and shot on 13th October 1815.

General Taylor also made the acquaintance of two old French soldiers whom he describes as a couple of fire-eating generals. General Vial, who resided in Antibes, was entertaining as his guest Marshal Clausel, who until 1837 had been Governor-General of Algeria. He and General Vial had held commands under Napoleon in Spain during the Peninsular War and fought their battles over again. Each maintained that the French soldiers of that day were immeasurably superior to their English opponents, but that they suffered from lack of generalship.

"But," General Taylor said, "you had Napoleon, and he was always looked on as a great general."

Marshal Clausel replied : "Perhaps when he fought against small men, but your Lord Wellington with his large nose smelt out all his secrets."

Marshal Clausel told General Taylor that before he relinquished the command in Algeria he had soundly beaten Abd-el-Kader and had entered Mascara in triumph. General Taylor made a note of the details of this guerilla warfare which he thought would be of interest to the gentlemen-cadets under his charge.

It was the report that Lord Brougham intended to make another visit to Cannes in April that decided the Carew party to make tracks for home. It was, in fact, General Taylor, and not Sir Walter, who suggested the move, although the latter was more than ready to fall in with it. The General had suffered from Lord Brougham's vagaries when he was Groom of the Bedchamber to the Sailor-King, whose "liver usually demanded calomel after an interview with the Lord Chancellor." He makes a note in his journal :

"Palmerston writes me that Brougham is making a perfect nuisance of himself, his political conduct is atrocious, he makes every effort to keep in with the Radicals, at the same time courting the Tories, but his sole aim is to make things as difficult as possible for the Government. That is Brougham all over, and if, as Palmerston hopes and prays, he takes himself off to France, which, of course, means Cannes, I have no mind to be drawn into any argument with him which would be unavoidable in the restricted society of this place."

Sir Walter and his party left for England on 20th March. A courier of a different type who would be more at home in the rumble with Henry had been found by M. de l'Arras. Sir Walter, as on the outward journey, insisted that he and General Taylor should travel outside, Lady Carew and Ellen being again left to wallow in the impurities of a closed carriage. Lady Carew was most anxious to visit Paris which, she said, "would make a perfect ending to the honeymoon." Sir Walter, whose only desire was to get home as soon as possible, at first made difficulties, but feeling perhaps that the worst was over and that he might for a change consult his wife's feelings rather than his own, let her have her way. After leaving Moulins, therefore, instead of going by way of Orleans, they followed the road through Nevers and Fontainebleau. This, of course, entailed a visit to the palace and they put up there for the night. Before the start next morning the courier reported that Paris was in a very disturbed state owing to the revolutionary activities of that consistent agitator Louis Auguste Blanqui, which might cause an insurrection. It was decided, therefore, to avoid Paris after all and visit Versailles where Lady Carew revelled in the beauty of the Trianons and Malmaison. From thence they travelled direct to Dieppe, arriving at Newhaven on 15th April, where they found the Haccombe carriage awaiting them.

So ended a " honeymoon " described by Lady Carew as " too heavenly for words," but by Sir Walter as " five months of infernal misery."

Chapter Nine

ATTEMPT ON THE QUEEN

AFTER her return from her continental honeymoon, Lady Carew received a letter from her father (who was always well up in doings of the day) describing a disagreeable court scandal which had occurred in March and which had a most unfortunate effect on the Queen's popularity.

General Taylor wrote :

" You will be sorry to hear that there has been some unpleasantness at court on account of a Lady-in-waiting to the Duchess of Kent, Lady Flora Hastings, whom you met in London and is about your age. She was a nice harmless little creature, but some evil-minded person suggested that she was with child ; the Queen said she must not appear at Court until the imputation was cleared. I believe that useless old humbug, Sir James Clark, insisted on her submitting to a medical examination which completely established her innocence. Her brother, Lord Hastings, very naturally was furious and demanded an audience of the Queen. Such things happen in the servants' hall, but not in good society. I blame Lord Melbourne for having permitted such a story to get about."

Lady Carew, who worshipped the Queen and could believe no ill of her, told the story to Sir Walter, who was singularly unsympathetic. " The Queen'll forget about it sooner than the other woman," he said.

Towards the end of 1838 Lady Carew gave birth to a son who was christened Walter Palk ; Walter, of course, after his father, and Palk after his Grandmother, who, as the only daughter and heiress of the Indian magnate, Robert Palk, had added the valuable property of Marley to the Carew possessions. Sir Walter took the advent of a son and heir as a matter of course, treating him as a puppy from a litter ; he was quite content to leave him in the charge of nurses and hirelings so long as he himself was not incommoded.

In the February of 1840 there was great excitement in the country over the marriage of the Queen, but since Lady Carew was attending to the new infant, she could not go and had to be contented with a letter from her father, who was present.

" The wedding on the 10th went off pretty well. The week before Prince Albert drove about the town with a mob shouting at his heels. On the wedding morning the route along which the royal procession was to pass was lined by Household Cavalry. The coach containing the Queen, the Duchess of Kent and the Mistress of the Robes arrived at St. James's Palace and was conducted by the Lord Chamberlain to the Chapel Royal. At a quarter to one the ring was placed on Her Majesty's finger. The royal couple then drove to Buckingham palace. Upon leaving the Palace for Windsor, she and Prince Albert were pretty well received ; but they went off in a very poor and shabby style. They travelled in one of the old coaches, the postillions in undress liveries, three other coaches with post-horses following."

Sir Walter's comments on hearing the letter read were brief. " Quite good enough for that German feller."

The even round of life went on at Haccombe for the remainder of the winter. Sir Walter was fully occupied with hunting four days a week and shooting the remaining two. The deep sunk valleys and precipitous hills provided some of the best pheasant shooting in the west, but the birds, as Fess, the head-keeper, said, " tuk a terrible lot o' killing." Sir Walter had a keen eye for the larder and market, the use of both tending to reduce running expenses.

This being the case, the indifferent shot was ruled out of any invitation to the big shoots and if any such had to be invited, because they were relatives or for any other reason, they were usually asked at the end of the season when there was very little left to shoot.

Such an occasion arose at the end of February and the first of the guests to arrive was an old Colonel of the Honourable East India Company's service, Colonel Albert Taylor, a cousin of Sir Walter, who saw as little of him as possible. The Colonel arrived in a decrepit station " fly " from Newton Abbot and emerged from it trailing a musket of very obsolete pattern. He was welcomed by Archman, the butler.

" Glad to see you again, Archman," the Colonel said.

" And so be I, sir," Archman replied, but he went on, " 'Tidn't as I may say no surprise, because I 'eard Sir Walter say to her Ladyship, ' I suppose us must ask Orlbert.' "

The next fly passenger required more handling—the Admiral, another cousin, whose bulk was more suited to an Admiral's cabin than a station fly. The red-nosed flyman heaved himself off his box to let his fare out, but he was not quick enough ; the fly shook with an internal convulsion and the window-glass shivered into fragments.

" Drat my whiskers ! " the flyman ejaculated wrathfully, " what a cantankerous old party. Who's to pay for my window ? "

Archman, who had experience of refractory patients in the shape of his master, was equal to the occasion.

" Easy, Admiral, easy, sir," he said, and to the waiting footman, " 'Enry, fetch that there screw-driver what Mr. Barker, the undertaker, left 'ere by mistake, and we'll soon 'ave the Admiral out."

The Admiral was in trouble again next morning at the opening of the shoot when installed on a support at an angle of about sixty degrees on the side of a hill. Archman again came to the rescue and cupping his hands he bellowed to the head-keeper,

" Sir Walter says please to put the Admiral's bath-chair to the bottom of the hill as he's liable to topple over."

The Admiral was duly removed, but the reduced elevation was not productive of any heavier casualties amongst the birds. There was a fine spirit of camaraderie amongst the shooters, beaters and keepers. The Rev. Thomas Carew, who held one of the family livings, did not find it incompatible with his ecclesiastical duties to take part in these friendly shoots. On this occasion he was obviously not up to his usual form and Fess, the head-keeper, rapidly appreciated the situation.

"Damme, Mr. Tom," he shouted, belabouring the ground with his stick, " do 'e go home and write your sermon, then take your gun and shoot they who don't listen to 'e ? "

As the spring weather got milder Lady Carew thought that the baby should be taken for " airings." The " airings " were of doubtful value since she, the baby, and two nurses with a warming-pan, drove in the closed barouche with both windows hermetically sealed. The four of them must have been nearly stifled by the time the drive was over, but they seem to have borne it with impunity. Lady Carew, who was a chilly person, was frightened that young Walter would take cold, and finally ordered a second warming-pan to be installed in the carriage. One day Lady Carew innocently asked her husband if he would accompany herself and the baby in a drive. He almost had an apoplectic fit.

"What," he shouted, " be smothered in a crowd of females and warming-pans ? Give me fresh air, for God's sake."

At the end of May Lady Carew received a letter from her father, asking her to come to Sandhurst for a few days. He was taking a party to the Ascot races, he said, and thought a change would do her good.

"You will, of course, bring your maid," he said in his letter, " and it would be most suitable if you came by the coach which goes from Newton direct to the Golden Cross Inn, where I will meet you with a carriage."

She and her maid, Ellen, went as inside passengers, and arrived, after a hot and uncomfortable journey, at the Golden Cross Inn, where to her delight she found her brother, Fitzwilliam, who had been sent by her father to bring her to Sandhurst. Fitzwilliam was also delighted to see his sister again, and confided to her that their father thought she needed a rest from Sir Walter and that was really the reason why he had not asked her husband too. Fitzwilliam added that he had heard that Sir Walter had been very tiresome of late. Lady Carew, who did not wish to give her husband away even to her brother, replied that he had been much as usual but she did not think he liked driving in a closed carriage with a child and nurses.

The horses in the chaise were rather better than usual for they only took five hours doing the twenty-nine miles to Sandhurst, arriving there at nine o'clock in the evening.

Lady Carew had a pleasant surprise when she learnt that they were to stay with Lord and Lady Palmerston in London for the races which were to take place on 11th June.

On 10th June there was an unpleasant scene when a boy named Oxford, aged about eighteen, fired two shots at the Queen. Lady Carew, her mother and Fitzwilliam were out walking when it happened and Fitzwilliam records in his diary :

" Mama, Ann and I had walked down Piccadilly, when we saw the Queen and Prince Albert driving in a low carriage up Constitution Hill. At about half-past six o'clock I noticed a man standing with his back to the Green Park fence ; he advanced towards the carriage and deliberately fired at the Queen. The postillions were taken aback and stopped. I heard Prince Albert say in a loud voice, ' Drive on.' The man who had fired said, ' I have got another,' and discharged another pistol which also missed its mark. Two peelers laid hold of the man and took him off to the police-house. The Queen was perfectly cool and not in the least alarmed. She then drove to the Duchess of Kent's house in Belgrave Square, I suppose, to assure her of her safety. The crowd followed her cheering."

The next day, the party went to Ascot in a coach and four. Lord Palmerston was determined to enjoy himself, " and," as he said to General Taylor, " leave those disagreeable people in the Cabinet to stew in their own juice for a day." He had been given a tip by Mr. Greville, the owner of " Alarm," for the Emperor's Cup and advised the others to back him heavily. Mr. Greville was a sound prophet for his horse romped home. Lady Carew, who had never backed a horse in her life, was triumphant as she had asked Fitzwilliam to put a shilling on " Alarm " but " for heaven's sake do not tell Walter," she said ; " although he gambles himself, he would be furious if he thought a lady did such a thing."

The only other member of the Cabinet present was Lord Minto of the Admiralty, who was there with Lady Minto, Lord Melgund and Lady Fanny Elliot. The Mintos came and joined Lord Palmerston's party at luncheon, and they had a very uproarious meal. Lady Carew and Lady Fanny Elliot found a great deal in common.

" Do you remember the last time I saw you here ? " Lady Carew asked Lady Fanny. " It was in 1832 when a man aimed a stone at the King, which took off a peeler's hat, and the King got so angry with the peeler for chasing his hat instead of the man who had thrown the stone."

Lady Fanny remembered perfectly and said, " You and your sister were here ; you wore a rose and she wore a lily."

The time passed very pleasantly with these recollections and they drove back to London very well pleased with their day.

Chapter Ten

LAUNCH OF THE *BEATRICE*

LADY CAREW was rather fully occupied for the next two years as she presented Sir Walter with two daughters—one Elizabeth, who was usually known as Bessie, born in 1840, and another Beatrice, commonly called B, who appeared in 1842. Sir Walter, perhaps thinking of his pheasants, designated it " the rearing season."

Another portent which appeared during the " rearing season " was the income tax at 7*d.* in the pound, which upset all Sir Walter's calculations. This entailed a loss of income to him not far short of £500, a sum which he had intended to spend on building a yacht. He apparently overlooked the fact that he still had about £20,000 per annum to spend, but decided that " what he lost on the swings he would make up on the roundabouts." He thereupon blocked up all the servants' windows in the house to avoid payment of the window tax, leaving the occupants in inner and outer darkness, except for such light as they were able to obtain by burning candles. As the housekeeper paid the candle bill, it is presumed that the added cost escaped his notice.

Sir Walter's rage against Sir Robert Peel, the author of " this dastardly income tax outrage," was intense, and when in January 1843 Mr. Edward Drummond, Peel's private secretary, was shot at and killed by a madman, named M'Naughten, Sir Walter merely remarked : " Pity it weren't that rapscallion Peel."

In February 1844 Sir Walter, having taken stock of his finances, decided that after all they would allow of his putting a yacht in hand. He was not the man to do things by halves, if it suited his own convenience ; and he accordingly obtained the services of Sir William Symonds, the Surveyor of the Navy, who had designed the *Victoria and Albert* steam yacht in the previous year, and requested him to design a sailing yacht of about 100 tons.

" None of your infernal engines in her, mind. I want fresh air and not to be smoked out by steam and soot ; it may do for the Queen and that German feller, but not for me."

The designs were sent to Veale and Sons, boat-builders of Torquay, who proceeded straight away with the yacht's construction. Out of deference to his youngest daughter she was to be called the *Beatrice*. Lady Carew was told that " if she so minded, she could choose the frillings and furbelows for the cabins and the saloon." This necessitated frequent excursions to Torquay, and gave Lady Carew and her youngest sister, Eliza, who was spending the winter at Haccombe, a congenial occupation.

On returning from one of these expeditions, on a Saturday, they were surprised to hear singing in the little church which was next door to the house. Lady Carew and her sister dismounted from the carriage and went into the church. There a most amazing sight presented itself. As they entered the church they were greeted by the sounds of Bishop Heber's hymn, " From Greenland's icy mountains," sung by a choir composed of the male and female domestic staff. They were being coached by two gentlemen, one in a black coat and the other in hunting pink. At their approach the singing stopped and Sir Walter shouted to his wife : "Just come in from hunting. Had a rare run. Jack Russell's staying the night and will take the service to-morrow ; wants the choir to run through their paces."

The little church was actually a parish church, but was regarded by Sir Walter as his own particular spiritual home which was perhaps excusable as the congregation consisted exclusively of

his family and their retainers. Church parade on Sunday mornings was an impressive, if somewhat formal, affair. Sir Walter
was a stickler for correct attire amongst the staff, the male portion
wearing livery, while the female contingent donned poke-
bonnets with dresses of a suitable dullness. Archman was the
choirmaster and Lady Carew officiated as organist at the organ-
harmonica, made by Mr. Evans and recently installed. It was
no fault of hers that on this particular Sunday, in the middle of
a hymn, the instrument, which had not yet attained perfection,
gave out. The choir did their best to sustain the rhythm, and
her Ladyship plodded manfully at the pedals with which, the
seat being too low, her feet were making faulty contact. Matters
improved somewhat when Archman adjusted the elevating
contraption or, as he described it, "wound her Ladyship
up." The choir were at their last gasp, but Archman was in
time.

"Now, m'lady," he whispered, "put some wind into your
bellows for the Amen."

The Rev. John Russell, never at a loss, went into the pulpit
and giving as his text "For this relief much thanks," preached
an excellent extempore sermon.

The building of the *Beatrice* proceeded apace and by the spring
of 1845, she was ready for launching. There was a great gathering of the clans for the occasion. Royalty was present in the
person of Queen Adelaide, who actually performed the ceremony. She was staying at the Imperial Hotel, Torquay.
Arthur Taylor, Lady Carew's brother, was serving as her equerry,
but it was his father, the General, who prevailed on her to
launch the vessel. Lord Palmerston was also present. Sir
Walter did not object to him since, as he was out of favour with
the Government, Sir Walter thought that perhaps he might be
got at to vote against the imposition of the income tax. Lord
Haddington, the First Lord of the Admiralty, considered that
he was entitled to attend by virtue of his position, but Sir Walter
thought him "a prying politician," poking his nose in where he

wasn't wanted. Georgiana, the third of General Taylor's daughters to do well for herself, had recently married Lord Willoughby de Broke who had a large estate in Warwickshire. They with the rest of the family and of course Fitzwilliam Taylor were amongst the party. The ceremony went off quite successfully ; Queen Adelaide broke a bottle of champagne over the vessel, and the Rev. Fitzwilliam, who having just taken Holy Orders, acted as chaplain, repeated the words " and may God bless all who sail in her."

The party afterwards adjourned to the Imperial Hotel for dinner at four o'clock, a somewhat protracted business. After the loyal toasts had been drunk, there followed in quick succession, toasts to the Earl of Haddington, to the Duke of Wellington and the army and to Her Majesty's Ministers. The last toast had an unfortunate repercussion, for Sir Walter, flushed with the launching of his new toy, ended up with " and damnation to the income tax." Lord Haddington looked down his nose, but Palmerston, who enjoyed himself when in opposition, rather unwisely said, hear ! hear ! Fortunately the remark was lost in the buzz of conversation.

Towards the end of August, a skipper and crew having been collected, Sir Walter determined to take the *Beatrice* for a trial run. It was to be a male party, Sir Walter saying he " didn't want any females fussing and fiddling and probably being seasick into the bargain." Sir Walter, Lord Willoughby de Broke, Mr. Fortescue, the Rev. John Russell and the Rev. Fitzwilliam Taylor made up the party. Sir Walter, who had an eye to the commissariat, determined that he and his guests should be done well, and took it upon himself to engage an expensive cook. Another reason for his unwonted generosity in the matter of the cook was the fact that Mrs. Haigh, who had been cook at Haccombe for the last six years, had given in her notice "not being able to put up with Sir Walter's cantankerous ways any longer."

The trip was not a very long one and the Rev. Fitzwilliam records in his journal :

"BEATRICE" R.Y.S.

From a painting in the possession of the author

" *25th August.* Got under way about noon. Fine day not much wind, had a tiring trip to Cowes ; found a rolling swell outside when Jack Russell was very sea-sick and could not eat any dinner which was as well as the new cook, Mrs. Hext, was so ill herself that none was prepared. Walter was so angry that he said he would get rid of her in Alderney where we go to-morrow.

26th August. Fine day and beautiful breeze. The cook got better and cooked such a beautiful dinner that Walter forgot his annoyance of yesterday.

27th August. We lay a course for Alderney. Two reefs down in mainsail and bonnets off foursail and mainsail ; not so much sea as we thought. Result, another excellent meal from Mrs. Hext. Got inside the pier at 8 p.m.

28th August. Sailed from Alderney at 9 a.m. foggy and disagreeable when we started ; cleared up about 12. Breeze freshened towards evening had to get in foregaff topsail in consequence of the topmast stay giving way and were obliged to take in jib topsail too. After dinner wind gradually died away just as we were getting into Torbay."

The party agreed that on the whole it had been a very successful trip, but the Rev. John Russell decided he much preferred hunting to yachting. They returned to Haccombe accompanied by Mrs. Hext, the new cook, two waiters having been paid off and discharged. Mrs. Haigh brought her Scots temper into play when Mrs. Hext walked into her kitchen.

"And who de ye reckon ye be, you miserable foreigner ? " she said, advancing on the new cook. " I'll no be insulted by the likes of you ; 'tis to be hoped ye'll like your new master so much as I do."

Sir Walter for once was defeated when the furious Mrs. Haigh came to interview him.

" Let me tell ye, sir," she said, " that you're six feet three of the varra worse stuff as I ever seed wrapped up in one bundle. Guid marning to ye, sir."

Sir Walter lost no time in sending the woman to the coach office at Newton Abbot.

In spite of Sir Walter's ban on " females " on the trial run of the *Beatrice*, there was nevertheless to be a ladies' day on board before the summer was over. The occasion was the Torbay regatta which took place in the middle of August. Lady Carew was anxious to display the glories of the new yacht and Sir Walter gave a grudging assent to her being the hostess on the day of the regatta. The Lord-Lieutenant of Devon, Lord Fortescue, and his beautiful young Irish wife were to be present, and they were bringing the old Marquis of Anglesey and his son, Lord George Paget, who had been a cadet at Sandhurst under General Taylor. Lord Fortescue and Lord Anglesey entertained the company with their reminiscences of Ireland, both having formerly been Lord-Lieutenant. Lord Fortescue related how, at the opening of the Ulster Railway in 1839, the engine blew up before the train ever started. Lady Fortescue fluttered the ladies somewhat by appearing in Wellington boots, which she said she invariably wore as she had been told England was full of snakes. Sir Walter interpolated one of his rare remarks in company, saying, " Rubbish ! Never heard tell of snakes aboard ship."

Lord Anglesey, endeavouring with true gallantry to bridge the uncomfortable gap in the conversation caused by this remark, launched into one of his interminable stories about the loss of his leg at Waterloo, describing his life had been saved by General Taylor pulling off his boots.

" Yes, Papa," Lord George Paget said, " we all know that, but 'twas nothing to do with snakes."

Lady Carew, sensing that the conversation was becoming somewhat strained, led the way to the saloon for dinner.

Mrs. Hext, who had been brought from Haccombe for the occasion, produced a magnificent six-course dinner. During dinner Lord Yarborough, a member of the Royal Yacht Squadron, whose yacht *Kestrel* was only a shade less magnificent than the *Beatrice*, persuaded Sir Walter to join the Squadron. Sir Walter, with proverbial caution, asked if it were expensive, and being assured that it was not, expressed his wish to become a member. Miss Burdett-Coutts and Mr. Charles Dickens, who assisted her in her good works, were among Lord Yarborough's party. Miss Burdett-Coutts was overcome with admiration at Lady Carew's decorations and considered her taste " quite perfect."

After dinner, during an interval between the races, Mr. Dickens was persuaded by Lady Carew to read portions of " your lovely work" the *Christmas Carol*. Mr. Dickens, who was young and ardent, was delighted to oblige his attractive hostess, and passed a very pleasant hour with the ladies, who preferred this type of amusement to the racing, with which they were somewhat bored.

It was during the last race that an exciting incident occurred which threw the racing into the shade. It had been rumoured that Mr. Green, the balloonist, who had already made several ascents, was to come over Torbay and descend at Torquay on that day.

It was a very hot evening and the party in the *Beatrice* were seated on deck, talking idly and watching the racing. Sir James Drummond's yacht the *Claymore* was just rounding the winning buoy. The Rev. Fitzwilliam's diary gives a description of what occurred. Being lately ordained, and in the stress of excitement, his phraseology is scriptural.

" Suddenly," he writes, " we heard a sound as of a mighty rushing wind above us ; looking up I saw what appeared to be an enormous envelope with a thing like a clothes-basket at the bottom, coming towards us. It seemed to be coming lower and lower and then there was a noise like a cannon shot, and we saw the basket bobbing about in the sea. ' God bless my soul,' Lord Anglesey said, ' sounded like gunfire ' and jumped out of his chair, leaving his wooden leg behind him, which rolled into the scuppers. Lord George Paget helped his father, who was swearing volubly, back to his chair and collected his leg. ' That must be the madman whom I saw go up in a balloon from

Vauxhall when I was at Sandhurst ! ' Lord George said, ' I'm told he landed in Nassau then, now he's chosen the sea.' The man, who turned out to be a Mr. Green, was hauled into the *Beatrice*, dripping like a seal, but not much the worse. He told us that the stuff made from coal which he used inside the envelope, blew up. Walter also blew up, and sent him to the galley to be dried."

After this spectacular finish to the regatta, the party broke up, Lady Carew receiving congratulations on having provided such a delightful entertainment.

Chapter Eleven

THE FOX-HUNTERS' CLUB

SIR WALTER considered that the *Beatrice* had proved to be a good investment, and after the Torbay regatta she was laid up for the winter. He lost no time in getting down to the more serious business of hunting, and on 2nd September held his first cub-hunting meet for the season at Haccombe. There were at this time about thirty packs of hounds in North and South Devon, all of them privately owned and financed by the masters. The farmers were great supporters of hounds, and so long as they could get their fun for nothing they encouraged the masters of hounds by preserving foxes. Sir Walter had kennels at Haccombe and Marley, the latter place embracing a large part of the Dartmoor country. John Beale, Sir Walter's huntsman, preferred the moor hunting and, as he said : " Dartmoor hunting is beautiful—if you could but see it ; they bogs be always in the way." Up to 1840, it had been usual to hold a hunting week at Chumleigh in North Devon which was a rendezvous for masters of hounds in North and South Devon. Sir Walter and that " Prince of Sporting Parsons," the Rev. John Russell, who held the perpetual curacy of Swymbridge, both brought their hounds and enjoyed a week of hard hunting followed by almost harder conviviality. Recently, however, signs of decay had set in owing to the dropping off of many of the supporters. In November 1845, it was resolved to found a new fox-hunting club to have its headquarters at the George Inn, South Molton, which would follow on the lines of the Chumleigh club.

The three gentlemen responsible for the new club were the Rev. John Russell, Sir Walter Carew and Mr. Trelawny of Coldrenick. Three such sponsors, all being notable M.F.H.s, guaranteed the success of the venture, the South Molton club being looked on as a kind of phoenix, rising with renewed vigour from the smouldering ashes of the Chumleigh club. All the country houses in the neighbourhood were thrown open to friends from a distance, but every available bed and stall was secured for weeks beforehand by gentlemen who preferred the freedom of a hostelry, untrammelled by their wives, to private hospitality. Needless to say, Sir Walter favoured this course and had arranged accommodation for himself, John Beale and the hounds. Lady Carew had received an invitation to stay with Lady Fortescue at Castle Hill, which was close to South Molton, and she gratefully accepted, thinking thereby to keep an eye on Sir Walter whom she was apt to mistrust, not without reason, on these bachelor hunting jaunts. Part of the railway from Exeter to Plymouth had been completed in May of that year so she and her maid travelled from Newton Abbot to Exeter by train, posting on to Castle Hill.

Lord Fortescue was Lord-Lieutenant of Devon and was engaged on the ¦duties of his office in London. Lady Fortescue, however, entertained a large house-party composed chiefly of the feminine sex.

The next day, 16th November, the meet was at Cuzzicombe Post and Lady Fortescue and her guests at Castle Hill attended in force. The weather was unkind and they went in two closed barouches. The Rev. John Russell and his wife were both mounted and Sir Walter viewed the Castle Hill carriages, filled with chattering women, with distaste. He approached Lady Carew's barouche and, taking no notice of the other occupants, said to her : " You had as well stayed at home. What's the use of coming hunting in a shut cab ? "

Lady Fortescue, who had got out of the carriage to speak to a friend, seeing Sir Walter, said, " Good morning, Sir

JOHN BEALE AND THE PACK

From a contemporary picture in the possession of the author

Walter, pray tell me where we can best see the hounds cast off."

Sir Walter looked at her Wellington boots. "Ah, Mam," he said, "where is your mount? You had best join Mrs. Russell, she'll put you right."

Lady Fortescue informed Sir Walter that she was not riding. "I have two carriages full of young ladies," she said, "and I have to devote my time to them."

"Don't you believe it, Mam," said Sir Walter. "Time is wasted on women, which you can give to hounds."

It is to be feared that Lady Fortescue and her "two carriages full of young ladies" saw little of the hunt that day, for Sir Walter, who was in a hurry to be quit of "this female flummery," called to John Beale to cast off the hounds, and they immediately found a fox in Twitchen Town Wood which they ran over Exmoor, killing him without a check in forty minutes. Mrs. Russell in a green habit, and the Rev. John, led the field. Another lady, Mrs. Horndon, was not far behind. The fox broke out over the moor wall, a fence big enough to stop a native red deer, but Mrs. Russell, seeing her rival just behind, determined to "set" that lady, and putting her horse Tickler at the barrier, sailed over it and, landing safely over the deep trench on the off side, went off with the leading hounds alone in her glory.

"Hold hard, damn you, Mam, let the hounds get ahead," Sir Walter bellowed, as he lumbered up on his strapping great mare. "Keep your wife in order, Jack," he added as an after-thought to the Rev. John.

The Rev. John Russell was by no means the only member of his cloth who followed the hounds; in fact there were several parsons in North Devon who kept packs of their own. The following week the Rev. John Russell's hounds were on duty, and hunted four days out of the seven. The Rev. John drew Sir Walter aside in the evening after dinner and said:

"I hear that old spoil-sport, the Bishop, is travelling round here on a visitation tour to-morrow, and he can't abide to think that any of his parsons go a-hunting. What shall us do about it ?"

Sir Walter, who had no love for Dr. Phillpotts, said, "Do ? What should us do but hunt as usual and be damned to him."

The next day the Bishop and his chaplain visited the parish of Hawkridge and drew a blank as the Rector, one of the hardest riders in the country, was otherwise engaged with the hounds. As the Bishop was leaving, the Rev. John's hounds crossed the road in full cry with several gentlemen in black coats in close pursuit. The Bishop said to his chaplain with due solemnity :

" Alas ! I fear this neighbourhood must have been visited by some dire epidemic, I never saw so many men in mourning before."

The Bishop no doubt said this with his tongue in his cheek, but the chaplain, who knew the country better than his Lordship, and since he identified the mourners, one after the other, as members of his own cloth and personal friends, decided that the best policy to adopt was "least said, soonest mended." The sequel came two days afterwards, when the Bishop called at Tordown, Russell's parsonage. Having received word from his friend, the chaplain, that it would be as well to be present, the Rev. John, against Sir Walter's advice, received the Bishop in his study. Parson Russell, always one to open an offensive, said to the Bishop :

" I am told, my Lord, that you object to my hunting."

The Bishop replied with a perfectly courteous smile : " Dear me, who could have told you so ? What I object to is that you should ever do anything else."

Sir Walter was highly amused when the Rev. John told him of the interview, and said : " One for the old curmudgeon, he flummoxed you proper."

The following week it was again Sir Walter's turn to hunt hounds and this time the meet was at Filleigh, next door to Castle Hill. It was on a Saturday, and it so happened that a battalion of the North Devon Militia were holding a practice exercise on Exeter Down. The house-party at Castle Hill appeared to be more interested in the military manœuvres than in the meet of the hounds, and the commanding officer was reviewing his battalion when Sir Walter and the hounds approached, drawing slowly up the Down. Suddenly, amidst screams of excitement from the ladies, a fox appeared, seemingly from nowhere, in the midst of the men. The Colonel, who was just as excited as everyone else, shouted out in a broad Devon dialect :

"There he go'th, boys, a lashing great shaver."

Then, forgetting the point at which he had ceased to give the word of command, he turned round and said :

"Where wor I, drummer-boy ? "

The boy, who had kept his head better than his Colonel, replied, "Present arms, sir," and the inspection proceeded.

Sir Walter, however, had the last word.

"Damme, sir," he roared at the Colonel, "what mean you by playing at soldiers and heading the fox ? Hadn't you the wit to know this was a hunting day ? Be off with you."

The Colonel thereupon followed the example of :

> The noble Duke of York
> He had ten thousand men,
> He marched them up to the top of the hill,
> And he marched them down again.

There was great glee that evening at the George Inn over Sir Walter's defeat of the British army. It was a lively party with six masters of fox-hounds present. Mr. Trelawny was in the chair and he records that Sir John Rogers and his brother Admiral Rogers, both hard-hunting South Devon sportsmen, kept the ball rolling with unceasing gaiety.

"We drank to fox-hunting several times over," he writes. "I sat next to Sir Walter Carew who stuck to his port like a man flooring his two bottles in orthodox style. The rest drank punch—Henley Rogers (the Admiral) and Sir John mixing the materials, Sir John favouring gin, and the Admiral as befitted a sailor, rum. After dinner there was a sale of horses by auction."

This seems to have been a usual end to the entertainment. Anyone could put up his friend's horse without even consulting him ; the rule being that the owner was only allowed one bid to protect himself. Consequently many members of the club found themselves in possession of horses they had not had the remotest intention of buying, the owners refusing to interfere by bids of their own. The method of procedure was simple in the extreme. A shilling having been dropped into a wine-glass and the horse named, the bidding was then started by the auctioneer to the club. In the event, Sir Walter found that he was the owner of a string of nags which John Beale, his hunts-man, said " he no more wanted than a cat wanted two tails."

The Rev. John had a respect for his head and slipped out early, and when pressed by Sir Walter to stay, said, " Hunting I tell you, Walter, is worth any sacrifice ; and if you sit up and get a headache, as you surely will, or if you don't you deserve to, you can't thoroughly enjoy it. So by your leave, good-night, gentlemen."

After the Rev. John had left, a somewhat disconcerting incident destroyed the harmony of the party. Sir Walter, perhaps letting his exuberant feeling outrun his discretion, made some uncomplimentary remarks about " that miserable old crow, Phillpotts." At that moment his cousin, Tom Carew, of Collipriest, also more full of wine than wisdom, walked into the room and overheard Sir Walter's observations. Not being friendly with Sir Walter, and professing for reasons of his own a great friendship for the Bishop of Exeter, he seized a large lump of butter off the table and hurled it at Sir Walter's head, saying, " There, take that and don't attack in his absence a better man than yourself."

Luckily for Tom Carew the missile missed its mark.

THE REV. JOHN RUSSELL

From a drawing by N. H. J. Baird

" You infernal young whipper-snapper," bellowed Sir Walter. " I'll teach you manners if no one else will," and he bared his arms which were like legs of mutton.

The chairman, thinking the affair| had gone far enough, signalled to the brothers Rogers, who hustled Tom Carew out of the room. Sir Walter, feeling the oncoming headache of which the Rev. John had warned him, thought discretion the better part of valour and also retired. The party then dispersed.

Lord Fortescue returned to Castle Hill at the beginning of December bringing as his guests, the Duke of Wellington and Lord Palmerston, the latter taking the opportunity to visit his constituency at Tiverton ; he was delighted to hear that Lady Carew, the daughter of his old friend General Taylor, was staying at Castle Hill and wanted to see more of the " sort of feller she'd married." The result of all this was that Sir Walter, on the invitation of Lord Fortescue, was reluctantly compelled to take up his quarters at Castle Hill.

The next day there was a small dinner party, Mr. and Mrs. Russell being amongst those invited. Lord Fortescue, in accordance with custom, asked the Rev. John, being the only clergyman present, to say grace. The reverend gentleman's mind was presumably elsewhere for he started " For what we are about to receive," and concluded " may the Lord give us good hunting." Mrs. Russell, overcome with confusion, curtly told her husband to sit down, saying he had completely forgotten himself.

The Duke of Wellington however was highly entertained and whispered to Lord Fortescue : " By God he's half in the pulpit and half in the pigskin." After this the meal went smoothly enough until the ladies retired. The gentlemen gathered round the table for their wine, and Lord Palmerston attempted a little conversation with Sir Walter, but without much success. He decided that the General had been right and that the man was an oaf.

On the following day Lord Palmerston went off to Tiverton,

and a meet of Sir Walter's hounds was arranged at Filleigh for the Duke of Wellington's benefit. None of the Castle Hill party, except Sir Walter, the Rev. John and his wife, and Mr. Trelawny, rode, and the meet resolved itself into what Sir Walter described as "a political stew-pot." Footmen circled interminably with "stirrup-cups" and eatables of various descriptions. The Rev. John was in a hurry to be off, but could do nothing until the master moved. Sir Walter, whose spirits had risen with the rounds of stirrup-cups, seemed immovable until John Beale, the huntsman, who had also had his fill, rode up and said to the master :

"His Reverence is in a fine pet to be off ; says you'll have a head fit to bust yourself with afore you start."

Sir Walter pulled himself together, crashed into a man carrying a trap of bottles, shouted, "Yoicks forrard," blew his horn and went off at a hand gallop, followed by the hounds. They found a fox, which they ran to ground. Sir Walter was certainly not feeling himself, for he called the hounds off, and told John Beale to take them back to kennels, a most unusual procedure for him. The Rev. John was furious, and rated Sir Walter in no uncertain terms for his lack of control in the matter of stirrup-cups.

"You dipped too deep, Walter," he concluded, "and as I told you, you'd pay for it."

Chapter Twelve

TAKING THE WATERS

YOUNG Walter Carew, left in charge of nurses and governesses, had got too big for his boots, and it was considered that the time had come for him to have some discipline instilled in him at school. In the middle of January 1848 it was arranged that he should proceed to Mr. Henley's academy for young gentlemen at Bath. This, as it happened, fitted in with Sir Walter's plans, for he had latterly been laid up, on and off, with gout. He had been advised by Dr. Winkle, the family physician, to abjure port, and undergo a " treatment of the waters." Sir Walter had no intention of substituting water for wine, but having heard from his brother-in-law, William Fortescue, that he also had been recommended the same treatment, he decided to accompany Lady Carew and young Walter to Bath. Much against his will he was persuaded to travel by the railway from Exeter, and on the 17th January Sir Walter, with his valet, Lady Carew and her maid, with young Walter, departed from the Exeter station. Rooms had been taken at the Lansdowne Inn and on arrival at Bath station Sir Walter and Henry, the valet, climbed into a surrey and were driven off to the inn. Lady Carew, Ellen, the maid, and young Walter were shepherded into a closed " fly " and taken to Mr. Henley's academy.

Young Walter, inheriting his male parent's feelings, objected strongly to being shut up with two women, and to show his disapproval tried to break the window of the " fly." On arrival at the academy the boy was dragged out of the fly by Lady Carew and they were ushered into a fearsome chamber known as the breakfast room.

Miss Henley, the sister of the headmaster, in her rustling black gown with bugles, appeared to young Walter as an ogress, and he turned for consolation to her niece, Miss Henrietta, whose more youthful appearance gave promise of more leniency. His intuition was right, for whilst Lady Carew was settling his fate with Miss Henley, Miss Henrietta beckoned to him and surreptitiously extracted from some hidden recess in her dress a penny packet of bullseyes. This was the usual formula adopted by Miss Henrietta on such occasions ; it certainly proved effective.

Sir Walter and William Fortescue had not wasted their time. Dr. Holland, physician to Prince Albert, was in Bath at the time and was staying at the Lansdowne Inn. Dr. Holland sized up his clients fairly accurately. Sir Walter's whole object was to get his doctor's decision on the wine question reversed, and he broached the matter at once with the celebrated physician, saying that he personally favoured a '24 vintage port.

" A most excellent wine, my dear sir," the doctor announced, " I always drink it myself, but in your case I would recommend a leetle lighter brand, a pint would do no harm to anyone."

This point having been settled to Sir Walter's satisfaction, he looked forward to the remainder of his stay with equanimity.

In March 1848 Lady Carew received a letter from her father telling her of the revolution in France and saying that he had met the King and Queen of the French, after their escape from France, at Newhaven and had accompanied the royal party to Claremont. The General added that the King had told him the story of his escape and the disguises that he and the Queen had adopted.

" It struck me," the General wrote, " that the King was undignified, having no feelings about his country, but thinking only of himself. He said of the French people, 'They have chosen their destiny, now I must uphold mine.' The Royal Family have no money at all, and beggary is staring them in the face. I am rather surprised at Palmerston's action in saying that the King could not stay at Claremont, as the Duke of Wellington went to see him and told him Claremont was the fit place for him. However, he is to stay after all as Leopold of the Belgians (who is the legal owner) told him he could stay there as long as he liked."

In April 1848 there was widespread excitement over the Chartist petition to be presented at the House of Commons on the 10th. There were repercussions in the provinces, and in Bath there were some incidents. On 9th April Sir Walter was being wheeled back from the pump-room to the inn by his valet when they were surrounded by a crowd of roughs, who evidently meant mischief. There were shouts of " Look at the old grampus ! We want universal suffrage, and to do away with the likes o' you."

Sir Walter, who, whatever his faults, was never lacking in physical courage, seized his stick and had his leg permitted would have leapt out of his chair.

" Damn this gout," he shouted. " Here, Henry, take this stick and charge the rapscallions."

Henry, whose paths had hitherto lain in the paths of peace, looked doubtful ; his prowess was not however to be tested, for at that moment a troop of the Somerset Yeomanry came galloping up the street and the hooligans quickly dispersed.

On 12th April Mr. Henley's school broke up for the Easter vacation, and young Walter travelled home with his parents. Lady Carew, who went to fetch him from the school, was this time received by the headmaster, who had but a sorry tale to tell of the boy's progress and general behaviour.

" I am sorry to tell you, Mam," Mr. Henley said, " that young Carew shows little aptitude for study or discipline. I have had to correct him more than once with the cane, but on the last occasion, with most unbecoming language, he seized the cane and threw it at me. I fear me I cannot keep such an irresponsible young gentleman at my academy, and I make bold to suggest that you enter him for the junior school at Eton which, I understand, is his ultimate destination."

Sir Walter on hearing this report was rather pleased than otherwise, and praised the boy's spirit to Lady Carew. He added that Mr. Henley was incapable of dealing with him and that he would put him in his old house at Eton.

On their return to Exeter the Carews were met by Bessie and B, and their governess, Miss Cole. Bessie and B were now aged nine and six respectively and were extremely forward young ladies. They were delighted to have Walter home again and were rather proud at his expulsion from Mr. Henley's academy.

The boy spent his holidays running wild; in the following year he was to go to Eton, and meanwhile he made hay while the sun still shone. Sir Walter had bought him a magnificent pony and he careered all over the country on it. Whilst on a visit with Sir Walter to the Rev. John Russell in North Devon he had become friendly with young Redvers Buller of Downes, who was also destined for Eton. The two young limbs were of much the same temperament, both were going into the army, they said, and young Walter said to Buller, " But we must have wars and plenty of 'em."

This friendship continued and in the summer of the following year the two boys went to Eton together.

Meanwhile Bessie and B, envious of the attention bestowed by Sir Walter on their brother, considered themselves rather neglected. Miss Cole was well enough, but she had not much conversation outside the schoolroom routine. If the weather was fine, Miss Cole took them for a boring walk, and occasionally Lady Carew took them for a drive in the closed landau.

" Mama is such a chilly person," Bessie observed, " and will hardly ever go in an open carriage. I should like to go with

Papa in the T. cart, but then he always takes Walter and leaves us behind."

There came a day, however, after Walter had gone to Eton, when they were taken a trip in the *Beatrice*. Bessie kept a diary from a very early age. She had made herself acquainted with all the technical terms appertaining to a yacht, and was better up in them than was Sir Walter. She airily discussed foregaff topsails, jib topsails and all the rest of them. On 16th June they went to Teignmouth regatta. In her diary she wrote :

" Got under way in Torbay at 10 o'clock, went for a sail as far as the Parson and Clerk, but Miss Cole was so horribly seasick we had to turn back and put into Teignmouth where we landed her like a parcel of dirty clothes and left her at Lady Sinclair's. Papa was very angry and said ' those sort of people do not know how to behave.' I was very sorry for Miss Cole as it was not her fault. Papa has not got a skipper yet and we had a pilot on board. He was rather a stupid sort of man and nearly ran us on the bar getting into Teignmouth harbour. It was rather rough outside so the regatta only took place in the estuary which was rather dull ; there were only stupid little boats taking part. B wanted to go in one so Lord Sinclair took her in his, then the boat heeled over so she got frightened and had to be brought back. Papa said she ought to be well shaken and she would never make a sailor. I made friends with the coxswain and he let me take the rudder which was great fun. Mama was sorry for Miss Cole, so she and B went ashore and they all went home in a fly. Papa said it was the best place for them. We had a beautiful sail back to Torbay with a nice breeze off the land. I enjoyed my first sail in the *Beatrice* very much indeed."

Chapter Thirteen

SEABORNE "EXHIBITION"

SIR GEORGE HAYTER had painted Ann Carew and Harriet Fortescue in their girlhood and they still look down over the years with all the attributes of their early beauty : Ann Carew with a peach-bloom complexion and hair the colour of ripe corn, and Harriet Fortescue, a striking brunette, exchanging their favourite flowers. Thus must they have appeared on an afternoon in the late April of 1851, when they were engaged in the same occupation in the saloon of the R.Y.S. *Beatrice*. They were rudely disturbed by the entrance of Sir Walter Carew, who bade them " stop fooling about " as the servants had to lay the table for dinner.

The truth was that on that particular day, there was a good deal of confusion aboard the *Beatrice*. In the first place, a new skipper had arrived to take over. Mr. Dove had been skipper under Lord Yarborough in his yacht *Kestrel* and knew exactly how things ought to be done. The mate, Mr. Jonas, was also a new hand, who according to Mr. Dove knew how things ought not to be done. The relations between skipper and mate, therefore, were not at the moment happy. Some of the crew of twenty were old hands but about half a dozen were survivors of the steamer *Royal Adelaide* which had been wrecked in the previous year off Margate. In the words of Mr. Dove they were a " set of useless land-lubbers," and the skipper therefore had his work cut out to make the *Beatrice* ready for sea.

The *Beatrice* was lying in her home port in Torbay, and Sir

Walter, much against his inclination, had a large party of ladies and gentlemen on board. It had been Lady Carew's idea that they should go to the Great Exhibition and afterwards visit young Walter at Eton for the 4th of June celebrations. Lady Carew had quite naturally proposed travelling by the railroad to London, but Sir Walter would have none of it. The South Devon railway had been opened the previous year and Sir Walter had had acrimonious arguments with Mr. Brunel, one of the directors, over the acquisition of land belonging to the Marley estate. Sir Walter was successful in so far as he obtained an injunction to restrain the directors from laying the track in front of his house unless a tunnel was constructed to hide the train from view. As a consequence, the directors and the shareholders (of whom Sir Walter took good care not to be one) found their dividends reduced. Sir Walter vowed he would eschew railroads like the plague. Hence his decision that if "this fool journey" had to be done, he would do it by sea.

This gave Lady Carew an opportunity to spread herself and she accordingly set about issuing invitations for the trip. The party consisted of her father, General Taylor, and her brother the Rev. Fitzwilliam, her two sisters Harriet Fortescue and Georgiana Willoughby de Broke and their husbands, and last but not least Lord Minto, who as Lord Privy Seal had ample time on his hands, and Lady Minto. There was an excellent French cook on board in the person of M. Perron, whom Sir Walter had purloined from the Imperial Hotel, Torquay, and an ample domestic staff presided over by Dally, the butler who had succeeded Archman. An untoward scene marred the departure. The irate proprietor of the Imperial Hotel, having discovered M. Perron's defection, appeared on the quay and demanded his return, offering him a wage considerably in excess of what he had previously given him. Sir Walter, however, knew a game worth two of that. Knowing that M. Perron was an artist at his trade, and being ever generous where his inner man was concerned, he clinched the affair by topping the proprietor's offer by £50, M. Perron no doubt thinking that employment under private ownership was easier money than working in a hotel. Whilst M. Perron was being hustled on board, Sir Walter aimed a Parthian shot at his furious opponent. "The highest bidder always wins," he shouted. "Good day to you."

After these tiresome preliminaries, the *Beatrice* got under way at noon on 26th April. The Rev. Fitzwilliam, who not long since had been inducted to the comfortable family living of Haccombe, constituted himself as diarist for the occasion.

"Fine day but a beam wind," he records, "had a long wearisome beat down to the Needles; found a rolling swell outside which finished off most of the ladies; they could not eat any dinner which was as well as the new cook, M. Perron, was so seasick himself that none was prepared. Walter furious, said he did not pay M. Perron to be ill; made do with some food prepared in the galley.

"*21st April*. Fine day and a beautiful breeze. M. Perron better and cooked such a beautiful dinner that Walter forgot his ill-temper of yesterday. Two reefs down in mainsail and bonnets off foresail. Not so much seas as we thought. Lord Minto and Willoughby fished for mackerel, but caught nothing except a great brute of a dog-fish which bit Lord Minto when he tried to handle it; the crew ate it.

"*23rd April*. Put into Dover. The Duke of Wellington, who is Warden of the Cinque Ports, came on board and had a chat with Father. Mr. Brett, who laid down a submarine telegraph between Dover and Calais last year, dined on board; he is a funny little man and looks more like a jockey than an inventor. The ladies had dinner by themselves, and the gentlemen got lively over their wine. One of Mr. Dove's 'landlubbers' also got lively, and chased Ellen, Ann's maid, the length of the deck. Walter ordered the man to be 'cooled off,' so Mr. Dove had him put into a sack at the end of a rope and dipped into the sea. Methinks we shall have no more trouble with *him*."

The next day there was a nasty choppy sea, and several of the passengers were again incapacitated. Some difficulty was experienced in entering the Thames estuary at Southend, necessitating a good deal of tacking. As the *Beatrice* came abreast of Southend pier she narrowly escaped collision with the warsteamer *Nemesis* coming down the river from Gravesend. The Rev. Fitzwilliam describes the alarming episode.

" We had run into a fog at the mouth of the river, the wind had died away to nothing, when we got away from the pier into the channel, the *Beatrice* had no way on her, and we were going astern with the current and drifting on a large merchant schooner. Walter was shouting at Mr. Dove, and he was going for Mr. Jonas. In the middle of all the row we heard bells ringing, and a churning of water and saw a large steamer bearing down on us. As she got closer we could see through the fog the bewhiskered Captain in a naval uniform on the bridge. He shouted something not very polite at Walter who was on the poop, and told him to get out of the fairway. Walter always answers back, and told the officer, he'd see him damned first. With a great splashing of water the steamer's machinery made her go backwards, and as she did so the wind got up. Mr. Dove, as quick as lightning, luffed and got the *Beatrice* clear. Lord Minto was so excited that he rushed up and shook Mr. Dove by the hand. Walter was rather sulky and said, ' No thanks to Dove, 'twas more by good luck than good management.' I thought myself that Mr. Dove handled the ship very well. After the excitement was over, M. Perron, if you please, had the audacity to send word that he wanted some brandy to settle his stomach. Walter said he was not going to waste brandy on a frog-eating cook and told one of the crew to take him some rum instead. M. Perron then said rum was no good and he must have a bottle of brandy or he could not stay in the *Beatrice*. Walter swallowed his medicine with a wry face and handed over the brandy. Methinks M. Perron is a bit of a twister."

The *Beatrice* was berthed at Gravesend, where the party split up. General Taylor and his two daughters, Ann and Harriet, had been invited to stay with Lord and Lady Palmerston, Sir Walter and Mr. Fortescue having been rather pointedly excluded. Lord Palmerston had sent his carriage for his guests ; Lord and Lady Minto and Lord and Lady Willoughby de Broke were content to travel to London by the South-Eastern line ; but Sir Walter inveigled Mr. Fortescue and the Rev. Fitzwilliam into driving with him in a phaeton which he hired at a livery stable. The expedition was not a success as the hireling nag was such a poor specimen of his class that he went lame and had to be left at Dartford. There they picked up a carrier's cart and after spending a wretched night at a roadside tavern, they eventually arrived at Sir Walter's favourite hostelry, the Golden Cross Inn at Charing Cross, all rather the worse for wear.

On 30th April Lady Carew sent a message to her brother asking him to escort her and Harriet to the opening of the Exhibition the next day, as Lord Palmerston had to accompany the Queen and Prince Albert, and General Taylor was going with the Duke of Wellington. Sir Walter had made it quite clear that he and Mr. Fortescue would not attend, Sir Walter saying that he " did not hold with that German feller wasting our money over glass houses." Therein Sir Walter misjudged the strangely acute business sense of Prince Albert, since the Exhibition left a surplus of £150,000 after all expenses were paid, although it did not, as anticipated, inaugurate a period of peace. Sir Walter regretted having come to London at all, and his toady, Mr. Fortescue, was, of course, in agreement with him. Sir Walter decided that he would prefer to pass the time at sea where he would be master aboard his own ship. Lady Carew and her sister were, he knew, going to stay at Compton Verney with the Willoughby de Brokes ; they would have the company of Fitzwilliam Taylor, and he and Mr. Fortescue might or might not join them, as the spirit moved them. Meanwhile they made their way back to the *Beatrice* at Gravesend.

Lord Palmerston had placed a carriage at the disposal of his guests, and on 1st May Lady Carew, her sister and Fitzwilliam

Taylor left the Foreign Secretary's house at 10 o'clock in order
to allow plenty of time to see the state procession which was due
to start at half-past eleven. Fitzwilliam Taylor was very proud
of his sisters. Ann Carew was superb in a grey and white silk
dress with pagoda sleeves and a bonnet trimmed with red and
white roses, covered with a gauzy veil ; Harriet Fortescue looked
very striking in a gown of green silk, as befitted her darker
beauty, with a coquettish little round straw hat adorned with
a single lily. The Rev. Fitzwilliam made copious notes in his
journal.

" ' The Rose and the Lily ' attracted a great deal of attention
as we drove along, and quite put their parsonic brother to shame
in his black coat and white choker. We took up a position in
Hyde Park which gave us a good view. At a quarter to twelve
we saw the state carriages approaching from the Green Park.
In the first was the Queen, Prince Albert, the little Princess
Victoria and Prince Edward. Then came the Prince and Princess
of Prussia and their son, and afterwards other carriages with
Lords and Ladies-in-waiting. After the Royalties had entered
the great Glass House, we followed almost immediately, and
then we heard the huge organ playing ' God save the Queen.'
It made such a shattering noise that it seemed as if it must crack
the glass. As the Queen moved to the middle of the building,
a spray of water flowed from a fountain in the roof. Two
gentlemen in front of us were gesticulating and shouting at
each other in an angry way. I found out that one was Sir
Joseph Paxton, who designed the plan last year, and was knighted
by the Queen ; the other was a Mr. Fox, who actually designed
the building and I suppose thought he should be knighted also.
(I think that he was in the end.) When the Queen had finished
opening the Exhibition, we walked round the different stalls.
They were all arranged for different countries. We saw Turks
making carpets, Belgians making lace, and some French cooks
were making delicious sweetmeats, most of which they seemed
to be eating themselves. We were very interested in Mr.
Talbot's photographic room ; he was explaining the quick way

he has invented of making photographic pictures, which can be made to appear quite clear on paper. We came across Father and the Duke of Wellington with the old Marquis of Anglesey and his son, Lord George Paget. The Duke I thought has aged a lot and looked very feeble. Lord George Paget was a cadet at Sandhurst under Father ; he tells me that he is going to be Colonel of the 4th Light Dragoons ; not bad at thirty-three years of age ! ' Methinks I have had my fill of this,' Lord George said to me, and Lord Anglesey, who heard his remark, said ' Egad and so have I, let's be away, George.' I managed to drag Ann and Harriet away, much against their will, and we went back to Lord Palmerston's, where he has been civil enough to ask me to stay. Papa is going back to Devonshire by the railroad as he has a meeting of Magistrates ; he says he cannot dilly dally any longer with Walter in the *Beatrice*.'

The Queen went several times to the Exhibition, and Lord and Lady Palmerston made another visit on 12th May, asking their guests to accompany them. The Rev. Fitzwilliam describes the expedition.

" We felt very exclusive," he writes, " going with the Foreign Secretary and not without reason as it turned out. There was a regular at-home of Cabinet Ministers ; we were introduced to Lord John Russell, Sir Charles Wood, the Chancellor of the Exchequer, and the First Lord of the Admiralty, Sir Francis Baring, who is an old friend of Papa's. M. Thiers, a French statesman, was also there, whom Lord Palmerston said he wanted to keep an eye on as France was very unsettled. The triumph of Ann and Harriet's day at any rate was being introduced to the Queen and Prince Albert. The Queen recognized Ann and Harriet from the portrait by Sir George Hayter, and said that he had painted her portrait when she was Princess Victoria. She and Prince Albert were most gracious and seemed very pleased with everything they saw."

On 4th May Lady Willoughby de Broke wrote saying that Broke was suffering from gout, and was in such a bad frame of

THE ROSE AND THE LILY OF DEVON
Ann, Lady Carew and her sister Harriet Fortescue
From a drawing by Sir George Hayter in the possession of the author

mind that she was afraid she would have to put the party off. Lady Carew, who was no stranger to a bad frame of mind when Sir Walter was afflicted with the disease, was naturally disappointed but decided that the only alternative was to return to the *Beatrice* and wrote to Sir Walter to that effect, saying that she had invited Sir Francis Baring, the First Lord of the Admiralty and an old friend of her father's, to join them, and hoping he would have no objection. Sir Francis, who had heard that the *Beatrice* had been designed by Sir William Symonds when Surveyor of the Navy, thought that this would be a good excuse for combining business with pleasure ; he also saw an opportunity of showing himself to his constituents at Portsmouth, whom he had neglected for some time. On 7th May, therefore, the party travelled down to Gravesend by the railroad.

They were only just in time, for Sir Walter, who had not received Lady Carew's message announcing her change of plans, was preparing to put to sea. He had just heard that the yacht-schooner *America* of 170 tons had arrived at Cowes and was challenging all comers to a race round the Isle of Wight. Sir Walter decided to test the sailing powers of the *Beatrice* against her American rival. He greeted Sir Francis Baring without enthusiasm ; he was not very partial to politicians, being imbued with the idea that in some subtle way they would take his money one way or the other, and he asked Lady Carew with some warmth what she meant by "bringing a prying purser on board." Sir Francis Baring, for the sake of appearances, submitted to be shown round the yacht by Mr. Dove. He expressed himself well satisfied with her general trim, and was much interested in the new elliptical stern.

There was a good deal of shipping in the river and Mr. Dove, not wishing for any repetition of the incident which had occurred off Southend, engaged a pilot and a tug for the outward journey. Sir Francis Baring said this was quite unnecessary, and sent word to the officer commanding the navy steam sloop *Warrior*, lying at anchor in the river, to take the *Beatrice* in tow. Sir Walter expressed no thanks to Sir Francis Baring for his well-meant and timely intervention, since he strongly resented " being tugged out by an infernal machine " ; during the passage down the river, he grumbled to Mr. Fortescue at being " smothered in smoke and soot." When the *Beatrice* was clear of the mouth of the river, the *Warrior* left her and Mr. Dove again assumed command.

Sir Francis Baring, quite unaware of Sir Walter's ill-concealed hostility, was prepared to enjoy himself and made himself very agreeable to the two ladies. He talked little of politics beyond saying that the Government had been defeated by fourteen votes over Mr. Hume's bill to limit income tax to one year. At this Sir Walter pricked up his ears.

" Serve 'em right," he said venomously. " Hume ought to be Prime Minister."

Sir Francis Baring, secure in the financial background of Baring Brothers and Co., had few feelings one way or the other, and had no intention of entering into a political argument with his host. He therefore contented himself by upholding the Prime Minister, saying, " Lord John Russell is generally considered to do pretty well."

The *Beatrice* pursued her way in beautiful weather and rounded the North Foreland whence they proceeded towards the Straits of Dover. Mr. Dove had gone below for a little rest, leaving Mr. Jonas, the mate, in charge. Mr. Jonas apparently justified the skipper's dictum that " he knew how things ought not to be done " by coming within an ace of running the *Beatrice* on the Goodwin Sands.

The Rev. Fitzwilliam writes :

" We must have been somewhere off Sandwich, and we were bowling along with a fine breeze off the land. Mr. Dove was below and Mr. Jonas was *supposed* to be the sailing-master. Mr. Dove had kept a course fairly close in to the land, but Mr. Jonas for some reason best known to himself altered course and headed out to sea. A fishing boat a little distance away was anchored and a man in her shouted something like ' 'Ware sands.' No one took much notice and then ahead of us I saw the water shoaling and a mark set up. I shouted to Mr. Jonas, but I think he lost his head as he did nothing. I then rushed below and called Mr. Dove, who ran on deck. He took in the position at once. ' Down mainsail,' he roared to the crew, and to the steersman, ' hard-a-port,' this brought the ship into the wind. He then dealt with Mr. Jonas, shoving his furious face close to the mate's. ' D'you see that mark? You half-baked lubber,' he shouted at him, ' that's the Goodwin Sands and no thanks to you we're not landed on 'em. Sir Walter will have something to say, I'll be bound.' Mr. Dove was right; Walter had a good deal to say, and it was a very chastened Mr. Jonas who appeared when he had done with him. He will be dismissed at Portsmouth."

Sir Francis Baring disembarked at Portsmouth, which he considered the wisest course, as he had heard that the Queen was in residence at Osborne House and he did not wish to be seen " gadding about by that sneaking notary Truro," [1] who was also there. After sending Mr. Jonas about his business, Sir Walter made straight for Cowes. The harbour presented a gay scene with the numerous yachts which had arrived to take up the *America's* challenge. The Queen had offered a cup worth £100 to the winner of the race and there was great enthusiasm shown, although the race proper was to take place at the regatta in August and this was only in the nature of a trial run. On the 15th May, the morning of the race, the Queen, Prince Albert and the young Prince Edward drove over to Cowes to see the start of the race. The owners of the yachts were presented to the Queen by Lord Ellesmere who was acting as Commodore of the Royal Yacht Squadron. Sir Walter, with ineffable condescension, informed the Rev. Fitzwilliam that he had no objection to being presented to the Queen, but had no intention of " bowing and scraping to that German feller."

[1] Lord Chancellor.

As the weather was unsettled, instead of following the course round the Isle of Wight, it was agreed to sail round the Warner Lightship, twice round the N.W. Black Buoy of the Middle, winning off Ryde pier. The Rev. Fitzwilliam gives an account of the race.

" There were six yachts entered," he writes. " The *America, Claymore, Urania, Crusader, Beatrice* and *Constance.* The preparatory gun was fired from the club-house at 10 o'clock. The wind was strong and puffy from the South-west with a weather-going tide. At half past ten the starting gun was fired and the crews of the racing yachts ran up their canvas and started for the Warner Lightship, the *Beatrice* taking the lead, closely followed by the *America* and *Constance.* M. Perron got so excited that he rushed on deck beating a saucepan against a frying pan, shouting ' *en avant la Beatrice !* ' Walter, who was infuriated by the noise, sent him below with a flea in his ear. Unfortunately the *America* passed the *Beatrice* to windward before reaching the Warner Lightship, which was rounded by the vessels in the following order : *America,* 1 ; *Beatrice,* 2 ; *Constance,* 3. The yachts then hauled their wind and laid their course to the N.W. Black Buoy of the Middle. The *America* kept the lead for the whole distance to Ryde pier."

Two days later the owner of the *America*, Mr. Louis S. Thatcher of New York, gave a dinner party on board to which the owners of the other competing yachts and their ladies were invited. On arrival the ladies were offered mint juleps, and the gentlemen bourbon whisky, which was handed round by negro stewards. Lady Carew and her sister at first sipped the drinks doubtfully, but later pronounced them to be very refreshing. Mr. William Henry Vanderbilt, who was engaged with his father, Cornelius Vanderbilt, in a coasting steamer business, was a passenger on board and made himself very agreeable to Lady Carew. She rather nervously asked Mr. Vanderbilt if the servants on board were slaves, and he replied : " No, we leave that to the South." The dinner was substantial enough in its way, though the hominy and flapjacks were not relished by Sir Walter, who thought the hominy was "good feed for horses"; he and Mr. Fortescue, however, rapidly acquired a taste for the bourbon whisky. At the end of dinner the host very wisely limited the toasts to two: the Queen and President Fillmore, which were drunk with acclamation. The party returned to the *Beatrice* having been much impressed with the magnificent accommodation in the *America*.

Sir Walter was laid low by a violent attack of gout and Mr. Fortescue was very seedy, suffering from what he called "Yankee doldrums." Dally gave as his considered opinion that the trouble in both cases was "that miserable rye liquor." Dally, who was usually competent when Sir Walter was "in a bad frame of mind," could do nothing right, and had a felt boot hurled at him during the course of his ministrations. Lady Carew, in spite of the discomfort caused to everyone by Sir Walter's attack of gout, decided that the undertaking had been well worth while. She had accomplished what she had set out to do and best of all had been informally presented to the Queen and Prince Albert at the Exhibition. What more could the heart of woman desire?

Chapter Fourteen

VOYAGE TO RUSSIA

AFTER the dismissal of Mr. Jonas, Sir Walter had experienced some difficulty in obtaining a mate for the *Beatrice*. In the middle of May 1852, however, Mr. Dove produced a man named William Hawke who had been fourth mate in the *Birkenhead* when she went down in February of this same year and had been one of the few survivors. He had just arrived back from South Africa at his home in Torquay and was glad to take on the job in a ship from his own home port. General Taylor, who was staying at Haccombe, said he would be very interested to hear a first-hand account of the wreck and persuaded Sir Walter to ask Hawke over. The General, the Rev. Fitzwilliam and Miss Bessie composed the audience and Hawke, nothing loath to relate his experiences, began his story which Fitzwilliam Taylor recorded in his journal.

" ' The *Birkenhead* was an iron paddle-wheel steamer,' he said, ' and sailed from Cork on January 7th with 730 souls on board. There were 350 men belonging to different regiments and a lot of women and children. Besides these there were 130 officers and ratings of the Navy. We got to Simon's Bay on February 23rd when orders came to proceed at once to Algoa Bay to land the drafts for the Kaffir War. On the same evening we continued the voyage. The night was calm and the sea smooth, the shore being about three miles away. I was watching the man casting the lead, and just about 2 a.m. on the 24th the man called out " 12 fathoms," but he had hardly spoken when we felt a sudden shock. The ship had struck on some sunken rocks. Water at once poured in and drowned several soldiers who were in their berths in the lower troop deck. When the shock was felt, Commander Salmond, the Captain, and the officers not on watch, rushed on to the deck. The Commanding Officer of the soldiers, Colonel Seton, called the officers to him and told them discipline must be kept up. The men obeyed as if they were falling in for inspection. One party was told off to work the pumps, another to help the sailors to lower the boats, and a third lot to throw the horses overboard. In the meantime the Captain had ordered the engines to be reversed. He couldn't have done a worse thing, for the ship came on the rocks again with another bump which knocked a great hole in her bottom and let in tons of water which put out the fires in the engine room. The sailors had got three boats lowered and passed the women and children into them ; the other boats were stove in and could not be launched. Colonel Seton stood in the gangway with a drawn sword to prevent any rush by the men ; none was attempted and all the women and children in the boats were saved.'

" The listeners were spellbound, and it was Miss Bessie who said, ' Go on, Mr. Hawke, please.'

" Hawke, who had warmed up to his subject, continued :

" ' About ten minutes after striking, the ship broke in two at the foremast and the funnel fell crushing some people and throwing into the sea others who were trying to clear the paddle-box boat. It was then that Commander Salmond gave a mad order ; he told all those who could swim to jump overboard and try and reach the boats. This made Colonel Seton wild with anger ; he told the men to do no such thing as even if they reached the boats they would swamp them and send the women and children to the bottom. Not a man stirred ; perhaps they couldn't swim, but anyway there they stayed. Just after this the ship broke again abaft the mainmast, and threw those clinging on board into the sea, which was full of sharks. I, with seven men of the 91st regiment, were more fortunate than the rest. We managed, completely worn out, to make a landing at Point Danger, and in the end were taken by H.M.S. *Rhadaman*

—thus to Cape Town. All the women and children were saved and 160 men of the Army and Navy, but 370 officers and men of the Army and Navy were drowned.'

" ' A very harrowing but heroic story, Mr. Hawke,' General Taylor said, when he had finished.

" ' Yes, sir,' Hawke replied, ' but I blame Commander Salmond for the loss of life. He should never have reversed the engines, but there, the poor man's dead, so I'll say no more.' "

In spite of such disasters and of the uneasy international situation in 1852, the life of the English privileged classes went smoothly on.

There may be among the old files of the Royal Yacht Squadron a record of the regatta held at Cronstadt in the summer of 1852 under the patronage of H.I.M. the Tsar. The unexpected and lavish hospitality extended by the Russians to their guests created a stir of excitement among the members of the Royal Yacht Squadron, and more especially in the minds of the privileged few at Haccombe who had been invited to join Sir Walter and Lady Carew in a trip to Russia in the *Beatrice* for the purpose of attending the regatta. In 1852, land values being a reality, Sir Walter, with a very sizeable rent roll, well-invested securities and income tax at 7*d.* in the pound, could afford to take his pleasure like a gentleman, and needless to say he did so.

Miss Bessie certainly was, and Miss B pretended to be, very keen sailors, and Miss Bessie kept the ship's log punctiliously. Mr. Talbot, whom Lady Carew had met at the Great Exhibition, had sent one of his assistants down to take a photographic picture of the *Beatrice* before she set out on her voyage. This necessitated a great deal of preparation, and Mr. Talbot's assistant popped in and out of a black canopy many times before the machine was set. The final picture, when it appeared on paper, gave a very fair idea of what the *Beatrice*, her passengers and crew looked like. Sir Walter does not appear to have suffered from shortage of man-power or labour troubles, since the picture shows the *Beatrice* as carrying a crew of 20 A.B.s, a captain and mate, to say nothing of a chef, scullions and other domestic retainers. There seems to have been a sharp dividing line between the cabin and the fo'c'sle ; in the photographic picture the crew are shown squatting respectfully on their hunkers, well forward, while amidships are grouped the passengers, including several ladies dressed in various degrees of elegance and holding parasols. Sir Walter himself, a massive figure of a man with mutton chop whiskers, stands firmly on the poop as if nothing short of a cannon ball would move him. The scene generally presents a perfect picture of Victorian complacency.

Meanwhile at Haccombe preparations were in full swing for the beginning of the great adventure. The servants were rushed off their legs ; ladies' maids were busy putting the last touches to their mistresses' luggage, which was loaded on to farm wagons, while footmen embarked on manual labour which was very foreign and very distasteful to their ideas of propriety. Dally supervised the packing up of the wine which formed a large part of the baggage. M. Perron, like Gallio, cared for none of these things and was content to watch his underlings stowing away kitchen utensils. The departure from Haccombe for Torquay, the port of embarkation, as described by Miss Bessie who was off her head with excitement, is reminiscent of the great Boer trek of 1835.

" *4th June.* Started from Haccombe at 12 o'clock ; our party consisted of Papa, Mama, B and myself, Uncle and Aunt Willoughby, Uncle and Aunt Forty, and Uncle Fitz. Papa has arranged that Dally, instead of being butler, will be Steward and Henry, the first footman, will be understeward ; the ladies' maids will be called stewardesses. Mama, B and myself went in one barouche, which Mama as usual insisted on being shut, though it was a hot day, and Uncle and Aunt Willoughby and Uncle and Aunt Forty went in the other, which very sensibly they had open. The servants went in two omnibuses and the luggage in three wagons. Papa and Uncle Fitz drove tandem."

Getting aboard seems to have been a leisurely business for

everyone except the servants, who were all hustled to their quarters by Dally—all, that is, except M. Perron, the chef, whose status did not permit him to be hustled by anyone. M. Perron followed in the wake of the house-party to the Imperial Hotel, where he doubtless partook of the elaborate six-course dinner which was served at three o'clock.

The first night up-channel proved to be an uncomfortable one for all the saloon passengers but Sir Walter, who had the digestion of an ox. The domestic staff, not having had the opportunity to gorge themselves on a six-course dinner, seem to have fared better, though M. Perron, the chef, was completely hors-de-combat; he would perhaps have fared better had he been content to be hustled aboard by Dally on an empty stomach. The next day brought little relief, and Miss Bessie writes: "All our party, except Papa, felt very poorly and kept to their beds. Poor M. Perron was so seedy that he could not prepare any food, which did not matter to us, but made Papa very angry as usual." Matters became so uncomfortable for all concerned that Mr. Dove was ordered to put into Yarmouth and this enabled Sir Walter to go ashore and get a square meal. Miss Bessie does not record how Dally and his staff fared. Presumably they made do with the crew in the galley.

It was not until the *Beatrice* was off the Norwegian coast and the yacht was becalmed for the best part of a day that the party really got into their stride. There was a hot sun and the ladies ventured on deck; most of them sought the shade of parasols and adopted the role of semi-invalids but a few indulged in a mild form of mackerel fishing at which they were not very successful and merely succeeded in hooking each other's bonnets. The "stewardesses" meanwhile were enabled to take a well-earned rest which they badly needed after ceaseless attendance on their mistresses.

Miss Bessie, who was an excellent sailor and had survived the buffeting as well as Sir Walter, took up her pen: "*9th June*. Fair wind, carried our squaresail until about midnight, when we came in sight of the Skaw Light." Miss Bessie is presumably making use of a writer's licence as she was usually packed off to bed before 10 o'clock. She continues the next day : " *10th June.* Very fresh breeze indeed, got down two reefs in the mainsail and the bonnet off the staystail. At two o'clock Papa made up his mind to run into Gothenburg."

Sir Walter was apt to make sudden decisions to run into any place to which his fancy led him, but the consequences sometimes proved disconcerting to those who carried out his orders. Mr. Dove protested that he could not enter the harbour without a pilot.

" The Swedes are very particular who enters their harbours," he said.

" Damn the Swedes," Sir Walter said, " an English gentleman can enter any harbour how or when he pleases."

But the Swedish authorities in this case proved that Mr. Dove and not Sir Walter was right ; they fired a warning shot over the bows of the *Beatrice*.

Miss Bessie writes :

" We were all very shaken : poor Mama had to be revived with smelling salts ; Dally told Papa that M. Perron was so upset that the dinner was spoiled, which upset Papa even more than the rudeness of the harbour people. When the pilot came, Dally had to give him three bottles of Papa's old brandy to make it right with him."

So far as the visit to Gothenburg was concerned the game seems hardly to have been worth the candle. According to Miss Bessie it was a drab place.

" We saw some horse-artillery exercising ; the horses were badly groomed and so were the soldiers. We saw a lot of common women with handkerchiefs tied over their heads, but only a few ladies in bonnets which are not nearly as smart as our ladies' maids wear."

Chapter Fifteen

THE CRONSTADT REGATTA

SIR WALTER, disgusted at the reception given to an English gentleman by Swede underlings whom he placed in a lower category than Devonshire turnips, decided that he would give the Danes a chance and make Copenhagen his next port of call. Miss Bessie, who studied the charts and knew her Shakespeare, Sir Walter being ignorant of both, insisted that they should put into Elsinore.

"Papa is interested in Danish pigs," she wrote, "but I tell him we must not miss seeing 'Hamlet's' home. He does not read much and I really believe until I explained, that he thought Hamlet was some sort of small pig. We chaffed him so much that he did what I wanted him to do."

There was quite a gathering of the clans in Copenhagen itself; two other English yachts, the *Claymore* and *Urania*, competing in the Cronstadt regatta, had arrived and a round of festivities took place. The visitors were treated with the utmost deference, "as an English gentleman ought to be," Sir Walter observed with complacency. He responded with what he considered to be generous hospitality on board, though Dally warned him that in his opinion the cellar was getting rather low.

"Get some more wine aboard then," Sir Walter said, "and don't let me hear you mumbling again that there ain't none."

Miss Bessie was thrilled and got busy with her pen.

"*14th June.* Anchored in Copenhagen harbour at three

o'clock. Lieutenant Prosellius of His Majesty's yacht came on board to welcome us on behalf of King Frederick VII, which Papa thought ' very civil of him.' Mama was rather doubtful and wondered if the King was quite nice as he had been separated from two wives and then married a lady who was not of royal blood. Then said Papa, ' If she asked us to dine, she will probably give us a better dinner.' "

Her morganatic Majesty apparently fulfilled all Sir Walter's expectations, and the gentlemen returned in the small hours well pleased with themselves. It was, of course, not etiquette to invite royalty to dine on board, but Lieutenant Prosellius and other officers of the royal entourage gladly accepted Lady Carew's invitation. Miss Bessie and B were too young to be present, but Miss Bessie gleaned all the necessary details from Dally.

" Covers were laid for twenty. Mama (with the help of M. Perron and me) had written a menu card in most beautiful French which I am afraid no one understood except Mama. Uncle Fitz being the only clergyman present, said grace. Lieutenant Prosellius, who speaks English, stood up, but the other Danish officers sat down and tucked their napkins into their stocks. Dally says they thought Uncle Fitz was translating the menu into English, and they did not really mean to be irreverent. There were ten courses, not counting side-dishes, and a great quantity of champagne was drunk. After the ladies had gone, some of the gentlemen got rather tipsy, and when they were getting into their boat, one of them fell into the water ; he was fished out with a boat-hook."

On leaving Copenhagen the *Beatrice* had as her consorts the *Urania, Claymore*, as well as a third yacht, the *Fairy Queen*. The opportunity was therefore taken to indulge in some practice racing in preparation for the Russian regatta. Miss Bessie and her sister thoroughly enjoyed it, but the elder ladies of the party, who liked to do their crewel work in comfort, were not amused. Miss Bessie notes :

"*19th June*. Got under way at three in the morning ; at seven, we began our little regatta which went on all day. Mama, Aunt Forty and Aunt Willoughby did not enjoy it much and went below. Papa chaffed them and offered to take them a ride in the penny steamboat from London to Greenwich when we got home. Mama said, ' At least we should get a whitebait dinner, but at this rate we shall get none at all.' Papa then told Mr. Dove to take in the square-sail and we stopped racing."

Whether Sir Walter did this to oblige Lady Carew, or was frightened at the threat of no dinner, is not related.

And so the *Beatrice*, with her cargo of landed gentry and delicately nurtured ladies, thinking of their dinner to-day and dreaming of whitebait dinners in the future, drifted through the Baltic Seas, past Bornholm Island and through the Gulf of Finland, arriving at Cronstadt on 24th June.

Miss Bessie thought the approaches to Cronstadt extremely dreary and obviously quotes from Count de Custine, the French general who had commanded the army of the Rhine in 1792 and who had been executed by the revolutionaries in 1793. She had been reading his account of a journey to Russia with Miss Cole, prior to the occasion.

"Cronstadt," she writes, "with its forests of masts, its sub-structures, and its ramparts of granite, finely breaks the monotonous reverie of the pilgrim, who is like me seeking for imagery in this dreary land. I have never seen in the approaches to any other great city a landscape so melancholy as the banks of the Neva."

This effusion must have been padding for the journal, since transport facilities of 1852 did not as a rule allow young ladies to do a round of great cities, nor would their parents have permitted it ; certainly not Sir Walter and Lady Carew, whose itinerary was seldom extended beyond Bath.

The cordial welcome extended to the pilgrims at Cronstadt compensated for the unattractive landscape and provided much copy for the journal.

" *24th June*. Found ourselves anchored in Cronstadt Roads. Prince Lobanoff and many gentlemen in attendance came on board with a message to Papa from the Emperor. We were all invited to breakfast on board the Royal steamer *Hercule*. It was a very wet day which was a pity, and it was also a very wet breakfast ; for we had quantities of champagne and sherry instead of tea, which the gentlemen preferred. The Emperor was not there, but his eldest daughter, who is not pretty, was in Prince Lobanoff's party. It was so wet that we didn't stay to watch the regatta, but went to Peterhoff where we found the *Beatrice*. Prince Lobanoff sent us off to her in a 16-oar boat. We were all invited to dine with the Emperor, and all our party, except B and myself, went. There were eighty people to dinner and Mama, Aunt Fortescue and Aunt Willoughby were the only ladies present. They said the gentlemen behaved very well, and did not drink a great deal, I suppose because the Emperor was there and he is a very stern man. Prince Lobanoff sent B and I a lot of lovely sweetmeats on gold dishes which he said we might keep as a souvenir of Russia. We thought this was very good-natured of him.

" *25th June*. Papa and Uncle Forty went to St. Petersburg ; Count Aperaxine came on board and offered to take us on shore, where we fell in with Prince Kotchchoubei on the pier, who was waiting to take us to the Palace in a carriage-and-four belonging to the Emperor. The palace is very beautiful but rather cold looking ; the Emperor keeps all his suite there, but he himself lives in a cottage in the garden which I expect is warmer. We then drove to the military parade ground where the Emperor was to review the troops. The Imperial Guard looked very smart in white uniforms, but were rather grubby round their necks. Prince Kotchchoubei then took us to the pavilion where the English guests were assembled, and we were joined by Papa and Uncle Forty. Prince Kotchchoubei introduced us to the Emperor who looked rather grumpy ; the ladies curtsied and the gentlemen bowed. The band of the Imperial Guard then played the Russian and English national anthems, after which the troops marched past. B and I decided that we liked the Cossacks best ; we could scarcely tell the difference between the men and their ponies, they were all so shaggy."

The most important event in the regatta festivities took place on 30th June when twelve yachts competed in the great race for the Emperor's Gold Cup. With the exception of his two daughters the ladies of Sir Walter's party were not regatta-minded and they gratefully accepted the invitation of the British Minister, Sir Hamilton Seymour, to accompany him to Moscow for a few days.

" *29th June.* Papa, B and I went to Cronstadt, having left Uncle Forty, Uncle Willoughby and Uncle Fitz in St. Petersburg. Papa sailed in the race not because he thought he had any chance of winning it, but to please the Russians.

" *30th June.* Took our stations early in the morning and started at 10 o'clock. The *Claymore* had the best start ; we got along well enough until the wind headed us. The *Georgian* passed us, as did the *Queen Victoria*, the Emperor's yacht. I think I never saw the *Beatrice* sail worse, and she came in nearly last. The yachts passed the flagship in the following order : 1. *Claymore*, 2. *Queen Victoria*, 3. *Georgian*. We gave the *Claymore*, who won the Emperor's Cup, three cheers. Mr. Dove, who, I am afraid, doesn't like losing a gold cup, was rather sulky and didn't join in."

After the race Miss Bessie and B, escorted by Lady Carew's maid, Gilbert, Ellen's successor, took a little relaxation on shore, and Miss Bessie has recourse to her journal.

" *2nd July.* Went to see the Hermitage Palace. It is very beautiful and full of pictures ; there is also a sculpture gallery. We then drove in a droshky to the Cazian Church, it is a very fine building ; as you go in at the door you pass a lot of beggars who bow at you and ask for money. We walked up to the altar. The rails before the altar and the shrine of the Virgin Mary are of solid silver ; her face is set all round with jewels as she is a patron saint. We saw the people come and touch the ground with their foreheads and cross themselves. It is not a

Catholic but a Greek church. When we told Gilbert this, she said, ' Greek or Catholic, 'tis all the same, I can't abide these old papists.' I'm afraid Gilbert was not enjoying herself. We intended driving to Lady Seymour's but found it was too far, so had a drive and came back. B and I had dinner at two o'clock and then drove with Gilbert and Mr. Sharp, who is the interpreter, first to the English and then to the Russian bazaar. All the things were dreadfully dear and as Papa had only given us very little money, there was no buying anything. We then drove to the Greek church where there is a tremendous quantity of silver. After tea we drove to the summer gardens and from there home.

" 3rd July. Went to a museum in the morning ; there is besides hosts of other things, the skeleton of a Mammoth, with an elephant by the side of it which makes the elephant look quite small. In the afternoon we went to two churches and went on to where the Emperor was to pass, but were too late to see him. We then went down to the Cazan Church where they were singing Mass. Gilbert made a scene and had to be hustled out. We went to see the Winter Palace and liked it much better than the other palaces. In the evening we went to Lady Seymour's where we met Mr. and Mrs. Otto Goldschmidt on their honeymoon ; she was Miss Jenny Lind, and she sang a most lovely song. We did not get home until 12 o'clock. Lady Seymour kindly sent us home in her brougham as it had got very cold. We were so ashamed of Gilbert having misbehaved herself at the Mass, that we made her go on the box.

" 4th July. In the evening we went to the house of Peter the Great and saw the stool and chair he had made and the boat he helped to build. The man who showed it to us called it the great-grandsire of the Russian fleet."

Sir Walter, perhaps nettled by the poor sailing qualities displayed by the *Beatrice*, determined to show the world at large that at any rate her cuisine, in charge of a talented French chef, was of the first order, and on 8th July gave a farewell dinner party on board. According to Miss Bessie there was a very distinguished gathering.

" At about four o'clock the guests began to arrive ; Prince Lobanoff and Prince Kotchchoubei arrived first ; then came Prince and Princess Bariatinsky, followed soon after by Prince Trubetscoy. Count Paul Bobrinski brought Monsieur and Madame Robespierre. Lastly came a dear old gentleman, Count Nesselrode ; he is a very distinguished man and was a friend of the great Napoleon. He was also a great favourite of the Emperor Alexander, but does not get on so well with this Emperor, who seems to be rather an interfering sort of man. The dinner lasted three hours and a half and a great deal of wine was drunk, especially by the visitors who seem to be very thirsty sort of people. Dally, who usually listens to every word, said that the only person he could understand was Papa when he swore at him, as everyone else talked French. Papa, of course, does not speak any language except his own, nor would he think of doing so."

Reactions on board next morning were varied and mostly unfavourable. Dally, on assessing cellar losses, rather sourly intimated to Miss Bessie that " Roosian princes and suchlike " had a larger liquid storage capacity than English landed gentry, which was saying a good deal. Miss Bessie later heard him ordering Henry, the under-steward, who was marshalling the empty bottles to " shy they dead Roosians overboard." Uncle Fortescue was not his usual self and was suffering from what he described in a somewhat mixed metaphor as " a ham-strung head." Sir Walter, who was not subject to this form of complaint, had nevertheless to pay forfeit with his feet and developed a sharp attack of gout. During these bouts Sir Walter usually succeeded in making everyone with whom he came in contact as uncomfortable as himself.

Miss Bessie writes :

" Such a to-do to-day whilst Uncle Fitz was reading morning prayers. There was a nasty swell and we found it difficult sometimes to keep our feet. Uncle Fitz had just got to ' deliver us from evil ' in the Lord's prayer, when the large family bible fell off the table on to Papa's bad foot. It must have hurt poor Papa very much for he made dreadful noises sounding like Amens, so Uncle Fitz had to stop. Dally said afterwards that it was tempting Providence and Papa when he had gout to read prayers on a choppy day. Some time after prayers, we heard a lot of popping noises astern, and we could see a lot of little black dots in the water. Uncle Forty thought they were seals and fired some shots from a musket at them, but did not hit any. I knew what they were as I heard Dally tell Henry to throw the dead Roosians overboard, so was able to chaff Uncle Forty."

On the next day the British Ambassador, Sir Hamilton Seymour, a friend of Sir Walter's dating from Eton days, called to say good-bye. He was accompanied by Prince Menschikoff, who brought a farewell message from the Emperor. The visit was of no particular significance to those concerned at the time, but in the light of after events, it is of more than passing interest.

In 1852, the European scene was already bedevilled by the dispute over the possession of the Holy Places in Jerusalem and Palestine, which were then, it must be remembered, within the Turkish Empire. For a hundred years France had had treaty rights to their possession but had never enforced them, until in 1850 Napoleon renewed the claim and received recognition of it from Turkey. Russia protested, since there was a far greater number of Orthodox Christians than of Latin Christians under Turkish rule but the protest was ignored. Early in the following year, 1853, the Tsar had a talk with Sir Hamilton Seymour about the situation which would arise when the Sultan of Turkey died. It was on that occasion that he used the famous phrase " the sick man of Europe ". The Tsar told Sir Hamilton that though he had no wish to see Constantinople in the hands of Russia he would never agree to a restoration of the old Byzantine Empire to include in its boundaries Greece and the Danubian States.

Sir Hamilton, on instructions from home, temporized and suggested that when the Sultan died, a conference of the Great

Powers should be called to settle the question. But in March, the Tsar sent Prince Menschikoff to see the Sultan and talk to him privately, omitting to call on the Minister for Foreign Affairs, Prince Fuad. Fuad immediately appealed to the French and British, both of whose ambassadors were absent on leave, but the British Chargé d'Affaires took it upon himself to summon the British fleet from Malta. The British Government ordered its immediate return, but Napoleon dispatched the French fleet from Toulon.

In May 1853, Russia occupied the two provinces of Moldavia and Wallachia and once more the British and French fleets occupied the Dardanelles.

In spite of a conference at Vienna in July, and a later offer from Austria to mediate between the parties, the Turkish army, under Omar Pasha, crossed the Danube on October 1853. Russia declared her intention of remaining " purely on the defensive," but in November a Turkish squadron was attacked by the Russian fleet at Sinope and virtually destroyed.

This " massacre of Sinope," as it was called, greatly inflamed British public opinion and in spite of the efforts of Lord Aberdeen to continue negotiations, war was declared on Russia by both Britain and France in March 1854.

These future events cast no shadow on the easy-going pleasure party in the *Beatrice* and Miss Bessie makes the following brief allusion to two of the actors in the drama.

" *10th July.* Sir Hamilton Seymour and Prince Menschikoff arrived in the Imperial barge to say good-bye to Papa and Mama. Prince Menschikoff sailed in the *Queen Victoria* in the race for the Emperor's Cup, and thought she should have won. The Emperor said he was glad she had not done so, as his gold cup was won by a subject of her namesake, our Queen Victoria. Mama thought this was a very nicely turned compliment. Papa was still very seedy and saw Sir Hamilton in his cabin ; he said he could not be bothered with any more Princes which was not such a good compliment. The gentlemen did not stay very long as they said they were very busy. Prince Menschikoff invited us to a farewell breakfast in the steamer *Hercule* to-morrow, which he is giving on behalf of the Emperor, to everyone who took part in the regatta. All of us are going except, of course, poor Papa."

The competing yachts were due to leave on July 11th, and the farewell breakfast seems to have been even " wetter " than the previous one on board the royal steamer. Members of the yachts' crews were also regally entertained by their opposite numbers in the *Hercule*, which possibly had some bearing on the mix-up that occurred when leaving harbour. Hilarity and bonhomie were the order of the day, and Miss Bessie was almost at a loss to describe adequately the thrills that took place.

" Our last day," she writes, " was too comical and exciting for words ; all the gentlemen except Papa and Dally " (bracketed, no doubt, for the purposes of the journal) " and even the seamen, came from the *Beatrice*. Papa would not have enjoyed it much as his temper was not very good yesterday, and to-day we were met by Prince Menschikoff and *four* other princes. We sat down to breakfast at eleven o'clock in the saloon. Everything was served on gold plates ; there was a large samovar of tea which no one seemed to drink except B and myself, so it must have been meant as an ornament. Everyone else drank champagne, which the gentlemen said was too sweet ; they drank a good deal of it all the same. B ate too much caviar and felt seedy afterwards.

" After breakfast we were garlanded with roses from the Emperor's palace at Czarskoe-seloe, and Prince Menschikoff proposed the healths of our Queen and the Emperor. When we got on deck the Russian gentlemen made the ladies dance a ring of roses, and Count Bobrinski made horrible noises through a speaking trumpet, pretending to be a Cossack trumpeter sounding the charge. The gentlemen became funnier and funnier and it was three o'clock before we got into our dinghy. The fun was not over even then, for who should we see but M. Perron with a garland of roses, seated in the stern, holding the tiller and behaving in the oddest way. B and I thought it very funny, but Mama was not amused, saying it was disgusting and he was intoxicated."

The trouble which occurred on leaving harbour arose from the truculence of the *Claymore*'s skipper. Inflated with his success in carrying off the Emperor's Gold Cup, he laid a bet in a fit of post-prandial exuberance with Mr. Dove that the *Claymore* would be first away and would continue to maintain her place against all-comers. Mr. Dove, who was still sore at the *Beatrice* coming in last, determined that at any rate she should be in first and devil take the hindmost.

Mr. Dove was certainly first off the mark, but as Miss Bessie explains, the manœuvre did not run strictly according to plan and caused a good deal of confusion.

" Mr. Dove was in a great bustle to be off," she writes, " and there was a terrific hullabaloo, avast here and belay there. It was blowing hard from the westward, and we found we were dragging our anchor and had got foul of the *Georgian* astern of us ; we were going astern fast and drifting on a large merchant schooner. There was an awful row going on between Mr. Dove and Mr. Hawke (the mate) and in the middle of it an old tub of a ferry-boat looked as if she was coming right into us, but she just managed, and only just, to go between us and the schooner ; had she been five minutes sooner, she would not have had room to pass as we were close to the schooner, whose jib-boom was swinging over our stern. The men somehow managed to let go another anchor, much to Mr. Dove's annoyance. It was half past six before we got under way under three-reefed mainsail, bonnet off, a reef down in the foresail, bonnet off the staysail and storm jib. When we got into the fair-way, we found that we were ahead of all the yachts, with the *Claymore* coming up some way behind. Mr. Dove was very pleased and shouted some rude remarks at the *Claymore* ; he seemed to have quite settled his row with Mr. Hawke. I am afraid, however, he had another row with Papa in his cabin, as he did not look best pleased when he came on deck again."

A day or two at sea seems to have put Sir Walter on his legs again and a more cheerful atmosphere prevailed. Sir Walter, in fact, was in high spirits, for he had just heard from his son, Walter junior, who was at Sandhurst, that he would probably receive a cornetcy in the 'Blues.' Even more exciting was the news that young Walter had arrived at Copenhagen with Sir Henry Wynne, with whom he was staying at the Embassy. A return visit to Copenhagen to pick up Walter was obviously indicated. Dally's tactful reminder that the cellar was somewhat depleted was an additional incentive.

The turbulent backwash of the Peterhoff Narrows had receded and the *Beatrice* drifted over calm seas to her anchorage in Copenhagen harbour. Miss Bessie and Miss B were off their heads with excitement at the prospect of meeting their brother, and wondered if whiskers, like mushrooms, would spring up in the night on a budding Household Cavalry man. The journal, with its pleasant background of romance, is, however, essentially factual :

" *17th July.* Wind fair, carried the square-sail all day, had a very nice cruise and anchored in Copenhagen at about four o'clock next morning. Such excitement about ten o'clock Sir Henry Wynne and dear, dear Walter came on board. Walter looked just the same but had not grown any whiskers. B and I hoped that when he kissed us we should feel Papa's nice bristly feeling, but I suppose he is still very young. Dally went off in a droshky to collect Walter's luggage from the Embassy and some cases of wine. Sir Henry Wynne took B and I for a drive in his carriage to the Rosenberg gardens which are very beautiful. The gardens are open to the common people, and there were a lot of rather dirty little children playing about. Suddenly we saw a go-cart drawn by a goat, which was led by a very smart-looking footman in green and gold livery, with another one behind. Someone who looked like a lady's maid or nurse was walking beside the cart. Seated in the cart was the most beautiful little girl about eight years old, wearing a little fur bonnet. 'That,' said Sir Henry Wynne, 'is the little Princess

Alexandra of Denmark.' [1]   She waved gaily to us as she went by."

The party, reinforced by young Walter, sailed from Copenhagen on 20th July.   Miss Bessie, strongly supported by her brother, expressed a wish to visit " the land of the midnight sun," and they persuaded Sir Walter to put into Christiansand, where they found the *Claymore* anchored.   A most cordial reunion took place which is noted in the journal.

" Sir James Drummond came on board from the *Claymore*, having brought the Emperor's Cup to show us ; it is very handsome, made of gold and enamel.   Papa insisted on filling it with champagne in which to drink Sir James's health ;   Sir James made a little speech and then proposed Papa's health on his recovery."

Miss Bessie thought the hospitality to be rather one-sided and her opinion was evidently shared by Dally ; for she adds :

" Dally thought it rather shabby to come begging with an empty cup, but he was not surprised as they keep a very poor table in the *Claymore*, he said, and only think of racing."

Time was limited, for Walter junior had to undergo a course of instruction before joining his regiment early in August ;   but the ladies were able to visit the Hardanger Fiord, and were much impressed with its beauty, while the gentlemen had some good fishing on the Torrisdad River.   Young Walter, although an excellent horseman in the cavalry style, did not distinguish himself as a driver, and came to grief with a pair of jibbing horses.

Miss Bessie writes :

" Papa and the three uncles set off in carioles for the Torrisdad River.   Walter was going to drive Mama, B and myself in a carriage and pair.   When we got into the carriage, Walter could not manage the horses ;   one pulled one way and the other

[1] Later to become Princess of Wales.

kicked in the opposite direction and finally both bolted. We very nearly capsized and ran into a hedge, when luckily the horses stopped. Papa and Uncle Forty caught some beautiful salmon which we had for dinner, prepared as only M. Perron knows how. They will make a nice addition to the menu."

Judging by the usual length of M. Perron's menus, the addition would seem to have been somewhat superfluous.

The *Beatrice* arrived off Yarmouth on 30th July, where Walter disembarked. On the homeward journey down-channel the party anchored for a night off Spithead, where the Queen was reviewing the fleet next morning.

"We had a beautiful view," Miss Bessie writes, "and the *Victoria and Albert*, with the Queen and the Prince Consort on board, passed close to us. We cheered as they went past; we saw the Queen quite clearly, and she bowed very graciously."

By easy stages the *Beatrice* proceeded to Torbay to take part in the August regatta. In her own home waters, amongst lesser fry, she in somewise retrieved her reputation. She had failed to carry off the Emperor of Russia's Cup, but she gained the Fortescue Cup, presented by the Lord-Lieutenant of Devon.

Miss Bessie concludes in a very cheerful vein : "We were all delighted, particularly Aunt Fortescue, at winning the Fortescue Cup which made a very good ending to our trip to St. Petersburg and the Cronstadt regatta."

Chapter Sixteen

THE CHOBHAM REVIEW

SIR WALTER CAREW was conservative in his choice of guests ; that is to say, he liked to have those whom he could handle easily and who were content to conform to the programme laid down, a programme designed primarily for his own comfort and amusement. This was the more necessary, he considered, in the confined quarters of a yacht, which did not permit of any deviation from his plans. The R.Y.S. *Beatrice* had been put into commission at the beginning of June 1853, and was now lying in Torbay, her home port, awaiting the summer cruise. The cruise to Russian waters in the previous year had been most successful, and since all the guests had been very amenable he had decided to make no change and the party remained much the same : the Willoughby de Brokes, Mr. and Mrs. Fortescue, the Rev. Fitzwilliam Taylor, Sir Walter and Lady Carew and their two daughters, Bessie and B. The only persons who viewed the voyage with distaste were the domestic staff who had been selected to accompany the party. Dally the butler and his subordinate Henry had come to the conclusion that their promotion to steward and under-steward in no way compensated for the discomfort of their cramped quarters in the *Beatrice* ; M. Perron, the *chef de cuisine*, cordially disliked the sea and everything appertaining to it, in particular the uncomfortable galley in which he was condemned, when not incapacitated by sea-sickness, to produce the six-course dinners on which Sir Walter insisted. Of the ladies' maids, Annette, Lady Carew's French maid who had replaced Gilbert and whose experience of the sea had been limited to crossing the Channel as a baby-in-arms, was the only one who showed any enthusiasm. She refused to be daunted by M. Perron's warnings of the horrors of *mal-de-mer*, and confided to Miss Bessie that M. Perron consistently overloaded his stomach, a fact of which that young lady was fully aware.

The Reverend Fitzwilliam Taylor, who was now the spiritual head of three comfortable family livings, although he was assisted by three curates who performed what little work the sparse congregations demanded, had some qualms as to whether he was justified in leaving his parishioners for a second year in succession, but was overruled by Sir Walter, who told him " to let those lazy beggars of curates do something to earn their living."

The itinerary, as originally planned, provided for a cruise in home waters, where by competing in the various regattas Sir Walter hoped to redeem the reputation of the *Beatrice*'s sailing powers, which had suffered an eclipse at Cronstadt in the previous year. On the face of it, this year's cruise did not open up such exciting possibilities, at all events to the ladies, as the Russian adventure, but there was a *pièce de résistance* in store for them at the end of the cruise—a visit to Ireland for the Dublin Exhibition, which was to be graced by the presence of the Queen and the Prince Consort. It was quite obvious that the visit would take place under the most favourable conditions, for Sir Walter had received a very cordial invitation from Lord St. Germans, the Lord-Lieutenant, who was a West Country neighbour. Lord St. Germans had written : " Come as early as you like in August ; we can offer you quarters in the Vice-regal Lodge until the Queen arrives on the 29th. After that, Lord Gough tells me he will be very glad to have you at St. Helens. You will be able to see royalty in all its glory very comfortably." The ladies were a good deal more enthusiastic over the invitation than Sir

Walter ; the proposed meeting with royalty left him cold, and although as a loyal subject he reverenced the Queen, he mistrusted the Prince Consort. Lady Carew, however, backed up by the rest of the ladies, decided that the situation demanded an immediate visit to their milliner, and the landau was ordered to take them to Torquay for a final consultation with Madame Morice (neé Morris), who had discovered that, as the leading *modiste* of a fashionable watering-place, the gallicised version of her name had brought in quite an influx of the Quality.

Already disquieting rumours of Russian intentions towards the Porte had reached the British Government, which, taking upon itself the guardianship of " the sick man," threatened the Tsar with a big stick but prevented itself from making war by abstaining from preparation, in fact it did nothing but form a camp for 10,000 men at Chobham. On 2nd June, Admiral Dundas received orders to sail for the Dardanelles, and in order to emphasize the " Entente Cordiale," the fleet proceeded to Bezika Bay with the French fleet. Amid all the flutterings of milliners and the distractions of discriminating between regatta costumes and ensembles suitable for royalty, Lady Carew received a letter from her father, General Taylor, then completing his last term as Lieut.-Governor of Sandhurst. The General, who obtained a good deal of inside information from his old friend Palmerston, now Home Secretary, wrote :

" Before you start on your cruise you must come here ; I have just heard that Sidney Herbert has ordered a large force of troops to assemble at Chobham on June the 14th as a warning to the Russians not to play tricks with us. The Russians, of course, will laugh at our large force of 10,000 men, but this government is made to be laughed at. There is to be a great review of the *might* of the British army which I think would amuse you to see. I believe that Walter and some of the Blues will be there. You could drive over quite easily from here."

Sir Walter, whose military history dated from the Waterloo era, which he considered had proved England's invincibility for all time, pooh-poohed the whole affair as "humbug." He had, however, a wholesome respect for his father-in-law, and with the added attraction of perhaps seeing young Walter, made no objection to the plan.

The tiresome cross-country journey to Farnborough by rail, with its interminable delays due to frequent changes of gauge, was abandoned in favour of making for Portsmouth in the *Beatrice*, and Sir Walter sent orders to the skipper, Mr. Dove, to make ready to sail on 30th June. The impressive cortège, headed by Sir Walter and the Reverend Fitzwilliam in the phaeton and followed by two landaus containing the rest of the party, arrived at the landing-stage at nine o'clock, the advance party of servants and luggage having been sent on ahead. Three flies, containing the ladies' maids, Madame Morice's assistants, and the band-boxes and articles of apparel for the ladies of which they were in charge, added to the congestion of traffic. Annette in a great state of excitement could not find her mistress and reported to Sir Walter that the ladies' wardrobes were "*toutes complètes.*" The latter told Annette to "go to the devil."

There was a considerable amount of shipping in the harbour that morning. A portion of the fleet had put into Torbay, among the vessels being the *Terrible*, flagship of Sir Charles Napier, with the First Lord of the Admiralty, Sir James Graham, on board. Sir Walter was far more interested in the American yacht schooner *America* of 170 tons, which had won the Queen's Cup at Cowes in 1851. She was considerably larger than the *Beatrice*, but Sir Walter had again accepted her skipper's challenge for a wager of twenty pounds. Three other vessels of the Royal Yacht Squadron were in harbour, the *Lancashire Witch*, *Gipsy Queen*, and *Urania*, the owner of the last named being Lord Ellesmere, a friend of Sir Walter's in his Oxford days. There was, however, some delay in leaving; for an invitation to the yacht owners had arrived from the flagship to attend a party in honour of Sir James Graham. Miss Bessie writes :

"Papa and Mr. Dove, who had been stamping their feet to get under way, were furious. I suspect Mr. Dove was really interested in the wager and was thinking what he would get out of it if we won. Papa flatly refused to go to the party, but we ladies thought it would be capital fun. Uncle Fitz and Uncle Willoughby took charge of us and we set off in the dinghy. Uncle Fitz, who had not rowed since he was at Oxford, insisted on taking an oar, and promptly caught a crab ; he looked very comical sprawling on the bottom of the boat with his clergyman's choker all anyhow. We got on board the *Terrible* and were taken to the Admiral's cabin. We were introduced to Sir James Graham by Admiral Napier. Sir James was a pompous stuffy sort of man who smelt of sherry wine, which he had dribbled down his coat. The steward offered us sherry and seedy cake. B was not used to drinking sherry, which made her hiccup, which we all thought very rude, but made Sir James Graham laugh ; he lifted his glass to her, saying, ' Your health, young lady.' We got back on board the *Beatrice* at half-past twelve o'clock."

The *Beatrice* won her wager against the *America*, though whether the result was due to the superior sailing powers of the former or the low cunning of her skipper must remain a debatable question. It is evident that Mr. Dove, who knew the stretch of coast between Plymouth and Portland Bill like a book, counted with some success on his opponent's ignorance of it, and that is borne out by Miss Bessie's account :

"Blowing great guns from the Westward, which seemed to please Mr. Dove. The *Beatrice* and *America* got off on an even start. When we got outside the harbour, Mr. Dove hugged the coast rather close we thought, and kept on the inner tack. We were under three-reefed main-sail, bonnet off, and a reef down in the foresail, bonnet off the staysail and storm jib. When the wind moderated Mr. Dove made as if to run into Teignmouth, where there is a strong current from the estuary coming over the Bar. We saw the *America* follow suit. Just then a heavy squall came on, so with us it was down squaresail in pretty quick time, and the foresail soon followed it. Mr. Dove tacked like lightning and we came out to sea. The squall died down, so we put on all sail again. The *America* was not so lucky and she seemed to be in difficulty near the Bar. By the time she got clear, we must have been two miles ahead, and she never caught us up again. We got into Cowes at 9 p.m. and the *America* arrived an hour later. The Skipper of the *America* came on board and Papa said that he was so unpleasant to Mr. Dove that he was ordered off, but not until he had paid the twenty pounds ! It seems to have been a case of all's fair in love and war. Got under way at 1 p.m. and beat down towards Yarmouth, where Papa and the gentlemen went ashore to get a decent dinner as M. Perron on his first day out had failed us again ; it is really too bad and we ladies have to starve. All the servants were very seasick after their rolling, except Annette, who was simply delighted that M. Perron's ' overladen ' stomach had taken him to bed. We afterwards ran on to Spithead, being passed by the fleet, and went into Portsmouth. In the evening the men came aft and sang glees whilst the ladies were busy arranging their dresses for the review at Chobham."

Sir Walter, as has already been related, abominated railroads and all their works and it was unfortunate that at the station he should have encountered Sir Francis Baring, one of the directors who had suffered from his insistence on a tunnel at Marley. Sir Francis however, with imperturbable aplomb, greeted him with " Welcome, the tunnel king."

Sir Walter, whose sense of humour was never marked, resented this coupling of his name with Mr. George Hudson, whose questionable activities in railway speculation had brought him under a cloud, and he refused to travel in the same carriage with the Member for Portsmouth. In any case, he was not attracted by the stuffy plush-lined carriages with canopied windows provided by the London and Southampton Railway Company for first-class passengers, saying they were " well enough for females and M.P.s " ; and he prevailed on the Reverend Fitzwilliam to join him in the purer air of a third-class open truck.

Miss Bessie described the arrival at the Farnborough station.

"Grandpapa met us with Lord Palmerston, who had been staying with him at Sandhurst. Grandpapa and Lord P. drove in the carriage with Mama, B and I. Lord P. had what he called a summer cold and B and I kept on watching the dewdrops which came and went at the end of his nose. Grandpapa had got us seats in the pavilion, which was full of very smart sort of people. We were introduced to the Duke of Newcastle, Lord Clarendon and Mr. Sidney Herbert. Grandpapa told us that Lord Palmerston and Lord Clarendon do not get on very well; he says that Lord Clarendon barks at the Russians but does not bite, while Lord Palmerston would like to worry them like a terrier."

This display of something less than a division to resist aggression was hailed with acclamation by the public as being a suitable instrument to administer salutary punishment to anyone unwise enough to attempt to "twist the lion's tail." That the component parts were of excellent material is true enough, and Lord Hardinge, the Commander-in-Chief, was rightly impressed by the bearing of the troops. Miss Bessie was carried away by enthusiasm and writes:

"The soldiers as they marched past were magnificent. The Foot Guards were fine tall men, but I really liked the Highlanders in their bonnets and kilts the best of the foot soldiers. The 11th Hussars in their cherry-coloured trousers were a very pretty sight; the 15th Hussars, who were led by Lord Cardigan, moved like machines and are supposed to be the smartest cavalry regiment of the line. Grandpapa told us that Lord Cardigan, when he was their Colonel, spent £10,000 a year on them. We had hoped to see Walter, but none of the Blues were here. Papa says 'he supposes they are coddling the Queen and that German fellow.' We went to the 17th Lancers' tent to luncheon and were entertained by Uncle Morris, who is second in command. We did ample justice to the luncheon, which consisted of six courses and side dishes, with sherry and champagne. Uncle Morris, who had forgotten to ask Uncle Fitz to say grace at the beginning, asked him to do so at the end. Uncle Fitz, who was rather sleepy said : ' For what we have received, may the Lord make us truly comfortable.' I am afraid B and I giggled a little."

The Brass Hats were on the warpath, and having inspected the seasoned veterans they decided to see how the potential officers were shaping. The Lieut.-Governor of Sandhurst had received a notification that the Secretary-at-War would hold an inspection of the gentlemen-cadets on July the 20th. This would entail a stay of some days at Sandhurst for the yachting party, and Sir Walter, who had come to the review under protest and preferred " a sail in the Channel to wallowing in a punt on the Sandhurst lake," announced that those who wished to do the latter could rejoin the *Beatrice* at Portsmouth on 31st July. All the gentlemen elected to remain with Sir Walter : the ladies went to Sandhurst. Miss Bessie and B foresaw a pleasant interlude in the company of young gentlemen as a welcome change from aged relations.

The gentlemen-caders in their review dress of scarlet made a very creditable display, and the Lieut.-Governor was warmly commended by Mr. Sidney Herbert and Lord Hardinge on the turn-out. The old Marquis of Anglesey, who was eighty-five, was present, and by virtue of his rank as Field-Marshal, was accorded the honour of taking the salute at the march past. After the parade the old gentleman was most affable, and arm-in-arm with General Taylor, chatted with Lady Carew. As usual, he reverted to the interminable topic of his lost leg, which had been with him figuratively ever since the battle.

" My good friend," he said, referring to General Taylor, " saved my life by pulling off my leg."

Miss Bessie and B thought the old man's senile remarks extremely amusing and got on famously with him.

The days passed pleasantly enough until the end of July, when the Royal Military College dispersed for the summer vacation. The time was fully occupied with picnics, field-days, and boating on the lake. Miss Bessie and B were both keen horsewomen, and the visits to the riding-school caused great amusement.

Miss Bessie writes :

" It was really very comical to watch the gentlemen-cadets flogging their nappy horses over the jumps or as often as not the Squadron Sergeant-Major flogging the horses one side of the jump and the riders coming off the other side. Some of the cadets will never be able to ride anything except a clothes-horse. On Thursday we all went and watched a sham fight on the Hartford Bridge Flats, which was capital fun. I was sorry for the gentlemen-cadets, who looked very hot and uncomfort-able in their high leather stocks and red coats. We had a picnic luncheon with lots of wine, at which some of the officers joined us and got rather tipsy."

On July the 28th the end-of-term ball was held in the riding-school. Miss B was considered to be too young to attend, but Miss Bessie, although not " out " in the strict sense, was allowed to go. She seems to have enjoyed herself immensely and is eloquent on the subject.

" My first ball," she writes, " and how wonderful it was ! Madame Morice has been most clever with my dress, a sprigged white muslin and green sash, with a white wreath in my hair. The band of the 71st regiment played beautifully. There were waltzes, polkas and quadrilles. I danced with a lot of gentlemen-cadets, most of whom trod on my toes. My favourite partner was a Mr. White, who is leaving this term ; he is a very amiable young man and very presentable. I asked Grandpapa about him afterwards, and he said that he was the best cadet in the College and that he would go far."

Sir George White fulfilled the Lieut.-Governor's prophecy, winning the Victoria Cross in the Afghan War of 1879 and eventually becoming a Field-Marshal. He was not to meet Miss Bessie again until forty-seven years later, when he was appointed Governor of Gibraltar after his successful defence of Ladysmith.

Chapter Seventeen

THE DUBLIN EXHIBITION

THE ladies duly returned to the yacht and Sir Walter who wanted to be off to take part in the Plymouth regatta, agreed with a somewhat ill grace to remain another day for the Naval Review at Portsmouth, at which the Queen was to be present. The *Beatrice* came near to being involved in disaster and Miss Bessie describes what happened.

" *11th August.* We were at Spithead when the ships saluted the *Victoria and Albert* with the Queen on board. All the men-o'-war then steamed away for the sham fight, and the noise of firing was tremendous ; the smoke was so thick that we could see nothing. M. Perron rushed up to say the galley was on fire, which I suspected rightly was an excuse for not cooking any dinner. All the maids started screaming until Papa told them to hold their noise and pushed them down the companion-way. When the smoke cleared we ran into Portsmouth harbour, where we anchored, and not a bit too soon, as vessels of every description were pouring in. It was blowing a gale, and before very long we found that we were dragging our anchor and had got foul of a cutter astern of us. There was a great hullabaloo as we were going astern fast and drifting on a large merchant schooner. In the middle of the row we heard frantic shouts of ' clear the fairway,' when, to our horror, we saw the *Victoria and Albert* bearing down ; she looked as if she must run into us, but she just managed to run between us and the schooner. Had she been five minutes sooner she would not have had room to pass as we were close to the schooner, whose jib-boom was swinging over our stern. As the *Victoria and Albert* passed, we saw the Queen quite plainly, a dumpy little figure in a billowing satin dress and poke bonnet, standing on the poop. A very red-faced angry-looking man roared at us, ' Have you no respect for the Queen ? ' Papa, who was just as angry, shouted back, ' Hold your tongue ! ' The Queen looked perfectly calm ; we heard afterwards that the red-faced gentleman was Lord Granville, the Lord President of the Council.''

The Plymouth regatta, interspersed with an archery meeting at Mount Edgcumbe, passed off very pleasantly. The *Beatrice* carried off the Royal Western Yacht Club Cup, and while Sir Walter and Lord Willoughby de Broke celebrated the victory afloat, the remainder of the party gained laurels on shore, the Reverend Fitzwilliam being awarded the gold medal presented by Lord Mount Edgcumbe for the best score at the archery contest. Miss Bessie writes :

" We all enjoyed ourselves at Mount Edgcumbe, where we met all sorts of notabilities, mostly from Devonshire. Lord and Lady Fortescue and Mr. Hugh Fortescue, Member for Plymouth last year and now Member for Barnstaple. They are relations of Uncle Forty, who says he is the ignoble branch of the family. There was a funny old clergyman, Mr. Russell, who keeps a pack of hounds and breeds terriers ; they call him ' The Sporting Parson.' He and Uncle Fitz are great friends, both having the same tastes. The Bishop of Exeter, Dr. Phillpotts, was also there ; Uncle Fitz does not get on very well with him ; I think because the Bishop tries to keep him in order, but does not succeed. A very happy day."

On 12th August the *Beatrice* rounded Land's End en route to Ireland. She dropped anchor in Kingstown harbour the next evening. Sir Walter's dislike of railways was considerably increased by the antics of the Kingstown–Dublin branch of the Great Southern and Western Railway Company. The line had been opened in 1844 with a great flourish of trumpets by the then Viceroy, Lord Heytesbury, but during its nine years of life the line achieved a marked degree of Irish instability. The train was scheduled to leave the Kingstown station at 11 a.m. on the 14th, and the whole party had taken their seats in readiness for departure. After two ineffectual attempts by the engineer to start, during which the train was sprayed by a shower of soot and sparks, the engine, with a succession of jerks, moved slowly out of the station. The Reverend Fitzwilliam, who was with Sir Walter in an open truck at the rear of the train, describes what happened.

" After the fireworks exhibition which smothered us with soot, the train went about half a mile, when it stopped. Suddenly we found ourselves going backwards and gaining speed down the incline. The guard, who was just in front, shouted, ' The coupling's adrift, I'll be jumping for it,' which he did to save his skin, not the coupling, leaving us to run down the hill. We ended up with a terrible crash into the buffers, which smashed our carriage to pieces. We found ourselves on the ground with the guard grinning at us. ' So ye got here first, bedad,' he said. Walter, who was more angry than hurt, blew him and his railway up very heartily."

The ladies and gentlemen eventually arrived at the Vice-regal Lodge in carriages from Kingstown, the servants having been left to get to Dublin as best they could by the railway. Whether they would arrive at all was, according to the guard, highly problematical, that functionary having doubts " wither the ould ingine houlds togither." His doubts were justified ; for less than half a mile out of Kingstown the boiler blew up, and Dally, who was in charge, had to charter two Irish cars for the remainder of the journey.

Lord St. Germans had done everything possible to provide for the comfort of the visitors, but he himself was detained by affairs of state at the Castle. In a note of apology to Sir Walter for not being there to welcome them, he wrote : " These pestilential Irishmen are a continual thorn in the flesh ; there is much unrest to deal with and I must try and get things quiet before the Queen arrives." Sir Walter, who had never tolerated any form of unrest in his own entourage, was unable to understand this failing in others and somewhat discourteously described his host as a "blattering humbug." That the authorities were taking no chances was shown by the presence of an armed detachment of the Royal Irish Constabulary, which ringed in the Viceregal Lodge. Sir Walter, on asking the sergeant in charge the reason for the guard, was told that "the Ribbonmen are out who are after the likes of your honour." Sir Walter knew nothing and cared less about Irish agrarian troubles ; the Ribbonmen were connected with the drapery trade, he shouldn't wonder, and he regarded the sergeant as a poor sort of Irish humorist.

On 25th August, Lord and Lady St. Germans gave a dinner party at the Castle. It was attended by Sir Walter and Lady Carew, Lord and Lady Willoughby de Broke, and the Reverend Fitzwilliam, who gives a short account of the proceedings.

"We set off to the Castle," he writes, "in a Vice-regal carriage with an escort of cavalry. The dinner was a stiffish affair ; St. Germans looked harassed and Lady St. G. looked prim. Besides us, was Richard Bourke (son of Lord Mayo) and his wife ; Bourke is a strong Tory and will have nothing to do with this government, but was Chief Secretary under Derby's lot ; he is now Member for Coleraine. Maziere Brady, an Irish attorney and now Lord Chancellor, and Mrs. Brady, both with brogues fit to slice with a butcher's knife. Sir George Brown, who is Commander-in-Chief for the time, and lastly the Papist Archbishop of Dublin, Cardinal Cullen, hatchet-faced like most of his brotherhood but a good trencherman withal and a nice taste for wine of which my mind there was little enough. St. Germans talked most of the time to Sir George Brown about shooting Ribbonmen, whilst Walter tried to talk about shooting pheasants. Altogether a poor sort of dinner which we were glad to see the end of."

In order to make room for the Queen and the Prince Consort who were due to arrive on 29th August, the Carew party vacated

the Vice-regal Lodge on the 26th. From there they went on
to stay with Lord Gough, and Miss Bessie makes a note in her
diary :

" Papa very cross at having to turn out for ' that German
feller,' as he rather disrespectfully calls the Prince Consort.
We went in the train from Dublin and got out at Booterstown,
where we were met by the St. Helens carriages. There we
found Lord and Lady Gough, Lord and Lady Raglan and Lord
and Lady Cathcart. Lord Raglan and Lord Cathcart were at
Waterloo with Grandpapa. Lord Raglan has only one arm,
having lost the other in the battle. B and I are very excited,
because we are all going to meet the Lord-Lieutenant's party at
Kingstown to welcome the Queen when she arrives in the
Victoria and Albert on the 29th. We are to go to the Exhibition
on the next day. Papa says that he is tired of Irish cooking and
will go back to the *Beatrice*, and as she is in harbour M. Perron
will have no excuse for not cooking ; he has persuaded Uncles
Fitz, Willoughby and Forty to join him."

The royal yacht duly arrived at Kingstown on the 29th and
in spite of underlying unrest was welcomed with enthusiasm.
As the royal party disembarked, the band of the 87th Regiment
struck up " God save the Queen," and the guard of honour,
amid the cheers of the crowd, presented arms. Miss Bessie was
equally enthusiastic.

" The Queen," she says, " came first, looking so happy, and
was followed by the Prince, who is tall and handsome, and the
Prince of Wales, a dear little boy in a sailor suit. We were all
presented to the Queen by Lord St. Germans ; she afterwards
got into a carriage-and-four and drove off to the Vice-regal
Lodge. After she had gone, a gentleman of her party, who
was looking severely at Papa, came up to him and said, ' Methinks,
sir, we met last in mid-stream with an unseemly exchange of
words ; for my part it is forgotten.' He then bowed and walked
away. It was Lord Granville, the gentleman who had shouted
at Papa from the *Victoria and Albert* at Portsmouth."

The house-party at St. Helens drove to the Phoenix Park on the morning of the 30th and watched a review of the Dublin garrison which had been arranged for the delectation of the Queen. They afterwards made a tour of the Dublin Exhibition, joining the Lord-Lieutenant and Lady St. Germans, who were in attendance on the Queen and the Prince Consort. Miss Bessie and B, under the ineffectual chaperonage of Annette, were allowed to form a party of their own with very nearly dire results. Miss Bessie describes the hair-raising experience to which they were subjected.

" It was raining very hard," she writes, " so we thought it would be capital fun to go to the Exhibition in a covered car, but it turned out to be anything but fun. The jarvey who shut us up inside had a very peculiar smell, which we supposed was natural to the common people. We started off at a terrible pace and narrowly missed several other cars. We heard a lot of swearing, but our driver took no notice and drove faster. We shouted to him to open the little window as we were nearly stifled, but instead of doing so he began to sing, while Annette, who was very frightened, started to scream. Suddenly the car stopped with a jerk and we were thrown into each other's laps. A policeman rushed to the door and let us out, when we saw one policeman sitting on the horse's head and two more dragging the driver away. The policeman was very excited and said, ' Glory be, your honour's safe ; 'tis the potheen has bit the spalpeen of a jarvey.' He came with us to the Exhibition Halls in the Dublin Society's grounds near Merrion Square. We were all a little shaken, as we might have been killed by the drunken driver."

In spite of their unpromising preliminary canter, the three girls managed to enjoy all the fun of the fair with the added attraction of trailing in the steps of royalty.

" We were just in time," Miss Bessie says, " to see the Queen and the Prince Consort enter the large hall. There was tremendous clapping, and then Lord St. Germans presented Mr.

Benson, the architect of the Exhibition, who was afterwards knighted. The Queen and the Prince then visited most of the stalls ; we were quite close to them all the time. The Queen was very interested in the bog-oak stall and bought some brace-lets ; I heard the Prince say, ' There is a young lady behind, Liebchen, who reminds me of you.' The Queen turned round and with a charming smile gave me a bracelet. I was so over-come that I can remember nothing except that when her dress rustled there was a lovely smell of lavender. We then went and ate ices at another stall, where we saw a little boy in a black velvet suit with a very stern-looking man. The little boy, when he saw us, waved and smiled, but was reproved by the gentleman with him, who led him away. We were certain that it was the Prince of Wales, who, Mama says, is very strictly brought up. We thought the photographic stall was very wonderful. Another inventor, Mr. Archer, was soaking gun-cotton in ether which he called collodion, which is still another way of making photographic pictures. The Queen was very interested indeed and so were we."

The ladies rejoined the *Beatrice* on 3rd September and Sir Walter decided that he had seen enough of Ireland. The next day, therefore, the yacht was " tugged " out of Kingstown har-bour and course was set for Devonshire. The return voyage passed without incident until the night of September the 6th when off the Lizard. At about 11 o'clock, a sudden squall off the land shook the *Beatrice* from stem to stern ; it lasted through the night and made all on board extremely uncomfortable. Miss Bessie makes a final note in her journal.

" We were all asleep, when we were awakened by a horrible rolling, everything creaking and tumbling about ; we rolled our side-lights in continually, and the roll continued to increase rather than decrease. Suddenly we heard a great scampering on deck and a cry of ' Man overboard.' B and I rushed up on deck in various attire. We then saw M. Perron lying on the deck in his night-cap looking just like a drowned rat. He had not fallen overboard but had been rolled into the scuppers and fished out by one of the men with a boat-hook. When the gale moderated, we made up our minds to decamp as far as possible and we arrived at Plymouth, having been literally rolled out of our summer residence."

Chapter Eighteen

PRELUDE TO WAR

THERE was a reunion of the Taylor family at Haccombe for the Christmas of 1853. General Taylor had arrived from Compton Verney, where he had been staying with the Willoughby de Brokes, and with him came his wife and daughters, Lady Willoughby de Broke, Harriet, Amelia and Eliza. All went merry as a marriage bell at the Christmas party and Sir Walter Carew was on his best behaviour. Then, in the following year came tragedy. General Taylor took to his bed with a feverish cold, which at first was not thought much of, but gradually turned to inflammation of the lungs. His favourite son, Reynell, who was home on leave from India, was sent for, and scarcely ever left his father's bedroom. The case was hopeless, however, and a few minutes before the end Reynell approached the bed and, saluting his father, asked in Hindustani, " Kuch hookum hai, sahib ? " (Have you any further orders, sir ?) The General replied in the same language, and on 8th January he died. The whole family attended the funeral in Denbury churchyard.

The General's death left a devastating void in the family circle. In his seventy-second year when he died, his whole life was full of incident, and it meant that a link with the past had been shattered.

Since the beginning of the year tension with Russia had been steadily growing ; in the previous December the allied fleets, at the request of the Porte, had entered the Black Sea. In March the Baltic fleet under Sir Charles Napier sailed and towards the end of March England and France declared war against Russia. There was an outbreak of "jingoism" in England, marked by patriotic songs and threats of vengeance against the Russians, in spite of the fact that the country was totally unprepared and there was remarkably little force to back up this ardour. It was in the early part of June that the Rev. Fitzwilliam received a letter from Lord George Paget, condoling on the loss of General Taylor and saying that he also had just lost his father, Lord Anglesey, who had died on 28th May. Lord George Paget wrote from Dorchester where he was commanding the 4th Light Dragoons. He suggested that as Dorchester was in reasonable reach of Haccombe, and as "it is a vastly dull place," that he should pay a visit and bring his adjutant, Captain Robert Portal, "who you will find to be a most delightful fellow." Lord George did not feel it necessary to explain how it was possible for the commanding officer and his adjutant to absent themselves from their regiment during a war, but apparently the question did not arise.

Lord George Paget and Captain Portal posted over from Dorchester, as it would have taken them about a week to come by the railroad, a journey which entailed about six changes on lines each having a different gauge. Lady Carew was delighted to see Lord George again and was much struck by the affability and good looks of his adjutant. Something of a matchmaker, she thought how nice it would be if Eliza, her only unmarried sister, got to like him, and she proceeded forthwith to exert every endeavour to that end. Her efforts were rewarded, for the two young people became extremely fond of each other, and after a week of picnics and croquet parties, ending up with a never to be forgotten dance at the Croquet Club-house at Teignbridge, the affair was well on its way to maturity. Although they did not get as far as a formal engagement since, as Robert Portal said, he might go to the war at any minute, it was nevertheless tacitly agreed that they were made for each other and would wait for more settled times. On his return to Dorchester

CAPTAIN PORTAL AND HIS HORSE " THE WAVE "

From a contemporary painting

he sent her a painting executed by a travelling artist of romantic tendencies, which depicted a troop of the 4th Light Dragoons on manœuvres in a Suffolk village in the summer of 1853. In the foreground is seated Captain Robert Portal and his horse " The Wave " ; behind him, scattered about in twos and threes, is his troop. The men have just off-saddled and are presumably at ease, if such a state of relaxation could ever be attained in the uncomfortable battle-dress of the time, made up of shakos, stocks and epaulettes. Eliza Taylor thought the picture beautiful and kept it as one of her most treasured possessions.

Captain Portal, during his sojourn in the Crimea, was a prolific correspondent and kept a diary, chiefly, no doubt, for the benefit of Eliza Taylor. He seems to have been immune from censorship and speaks with engaging candour, throwing an interesting side-light on the war in general and on the ineptitude of the home administration and of the commanders in the field in particular. But in the summer of 1854 the 4th Light Dragoons were still vegetating in Dorchester, and the presence of a smart cavalry regiment, under its aristocratic Colonel, considerably livened up the atmosphere of the old town. Military ardour which rumours of war had aroused throughout the country was at its height and many a Dorset farm lad, attracted no doubt by the glamour and dash of the 4th Light " Plungers," took the Queen's shilling and in due course found it to be a harder earned reward than any he had come by on the land.

Orders arrived on 1st July for the 4th L.D. to mobilize. This long overdue operation resolved itself into the formula " wait and see " ; for there was practically no wartime requisite available to be mobilized. There was no lack of spit and polish or of burnished horse accoutrements, but there was a lamentable deficiency of the horses themselves. However, this difficulty appears to have been solved by the simple expedient of collecting from other cavalry regiments likely to be left behind. There was no shortage of horseflesh among the officers, for they provided a generous quota of the establishment. Captain Portal had six of his own, but he did not feel called upon to make good the deficiencies of an incompetent and lethargic government :

" ' The Wave ' is too valuable to take," he writes. " I have been lucky enough to sell her to Her Majesty as a brood mare. The rest I am selling to Tattersall's, except ' Paddy ' who goes with me. The muddle and neglect are dreadful, but we are in a great bustle, except Lord George Paget who is very down in the mouth ; leaving his young wife is telling vastly on him. Most of the officers are in London saying good-bye, and I hope to do the same in a day or two. I shall then insure my life so that I may be able to raise enough money for all bills before I go."

Mobilization, or rather improvisation, having been completed, the 4th proceeded by route march on 10th July to Plymouth, the port of embarkation. The march took the form of a triumphal procession ; Portal had, of course, sent word to Eliza Taylor of the date he expected to reach Plymouth, and she and Lady Carew were there to meet him. Portal writes in his journal :

" I never saw people so excited at our departure ; in every town and village there were triumphal arches, gaily dressed ladies waving handkerchiefs and giving the men flowers, and flags waving from every house. The men are in great spirits, blew imaginary kisses at the ladies and cheered them lustily."

Embarkation took place amid equally vociferous crowds ; Lady Carew and Eliza Taylor had been invited to a farewell luncheon on board the *Simla*. The somewhat forced gaiety during the meal, perhaps induced by a generous supply of champagne, gave way to depression among those left behind. Eliza Taylor, at all events, completely broke down when the band played that soul-haunting melody, " The girl I left behind me," as the troopship slipped her moorings in the Hamoaze and amidst rousing cheers from the troops on board, to the strains of "Cheer, boys, cheer," steamed slowly round the green slopes of Mount Edgcumbe into the Channel.

Lord George Paget and Portal were much impressed by the spacious accommodation on board for officers and men, but apparently little thought had been given to the comfort of the horses. Portal writes : "The *Simla* is a most splendid ship ; the saloon is 80 feet long and 25 wide. The cook is a capital one and the food most abundant and good." Presumably he was speaking for the officers, since there were constant complaints from the men of the inadequacy of the rations. He goes on :

"They give us champagne and claret twice a week, so the roughing has not begun as yet. Even Lord George is beginning to recover his spirits a little ! The horses, poor beasts, go quite mad from the heat, standing as they do close to the engines all day and all night ; what forethought on the part of the authorities."

Gibraltar was reached in three days and twelve hours, " the shortest passage ever made at 13 knots an hour." And so, with the sea like glass and the sun like fire, the *Simla* made her way to Malta, thence through the Dardanelles to Constantinople, finally arriving at Varna on 1st August. The roughing had begun. Portal was not slow to appreciate this as may be gathered from his first letter home after landing.

"We are in the most uncomfortable situation possible, no food for the men, no forage for the horses. This morning at 4 a.m. my servant Richard, having just received my ration of coarse beef, came into my tent with it on a tin plate ; the tin and the meat were crawling with maggots. ' Here, sir,' he said, ' is your dinner for to-day.' I shouted, ' For heaven's sake, take the beastliness out and bury it.' Lord George cannot stand the food ; it makes him quite sick ; he had joined my small mess, but is now taking up his quarters with Lord Raglan ; I am glad for him, but sorry for myself."

Cholera had already broken out amongst the troops already at Varna, and Portal writes on 17th August :

" The dreadful mortality is having a most unhappy moral effect on the troops ; from the highest to the lowest, one hears nothing but growls and grumbles, and officers and men complain that they are brought out here to do nothing but die of cholera. What think you of thirty men out of three hundred dying in one regiment, the 5th Dragoon Guards, in 10 hours, fifty men on board of our men-of-war in about the same time, and two hundred on board one of the French ships in an equally short space ? Never did the army need a Wellington and the navy a Nelson so much as now, and that is what all feel, both soldiers and sailors. The fleet have not even yet got the soundings round the Crimea, and yet we talk glibly of landing 100,000 men there under fire. I saw some of the Guards yesterday ; they looked more like wraiths, so thin and emaciated as they were."

The 4th Light Dragoons were lucky inasmuch as they suffered comparatively few casualties from cholera ; but as Portal says, this was more by good luck than good management, and no credit need be given to the medical or any other authority. Portal had very little reason to give credit to anyone, but at any rate the 4th were sufficiently fit to make a landing in the Crimea on 14th September ; and on the 20th, after a forced march, they " were in time to see the battle of the Alma through their glasses." His comments are terse : " The battle was won by the English infantry ; the cavalry were not engaged at all ; the French did little or nothing, and the English and French Generals even less."

Chapter Nineteen

ONE OF THE SIX HUNDRED

THE victory of the Alma, it seems, gave rise to some wishful thinking on the part of the high command, who seemed to consider the war already won; for Portal writes next day :

"We are at this moment encamped safely in the Russian lines, and to-day the work of burying the dead is going on ; our wiseacres consider Sebastopol as ours ; I doubt it. I saw Hughy Drummond for a moment ; he was in great spirits ; he had two balls pass through his bearskin, and three into his horse, which was of course killed. He, however, shot five Russians with his revolvers. Having finished burying the dead, we are now collecting the wounded, of which there are an enormous number ; the French had no wounded to care for as they killed every man they found not dead ; they say it was done by their 'indigène' troops ; even so, it sickens and horrifies one, and yet no protest is made. Sebastopol is *not* ours, nor will it be until we learn the rules of war."

Portal, who was a shrewd observer and from being in touch with Lord George Paget heard much that the average regimental officer would not, was firmly of opinion that, had the victory been followed up, we might have been in Sebastopol, thereby voicing the opinion of later eminent historians. "But," he says, "it was not to be, for we were commanded or, rather, countermanded by a pack of old women who would have done better in their drawing-rooms."

The rising barometer of hope fell after the Alma, and a period of despondent inaction followed. Portal, writing before Sebastopol on 10th October, says :

" We do nothing of any use, but when this happens, the Generals are most active ; a venerable old gentleman was on the warpath last night, by name Sir George Brown and Commander of the Light Division. He was inspecting the vedettes, and after passing the vedettes of several regiments, he drew a blank in the line of communications ; his A.D.C. said, ' It must be a mistake, sir, of the Officer of the 19th ; he cannot have brought his vedettes as far forward as he ought.' Sir G. Brown said, ' We will soon see, for we will ride in and see if we can meet with them.' He had not ridden a hundred yards when one of the vedettes of the 19th challenged (as they all do). Sir G. Brown called out, ' General Officer, all right,' but it was all wrong, for the man gave the alarm and about a dozen shots were immediately fired at the advancing General. He took off his cocked hat and waved it to them, which by the moonlight he thought would be seen, and so it was, for some of the vedettes shouted, ' He's cheering his men on ; fire quick, boys ! ' Luckily the old fool was not hit, but his A.D.C. was shot through the skirt of his coat. The men in the 19th were not to blame, for no one in their senses would ever go at night outside the vedettes. We are greatly disgusted with *The Times* of 2nd October, giving after Alma an account of ' the taking of Sebastopol ' ; it is really too bad that the public should be imposed on in this manner."

Mr. Russell, *The Times* correspondent, whose policy was to expose the true facts, presumably had not made his voice heard when this was written. Portal met Russell on many occasions, in his official capacity as A.D.C. at embryo ' Press Conferences,' and also informally ; he was entirely in sympathy with his activities, except on one occasion, of which he has something to say later.

The comic futility of one general was but a curtain-raiser for the tragic futility of others, with the epic of Balaklava as an immediate result. Portal, who took part in the famous charge, describes the action from the standpoint of a soldier on the spot, and his words are therefore perhaps as worthy of note as the utterances of later diligent searchers after the truth.

His account is contained in a letter written to his mother on 26th October, the day after the engagement.

" You will probably have heard before this by electric telegraph of the fearful loss the Light Cavalry Brigade sustained yesterday, but I want to assure you of my safety, thanks to God Almighty, as I conceive that every soul that returned alive was saved by a perfect miracle. The upshot of the affair was this. Yesterday, just as daylight broke, we suddenly heard some of the guns from the Turkish earthworks firing at the enemy, who were evidently advancing on Balaklava ; no sooner did the Russian infantry advance steadily up the first of the hills, than we saw all these curs of Turks running down the hill on the other side, leaving everything, including their guns, behind. We only had one infantry regiment and a few marines besides the cavalry down here, and we thought that Balaklava would be taken before any help came from the front, as the Russians were advancing rapidly. On the heights in front of the harbour we had some heavy guns in position, and in front of the gorge that forms the harbour were drawn up in line the 93rd Highlanders. A large body of Russians came over the hills they had just taken from the Turks and advanced against the 93rd, who did not move an inch, but poured in such a heavy fire that the Russians retired. About 3,000 Russian cavalry charged the 93rd, who formed square and poured volleys into them which sent them about their business. They formed up again, however, and advanced towards our heavy cavalry, who immediately went at them and routed them, the men cheering and cutting away like demons. About an hour afterwards, we saw that the Russian cavalry had formed up in line across a plain with hills on both sides of it about a mile from where our light cavalry was stationed. I was with Lord George Paget, and nearby were Lord Lucan and Lord Cardigan. Suddenly up dashed General Airey's A.D.C., a certain Captain Nolan, who told ' Look-on ' that the General desired the Light Cavalry would attack to their front at once. Lord Cardigan said : ' It seems madness to attack at such a distance without infantry and artillery support, and Lord knows what they may have stationed among the trees on the sides of those hills.' Nolan went off in a huff saying he would get a written order from the General (Airey) and soon afterwards returned with one which he gave to ' Look-on ' ; it said that the Light Cavalry were to attack.

" The 13th, 17th and 8th then advanced, followed at 400 yards by the 4th and 11th. We went at a steady pace at first, and then we saw all the Russian cavalry retiring, so all the men cheered and went on at a gallop. When we had ridden a quarter of a mile from our starting-point, a most fearful fire opened on us from the hills on both sides of us (Lord Cardigan was right for once) ; grape, shells, and minié balls fell like hail all round us, to say nothing of 18-lb. shot which whistled through our ranks dealing death and destruction all round. However, on we still kept going, knowing not whither, till at last we had got so far that we had crossed through this cross-fire and found ourselves in the middle of all the Russian cavalry ; we also found nine guns retiring, killed all the gunners, and would, had we had plenty of support instead of none, have brought all the guns back with us. As it was, we soon found we were in a regular mess, that the Russian cavalry were forming up in our front and rear, and that we were being hemmed in on every side. After going right through a regiment of Cossacks, a regiment of Lancers, and another regiment of Blue Hussars, we retired in perfect order towards our original position ; of course at full gallop. To do this, we had again to pass through this murderous cross-fire I have told you of ; if anything, the fire was more severe than before, and neither I nor anyone else who saw what we had to do, thought that the few left of us would ever get back. By a perfect miracle I was not touched except a piece of shell caught me in the back, and my horse ' Paddy ' was shot through the fleshy part of the leg, but he brought me back, nevertheless. I numbered in my troop this morning ten mounted men ; in round numbers we mustered on parade 700 men ; last night we numbered 180. Captain

Nolan was killed by the first shell, and we think it was a judgement on him for getting us in such a mess. Lord Lucan is
dreadfully cut up about it (not so much as his Light Brigade !) ;
he says he can show the order in writing, which is his only
comfort. Poor Morris, who commanded the 17th Lancers was
shot in the head. I passed him lying on the ground when we
were in full gallop, but of course could do nothing. It was
altogether the maddest and most extraordinary order ever
given to cavalry and an inquiry is to be instituted at once. Lord
Raglan, who came down to our Headquarters last night, was
furious and said loudly, ' The cavalry have been wantonly
sacrificed.' I slew one Russian by running him through the
vitals with my sword, and I think accounted for several
others."

Such was the ungarnished account by one of the few survivors
of the action. There was little sentiment apparent in the minds
of those who, three days after the action, ordered that the effects
of the officers shot should be sold by auction. The death-rate
of officers had been high, but excitement over their effects was
apparently equally so ; for, says Portal, " Everything sold in
the most absurd way, so destitute of necessaries is everyone ; a
knife and fork of the commonest kind made 45s., and an enormous sum was made." It is not stated who received those considerable sums, but from all accounts it seems doubtful if the
dependants of the deceased officers benefited to any extent.
Portal was touched by receiving a useful addition to his ward-
robe, which came to him as a gift, for, he writes, " that excellent
Mrs. Duberly, wife of one of the ships' Captains who has been
very kind to the officers, has just sent me from the store on the
ship, a warm pea-jacket. It is really very good of her ; it is
impossible to get them anywhere for any money."

Portal took part in the Battle of Inkerman on 5th November,
but, being meticulously truthful, is not very discursive ; for he
says in effect that the truth was impossible to arrive at. It is
interesting to note that the late Sir John Fortescue came to the

same conclusion when he wrote that "the sequence of events cannot be surely determined." Portal's short but forceful comments on the battle are again to be found in a letter to Eliza Taylor written on 25th November. He is as usual not flattering to the high command.

"Not once since we landed has Lord Raglan shown one particle of military knowledge, and yet he is made a Field-Marshal. The battle was won by the officers and men solely and wholly; the only orders received that day were by one Division, who were ordered when under a galling fire to lie down; a moment afterwards an A.D.C. ordered them to advance. These are the only orders I can hear of that were issued and received on that day. We hear of enormous reinforcements coming from France; I wish they would reinforce us with a new Commander-in-Chief, and put this one in petticoats and send him home. As to Lord Cardigan, he has as much brains as my boot, and is only equalled in want of intellect by his relation Lord 'Look-on.' Without mincing matters, two bigger fools could not be picked out of the British Army to take command."

Portal was much annoyed that this letter was held up in the Field Post Office for some time. A mild form of censorship had apparently been imposed, which would seem pardonable in view of the contents. He writes on 2nd December: "Lord Raglan sent his despatches by the French boat from Chersonese, and I am told stopped this mail to prevent private letters arriving in England at the same time as his despatches, and telling the truth; it looks very like it."

This may or may not have been so, but anyhow such action was not destined to prevent the truth from being exposed through other channels, though possibly not for the reason given by Portal, who says: "Mr. Russell, 'Our Correspondent,' has quarrelled with Lord Raglan, so we shall see the truth appear at last. He is a most amusing, clever man and great fun; I have met him many times on board ship at dinner." From whatever cause, the amusing, clever man appears to have quickly fulfilled all expectations; for Portal, writing soon afterwards, says:

" The article in *The Times* of 23rd December is a glorious one, and if it had been written a month sooner it would have done the army an immensity of good and saved thousands of lives; now an attempt is being made to improve matters, but I fear too late."

Christmas was a dreary affair for both officers and men of the 4th L.D. The dull routine of picquet duty went on, unlivened by any seasonable fare. The Commander-in-Chief, impelled no doubt by the kindliest motives, paid one of his rare visits to the troops shortly afterwards, but his well-meant effort evoked no particular enthusiasm. According to Portal:

" Lord Raglan yesterday saw a man in the regiment cutting some wood, and said to him, ' Well, my man, I suppose you are pretty comfortable ? ' ' Never so uncomfortable or so miserable in my life,' says the man. ' Well,' says Lord Raglan, ' you got a good dinner on Christmas Day, didn't you ? ' ' All I got on Christmas Day was a pound of charcoal; that's all I got.' Lord Raglan moved off and did not speak to any more soldiers on his visit."

Portal was a little cheered by receiving a present of some brandy from his brother, but even this was tempered with gall, for he says in his letter of thanks, " The brandy warms one, but you might give a hint to Mr. Fortnum or Mason, or both, not to send brandy in a tin vessel, as it turns completely black, and if you offer a friend a glass of it, he supposes that ink is the fluid you are offering him."

The way of the ordinary soldier in the Crimea may have been hard, but the path of the rich and influential officer seems to have been made smooth. Lord George Paget, considering that honour had been satisfied after Balaklava, prevailed on Lord Raglan to allow him to return home. Portal was distressed at certain uncomplimentary remarks made about his friend, and in a somewhat naïve passage in a letter to his mother takes up the cudgels on his behalf :

" As to Lord George, how could a man, desperately in love with a young wife, remain out here in misery, having proved to the world that he was ' no coward ' ? Every one of his own family in England is down on him, not knowing the true facts. In truth he never liked soldiering ; he happened to be an M.P. and a Colonel, so he could be as little as he liked with the regiment, and so things went on smoothly enough, but when it came to real soldiering in the Crimea, with every discomfort and misery to endure, with a wife at home on whom all his thoughts were fixed, he found he was not strong enough to resist the opportunity of getting away. He certainly left here with the intention of selling out for regulation price (as no one, of course, gives more now) as soon as he arrived in England."

Even if Lord George had obtained the regulation price he would have been a heavy loser ; for according to Portal, the privilege of becoming colonel of the 4th Light Dragoons had cost him £15,000. His Lordship, however, found an easier way out, whereby he was able to retain his investment and dwell for some time in comfort first in England and then in Constantinople with his young wife.

Chapter Twenty

JOURNEY TO CONSTANTINOPLE

LORD GEORGE PAGET, as has been related, had been luckier than most officers and had returned to London to join his wife. He apparently found life, in spite of the war, to be "pretty tolerable with lots going on." In the country the usual pursuits continued and at Haccombe the shooting season was in full swing. Partridges were plentiful and Sir Walter Carew had no reason to complain of the bag up to the middle of October. Pheasants, of which he had reared upwards of six hundred, had also done remarkably well and the first big shoot was to take place on 10th November. The war in the Crimea was a far cry from Haccombe, and until then had not unduly interfered with peace-time activities at home.

Sir Walter, having visited Russia in 1852 with the inherent jingoism of his tribe, took a poor view of the inhabitants. "That fellow Menschikoff" whom he had met at Cronstadt "and his gang of Princes and Counts was at the bottom of it," he shouldn't wonder, and left it at that.

True his son Walter, a cornet in the Blues, was in Scutari as A.D.C. to Lord William Paulet, the Military Commandant there ; but Lord William had promised Sir Walter that he would keep an eye on the boy, so there was little need to worry. It was "that miserable Shylock" Gladstone who gave him his biggest headache by doubling the income tax "to meet the expenses of the war" ; it now stood at one-and-twopence in the pound. The landed gentry of 1854 had evidently not taken kindly to any form of austerity.

Lady Carew regarded the war more seriously. First and foremost, of course, there was Walter ; then her brother Arthur in the artillery was also at the seat of war. Her sister Amelia was staying with her, and both she and Lady Carew were anxious as they had had no word from William Morris, Amelia's husband, since he had been in the Crimea. William Morris was commanding the 17th Lancers and he had been a great friend of the family since he was a boy ; he had finally fallen in love with Amelia and had married her in 1850. Lastly there was Robert Portal, their sister Eliza's young man, who was A.D.C. to Lord George Paget, commanding one of the Light Cavalry Brigades.

The shooting party assembled at Haccombe consisted for the most part of relations : Lord and Lady Willoughby de Broke, Mr. and Mrs. Fortescue and Mrs. Morris. Another guest was Sir Fleetwood Pellew, a fire-eating Admiral who in 1853, while commanding on the China station, had staged his third mutiny by his arbitrary severity and had in consequence been sent home. Sir William Parker, the Commander-in-Chief at Plymouth, completed the list of adults. Sir Walter's precocious daughters, Bessie and Beatrice, represented the younger generation. Lord Palmerston, the Home Secretary, another very old friend of Lady Carew's father, was at this time visiting his constituency at Tiverton ; he had also promised to come if, as he wrote in an outburst of frankness to Lady Carew, " I dare leave Aberdeen and the rest of 'em to deal with Russia in the only way she understands."

The shoot which took place was on the whole a successful one, although it was not graced by the presence of the Home Secretary. Details of the action at Balaklava on 25th October had begun to trickle in and Lord Palmerston was summoned to London. Whatever may have happened in the Crimea, the Haccombe pheasants defeated the efforts of the fire-eating

Admiral, who put the blame on his host's port, which, he told Manning the head-keeper, caused him to "splice the main-brace too free," making him see spots instead of birds. Sir Walter, whose sense of humour was never very pronounced, was not amused and swore that never again would he ask that "miserable old tippler" to shoot.

Two days later, the war was brought nearer home to Sir Walter. The guests, except for Amelia Morris, had all departed. Sir Walter had come in to breakfast, which with him was a solid meal of the mutton chop description. Dally the butler met him "with a face as long as your boot," to say that Mrs. Morris had been taken "very queer" and that her Ladyship was "in a pretty fash too." Sir Walter could not abide "women's tantrums," particularly at breakfast-time, but supposed he must see what the trouble was about. Lady Carew, it appeared, had received a letter from Lord George Paget, who had taken part in the charge of the Light Brigade at Balaklava and was now home on leave.

"I grieve to tell you," the letter ran, "that poor Morris was badly wounded by a sabre cut in the head, at the head of the 17th at Balaklava. He is now in the hospital at Scutari, and I fear he is in a sad way. I believe that his wife is with you, so doubtless you will break it to her as gently as possible. Pray do not be too perturbed about the reports in *The Times* newspaper of the bad conditions of the hospitals. That they *were* true, there is no doubt, but Sidney Herbert has woken up to the fact and is doing what he can to improve things. He has sent out a Miss Nightingale with a party of nurses, who arrived the day before I left and went to Scutari. Now, as I am shortly taking my wife to Constantinople, I have a proposal to make. Mr. Inman, the shipowner, has arranged a trip to take a certain amount of 'sociable families' to the seat of war and I have engaged our berths. Why do not you and your family and Mrs. Morris join us ? Mrs. Morris could then be with her husband and you would be able to see your son, who is not likely to be moved, though I am told he has tried without success to persuade Lord William Paulet to release him for active service. Pray let me know what you think of my plan."

Sir Walter, as might be expected, thought less than nothing of it.

"Constantinople," he said, "which is full of Turks and mangy curs, is no place for a pack of women."

Lady Carew and Mrs. Morris naturally took a different view —Mrs. Morris desiring to be near her husband and Lady Carew to see that Walter remained where he was, out of harm's way. The decision was finally clinched by Miss Bessie, who had a way with her father ; she insisted that of course they could not leave " poor Uncle Willie alone in that horrible place and that Walter wanted a good talking to." It was finally decided that Lady Carew, Mrs. Morris and Miss Bessie should go, leaving Miss Beatrice to keep Sir Walter company. Annette, Lady Carew's French maid, would accompany the party.

The *City of Glasgow*, which so far had not been requisitioned by the Government, was an iron paddle-steamer of 1,500 tons and had been built for passenger traffic in 1850. Trade being slack, the Inman Company had evolved the novel idea of running a tourist ship to Constantinople while the going was good. She was scheduled to sail from the East India Docks on 15th December. The company's speculation appeared to be justified, for every berth was booked. Since the cost of the trip, including board and accommodation for a fortnight, was only £5 per head, that was not, perhaps, surprising. Sir Walter, although disapproving in principle of the expedition, unbent so far as to accompany his family to London to see them safely embarked.

It might have been imagined that a regiment was moving overseas to judge by the impedimenta that cluttered up the two vehicles on the day of departure from Haccombe. The party drove to the Exeter station : the ladies in the closed landau, Sir Walter on the box of the omnibus, with Annette inside. The line from Exeter to Bristol was at that time on the narrow-gauge system, which necessitated a change at Bristol on to the Great Western broad gauge. Lord and Lady George Paget had offered to put up the travellers at their house in Park Lane, and their carriage met them at the Paddington terminus. Lord George, knowing Sir Walter's aversion to a closed carriage, had come in the phaeton. The conveyance of the vast amount of luggage was arranged by commandeering an empty Barclay & Perkins brewers' dray. It was Miss Bessie's and Annette's first visit to London, and they were thrilled at the volume of traffic; their excitement reached fever point when a battalion of the Guards, bound for the seat of war, passed them with the band playing "Cheer, Boys, Cheer," and the enthusiastic crowd joining in the chorus.

"*Voilà*, Mees Bessie," Annette exclaimed, "how comic are the hairy bonnets and red jackets to the red *pantalons* and blue jackets of our soldiers."

Mrs. Morris had naturally been in an agony of suspense about her husband, but before leaving London she was much cheered by a letter from him written in hospital saying that he was much better and begging her not to worry.

"My improvement, I do believe," he wrote, "is mainly due to Miss Nightingale and her ladies. Although they only arrived on the 4th, they have verily created order out of what was nothing less than chaos. Miss Nightingale is the guiding light, the other ladies are very worthy, but stars of a dimmer radiance."

The hundred or so "excursionists" who embarked in the *City of Glasgow* were, of course, extremely exclusive; drawn from the leisured classes who could afford the time and money to spend a winter season in Constantinople. Miss Bessie, a punctilious diarist, gives her first impressions.

"It was a terrible scramble to get on board," she writes; "the docks were crowded with common people and there were a lot of horrid little boys who got in our way. Luckily Papa is so big that he pushed a way through for us. This annoyed the crowd, who shouted, '' 'Ware the old bull—he's off to charge the Roosians.' The *City of Glasgow* looks rather a dirty sort of ship, and as we got on board we were covered with a shower of smuts from the funnel, which got into our eyes. We were told that the engineers were getting steam up. Papa soon got tired of what he called 'this filthy coal barge' and said good-bye. We afterwards shook down pretty well or squeezed up, as we four ladies have to sleep in a cabin the size of a dog's kennel at Haccombe. Lord George has got us a seat at table near the captain, who is a shaggy sort of man with enormous whiskers. We were introduced to Mr. Augustus Stafford, Mr. Delane of *The Times* newspaper, and the Duke of Newcastle, the Secretary for War. I asked Lord George why the Duke looked as if he always had a pain, and Lord George said because he had made such a mess of things. We have luncheon at twelve and dinner at four; the ladies pour out tea at half-past six o'clock; some of the gentlemen come in, but most of them like something stronger."

The *City of Glasgow* put in at Malta to pick up mail, arriving there on 27th December, having kept up an average speed of about eleven knots. The time seems to have passed pleasantly enough, the captain and ship's officers having been instructed to keep the " excursionists " amused, charades and deck croquet being much favoured by the younger members of the party. Miss Bessie says:

" It was all very strange being on a steam packet; we could not sleep at first owing to the noise of the engines and the thrashing of the paddles, or as Papa called them, the mill-wheels. It was very rough in the Bay of Biscay, with a howling gale from the east, which the captain called a Levanter. The ship rolled in a very frightening way, and poor Mama and Annette were very sea-sick. The captain said the ship was short of ballast, which was not much comfort to Mama and Annette, who were also suffering in that respect. We were thankful when we were through the Straits of Gibraltar and got into smooth water.

" *24th December.* In the Mediterranean. It has become quite hot, and Mama and Aunt Amelia are able to do their crewel work on deck. Lady George and I amuse ourselves by playing a sort of croquet on the deck. Just after luncheon, when we were off the Galatea rocks on the African coast, we were all greatly alarmed by a loud shout of 'Fire, Fire!' It turned out that that stupid Annette had hung out some of Mama's underclothes to dry near the engine and they had caught fire. Luckily it was soon put out, but the sort of turn it gave everyone on board can be imagined, as had the ship really been on fire we might have run on the rocks."

Malta was reached on 27th December, and Miss Bessie describes it as "the most curious and prettiest town I ever saw." This, of course, entailed a visit ashore, where, according to the diarist,

" we were surrounded by a crowd of soldiers sent by the Bey of Tunis and on their way to Constantinople. They shouted lustily at us and pointed at Mama, Lady George, and Aunt Amelia, who were wearing thick veils. Lord George, who was behind, hustled us into a closed carriage and told the man to drive quickly to Floriana Barracks, where the 20th regiment was quartered. When we got there, Lord George explained that the soldiers, who were Mahomedans, thought that Mama, Aunt Amelia and Lady George were ladies of the harem."

In view of the uncertain elements that were roaming the town, the veiled ladies were not again permitted by their male escort to go on foot, and their sight-seeing was confined to the view from the windows of the closed carriage in which they were driven back to the ship. They left that night at eleven o'clock for Constantinople.

Miss Bessie records the arrival there.

" *Golden Horn, Constantinople, 2nd January.* We anchored here this morning. Admiral Boxer, Lord William Paulet, and our dear Walter met us on board. Walter brought a message from Uncle Willie to say that his improvement continued and that he was being well looked after by Miss Nightingale and her nurses.

Lord William Paulet has asked us to stay with him in his house at Scutari. He had a carriage waiting, so we drove straight to his barge and crossed over to Scutari. His house is a most splendid one standing on the shores of the Bosphorus. I think that we shall be very comfortable as there are plenty of servants ; no one would think that we were actually at the seat of war. Aunt Amelia went at once to the hospital. It is delightful seeing Walter again ; he looks so smart in his uniform and his whiskers have grown beautifully."

Despite the war, Christmas was celebrated at the base with all the customary festivities, and Lord and Lady Stratford de Redcliffe gave a grand New Year's ball at the Embassy. Miss Bessie was not yet " out," but she and Annette were allowed to watch the proceedings from the Minstrels' Gallery. Colonel Morris had been granted sick leave to England, and he and his wife were awaiting a homeward-bound ship. Miss Bessie from the gallery notes :

" We had a lovely view of all the company. As Lord and Lady Stratford led the way into the ballroom the Rifle Band played ' God save the Queen.' They were followed by Lord Lucan, or Lord Look-on as Lord George calls him, and Lord Cardigan, both looking very grumpy. Lord George told me that they were being sent home because of the ' mistake ' at Balaklava, and he said a good thing too. Lord William Paulet was talking to Sir Colin Campbell, who is back from the front. Lady Stratford was wearing a most beautiful dress of corded apple-green taffety, and Lady George looked very well in a graceful dress of light-grey foulard. Mama danced a quadrille with Lord Cardigan. She told me that he danced tolerably but smelt of wine. There was quite a sensation when Omar Pasha, the Turkish General, entered in a most gorgeous uniform. He was accompanied by Mushaver Pasha, the head of the Turkish Navy, who was dressed like a Turk, but I was told afterwards that he was an Englishman, Admiral Adolphus Slade. There was a fierce-looking little Frenchman, who I found out was General Pélissier, who is to be the new Commander of the

French troops. Annette quite forgot herself when she saw a French uniform and shouted, 'Bravo! bravo!' and I gave her a sharp slap. I noticed that Walter seemed to be a great favourite with the young ladies."

Although the dreary vigil of the troops before Sebastopol continued, and the death-rate continued to mount, in Constantinople the privileged few managed to enjoy themselves during the winter. Young Walter, much to his mother's delight, had not succeeded in finding his way into the trenches. It was presumably in order to keep a watchful eye on him that she and her daughter stayed on at Scutari. There were hopes of an early peace when news came of the death of the Tsar Nicholas on 2nd March. Lady Carew had received a letter from her brother Arthur who wrote:

" So peace seems certain now, and indeed by all accounts it seems so certain that I quite hate to hear any musketry firing. Fancy poor fellows being shot just at last within a few days of peace being declared—horrible! Oster Sachenn, who now commands at Sebastopol, says he will not fire another shot when he hears that the Emperor is dead."

The hopes of the optimists were a little damped when it became known that Alexander II had announced his intention of following in his father's footsteps and driving the allies into the sea, but Lord Stratford de Redcliffe, who was presumably conversant with current affairs, had pronounced Alexander to be " a pacific nonentity who would not go far." The oracle had spoken. At all events he considered that an " excursion " to the Crimea to view the battlefields would be a welcome diversion, the more so since Admiral Lyons was sailing in the *Leander* to Balaklava in the middle of April and had invited Lord Stratford de Redcliffe and a party of friends to accompany him.

Chapter Twenty-One

CRIMEAN EXCURSION

ROBERT PORTAL was very excited to hear of the Carews' arrival in Constantinople, but disappointed that Eliza Taylor had not come with them. In a letter to her he had written :

" Would that you had come with the Pagets and Carews, but I suppose that would have been expecting too much. I don't think Lord George has the smallest intention of coming up here for the present when he can live comfortably in Constantinople ; he sees no object in coming here to command fifteen horses. Whether Lord Raglan will see it in the same light remains to be seen. You were very good to send me a lock of ' The Wave's ' hair ; do remember that ' The Wave ' is a lady and not a gentleman, so don't call her ' him ' whenever you mention the female."

During February and March, which marked a period of even more futile inactivity than usual, a state of tension existed on the heights of Balaklava, fostered by a faulty intelligence service which anticipated Russian attacks but regarded any offensive on the part of the Allies as impossible. The nerves of the responsible commanders were distinctly frayed. This state of affairs did not add to the comfort of the troops in the immediate neighbourhood, and Portal, who had entered into a correspondence with Miss Bessie, cites one or two instances.

" Yesterday morning," he writes, " at 1 a.m., all the regiments of Balaklava turned out as an attack was expected every minute on our extreme right on the high ground overlooking Balaklava by a force of 25,000 Russians ; all the ships in the harbour were ordered to be ready to land their crews at a moment's notice. Needless to say the attack never took place. It is said that the Russians, hearing our men marching up, retired ; but my own impression (founded on fact) is that old Sir Colin Campbell, who commands here and who I believe is an excellent officer, had a dream in which he saw visions of Russian hordes advancing against him, awoke suddenly fancying it was a reality, and acted on it."

It was during this period that *The Times* correspondent fell from grace in Portal's eyes and as he says " made an infernal nuisance of himself." He favours Miss Bessie with some more gossip.

" The Cossacks, the other night after dark," he wrote, " chased Mr. Russell of *The Times* as he was returning from dining in the heights, on his way across the plain of Balaklava. He immediately made a report of it to Sir Colin Campbell, who ordered out 100 cavalry at once to patrol the plain all night. This is done whenever Mr. Russell wants to get after-dinner information, which means every night, so you may fancy that the cavalry wish the Cossacks had carried Mr. Russell off somewhere else. Fortunately I now have little to do with these newspaper patrols as I have been made A.D.C. to the Commanding Officer of the Division."

With the advent of spring, spirits at last began to rise, leading Portal to write : " All sorts of new and interesting tricks were tried on the Russians." He recounts one of these " tricks " in a letter dated 13th April :

" We are still hammering away with our guns at Sebastopol, and I fear with no great success ; the number of reports that fly about in every direction are about as reliable as our shells—they never hit the mark ; and if they do the result is negligible. Some of our men, who were in a pit only ten yards from the Russians, got so tired of this sort of thing that they determined to bully the

Russians, and not exactly knowing how, at last hit on a grand notion. The old toper in the party had a bottle full of liquor which was speedily drained of its contents ; they then filled the bottle full of powder, put a small paper fuse into its neck, lighted it and tossed the bottle into the middle of the Russian pit. The effect was instantaneous as it burst, and no doubt scratched and frightened them all. However, the Russians hoisted a cap in the air on the end of a musket and whirled it round to show they were not all killed."

The ten days' bombardment of Sebastopol proved quite in-effective, but apparently undisturbed by its failure Lord Stratford de Redcliffe, the British Ambassador, invited a party of ladies from Constantinople to visit the seat of the war with him. Young Miss Bessie was naturally thrilled at the prospect of a visit to the front, and notes in her journal :

" *20th April*. This morning we embarked in the *Leander* man-of-war ; our party consisted of Lord and Lady Stratford de Redcliffe, and two Miss Cannings, Lord William Paulet and of course Walter, Mr. Kinglake the eastern traveller and Mr. Russell of *The Times* newspaper and lastly Lord and Lady George Paget. The officers turned out of their cabins for the ladies so we were much more comfortable than we were in the *City of Glasgow*."

The officers were doubtless extremely uncomfortable and it is probable that remarks not exactly complimentary to the picnic party were passed in the ward-room.

The cruise up the Black Sea passed very pleasantly, inter-spersed with glee-singing by the crew, who in the evenings came aft to amuse the company. Balaklava was reached on 26th April and Miss Bessie writes :

" We anchored here this morning ; the harbour is a beautiful sight, filled with shipping, and on the heights beyond is a vast plain of canvas stretching as far as the eye can reach. There is great excitement as the *Harbinger* had arrived bringing the 10th Hussars from India ; the 10th was Grandpapa's old regiment, how he would have loved to see them. We had a beautiful view of them disembarking ; they are all mounted on Arab horses, most beautiful creatures and in the finest possible condition. We hear that Miss Nightingale is at Balaklava visiting the hospital and that she is not very popular with the medical officers, as she is very severe with them."

The month of May proved to be highly entertaining for the " excursionists." Lord Stratford de Redcliffe was staying with Lord Raglan at his headquarters and most of the officers and crew had gone ashore to man the sailors' battery on the heights. Lord George Paget apparently had carte blanche aboard and played the part of host to perfection. Miss Bessie's excitement at being to all intents and purposes at the front was intense, and she voices her feelings in her journal.

"We are having capital fun," she writes. "Lord George arranges something different for us to see each day. Yesterday, the 20th, was celebrated as the Queen's birthday and we all went ashore and saw a parade of the cavalry near the Monastery of St. George. Lord Raglan, Lord Stratford, General Pélissier, and Omar Pasha were there with a brilliant staff and half the officers in the Crimea. To-day we rode out a large party and Robert Portal showed us the ' Charge ' ground where Uncle Willie was wounded. Mama stayed on board with Uncle Arthur who had come down from the camp. In the evening we had a late dinner ; afterwards we listened to the Rifle band which played beautifully. Walter flirted dreadfully with the youngest Miss Canning. I think she is very forward and do not like her much. Mama thinks she is very unladylike and spoke to Walter rather severely afterwards, to which I am afraid he did not pay much heed."

It is not to be supposed that Miss Bessie, who was not without personal attractions and was, moreover, the daughter of a wealthy landowner, had been without admirers during her stay in Constantinople. Lieutenant Grey of the 11th Hussars, " whose cherry-coloured trousers are most becoming," was one of the worshippers at her shrine, and they had kept up a more or less regular correspondence. He had been taken prisoner when on a reconnaissance under Sir Colin Campbell in April, and while at Balaklava Miss Bessie received a letter from him announcing the fact with an enclosure from Prince Menschikoff. Miss Bessie in a fit of girlish enthusiasm had written to Mr. Grey saying : " Now mind, dear Charles, that when you take Menschikoff prisoner, be sure and send me one of the buttons of his coat." This letter had been sent to Menschikoff for censoring. Before sealing up Grey's letter he enclosed a note of his own regretting that he could not comply with all the young lady wished, but he begged to enclose her one which he had just cut from his uniform coat. The button arrived neatly wrapped in silver paper. Miss Bessie was highly delighted with this memento of the Russian Commander-in-Chief and had it made into a brooch which long out-lived the memory of Lieutenant Grey and his cherry-coloured trousers.

The " excursionists " left Balaklava towards the end of May to an accompaniment of cheering and a medley of military music. This was not primarily, as some might suppose, in thankfulness for the departure of a tiresome lot of sightseers, but in celebration of the almost bloodless capture of Kertch by the Allies on 24th May. Doubtless, however, the dual event was hailed by the men in the trenches with equal satisfaction. The return journey to Constantinople was made in the transport *Robert Lowe*, described by Miss Bessie as " a very poor sort of ship with small steam power, having only what they call an auxiliary engine which pushes her along at the rapid rate of about four knots." There were several wounded men on board in charge of untrained orderlies, no medical officer being apparently available for the service. Lord Stratford de Redcliffe, who was also returning in the *Robert Lowe*, complained to Dr. Hall, the principal medical officer, of this lack of consideration, but whether on his own behalf or on that of the wounded men is not recorded. Dr. Hall, whose temper had become sadly frayed in his dealings with "that interfering female" Miss Nightingale, who had herself been down with a bad attack of fever, was in no mind to be dictated to even by Her Majesty's Ambassador and refused to take any action. Lord George Paget was remaining in the Crimea in view of his likely appointment to command a Light Cavalry Brigade, but Lady George returned with the rest of the ambassadorial party to Constantinople. Miss Bessie took a jaundiced view of the return trip.

"We were really quite uncomfortable," she writes. "Mama, Lady George and I were squeezed into a stuffy hole amidships near the engine ; Annette had to sleep on a mat outside. We could not sleep owing to the groanings of the poor men and the quarrelling of the people who were supposed to look after them. Lord Stratford was very grumpy although he had the best cabin on board the ship. We were all very thankful when we got back to Scutari."

At the beginning of June, Lady Carew received a letter from Sir Walter intimating that her stay with "Turks, infidels and cur-dogs" had been prolonged quite long enough and that she had better return home for a summer cruise in the *Beatrice*, which he had put into commission early in June. He told her that Lord Ellesmere, who was, like himself, a member of the Royal Yacht Squadron, had arrived at Constantinople in his yacht and would be delighted to accommodate her on the homeward voyage. Lord Ellesmere, who as Francis Egerton had been Secretary for War in 1830, had gone to Constantinople in an unofficial capacity, presumably with the idea of seeing for himself what a mess the present holder of the office was making of the job. He had just been made a Knight of the Garter for his services to various learned societies, and had been invited to stay at the Embassy. Knowing Lord Stratford de Redcliffe, however, he had declined, preferring to stay aboard his own yacht, which was equally comfortable and free from ambassadorial pomposity.

Lord Ellesmere had arranged to leave Constantinople in the early part of June. Two days before the day of sailing young Walter, very conveniently in the opinion of Lady Carew, met with an accident which, though not serious, was sufficient excuse for him to be granted leave to England. The mishap occurred when he was out riding with Miss Canning, his horse putting its foot into a hole and giving him a fall which broke his wrist. The accident might well have happened to anyone, but Miss Bessie, with sisterly suspicion, writes : " I think Walter was paying too much attention to that minx Miss Canning and not enough to his horse. Mama is quite pleased, as she thinks Walter will be out of the way of the Russians and Miss Canning."

The R.Y.S. *Urania* was extremely well found, and presented a welcome contrast to the discomforts suffered in the *Robert Lowe*. Miss Bessie, who was well read, at once found favour with Lord Ellesmere, who lent her his various works to read during the voyage.

" We are a very small party in the Saloon," she writes, " Lord Ellesmere, Mr. Stafford, Mama, Walter, and myself. Lord Ellesmere is very clever and interesting and most kind. He writes most lovely verses and I am now reading his *Donna Charitea*. Mr. Stafford is a rather serious sort of man. He has been helping Miss Nightingale in her ministrations in the hospitals. I do not think that he quite approved of the ' sociable families ' coming to Constantinople with so much misery going on, but he is always very polite to us."

The voyage home was somewhat tame after the excitements at the seat of war. Walter was rather disgruntled at being sent home with a broken wrist caused by the fall of a horse instead of an honourable wound like " Uncle Willie's " received in battle. He was inclined to blame his mother for having got round Lord William Paulet, who told her that he was " quite sick of the whole thing " and was thinking of going home himself. Leave seems to have been arranged without any fuss or bother for officers of the higher command. Lady Carew for her part thought that she had handled the matter very successfully.

The *Urania* arrived at Plymouth on 5th July to be met with the news that Lord Raglan had died of cholera on 28th June ; the victim, as Augustus Stafford put it, " of England's unreadiness for war." As the *Urania* made her way to her mooring in the Hamoaze, Miss Bessie, who was keeping a sharp look-out, spotted the *Beatrice*'s burgee, and through her glass was able to make out the massive figure of Sir Walter on the poop. He at all events was ready for the fray, and the Crimean excursion soon resolved itself into the summer regatta season.

Chapter Twenty-Two

FAREWELL TO CRIMEA

PORTAL had been very sorry to say good-bye to Lady Carew and Miss Bessie, as their visit had proved a welcome relief to the monotonous existence which the troops had lately led on the heights watching Sebastopol. He sent many messages to Eliza Taylor, and begged them to assure her that he was longing for the day when he would see her again.

Just after they left he felt impelled to write to her :

" I was very sorry to see the last of your sister, since she reminded me of you. Bessie is delightful and seems to have thoroughly enjoyed her visit to the seat of war. Last night I dined with Mrs. Duberly who had a party to meet Omar Pasha. Mrs. D. has made herself quite comfortable, goes everywhere and does everything."

Portal, however, was getting more bored with the curiosity-mongers who thronged out to the Crimea than with the ineffable monotony of the life itself. He goes on :

" Picnics are the order of the day, and the ' Amateurs,' or as we call them the ' Sympathizers ' who are a perfect nuisance, are beginning to arrive rapidly. Sir Thomas Whichcote and Philip Dundas have arrived and they all seem to think it capital fun which is more than we do. They are now advertising special ships to take so many ' sociable families' to the Crimea and back at £5 a head. Did you ever hear such nonsense ? "

This luxury shuttle-service was a great boon to the

" Amateurs," but its amenities do not appear to have been extended to the " professional " sick or wounded soldiers. The fluttering of the gaily coloured butterflies over the battlefields provided a more pleasing picture than the flocks of carrion crows which usually frequented them, and Portal, being human, and of a sociable disposition, appreciated this ; but he was nevertheless disgusted at the futile frivolity, for he says :

" The men cheer the ladies whenever they see them, but I think this amusement is out of place when there is so much misery. Eight hundred men were taken down sick to Balaklava yesterday ; several were found dead when they took them out of the ambulance carts ; the French have hitherto lent us their carts ; they have now declined to do so as they want them themselves, so our men will have to remain on the heights and die in their tents."

Meanwhile in the trenches before Sebastopol, the struggle for the subjection of the city continued with unabated violence. General Pélissier, on taking command of the allied forces, had accepted Lord Raglan's proposals for carrying on the siege by direct attacks. Both commanders agreed that the key of the place was the Malakoff and decided that by simultaneous assault, the Quarries under the Redan, and the Mamelon in front of the Malakoff, should be wrested from the enemy. The merry month of May was followed by a tragic June. The French on 7th June were partially successful inasmuch as they captured the Mamelon, but through a hopeless confusion of orders and lack of any co-ordinated plan, we suffered severe casualties in an unsuccessful attack on the Redan. Portal writes :

" muddle everywhere ; it is really too horrid and awful to think about, and yet all the sightseers talk of the attack on the Mamelon and Redan as if they were going out rabbit shooting. All the time that this fearful slaughter of the French and ourselves was going on, those looking on and the soldiers not engaged, cheered like demons and the Rifle band was playing lively airs in front of their encampment overlooking the whole scene."

An even more tragic farce followed on the 18th; both the Malakoff and the Redan were still in the hands of the Russians, and General Pélissier realized that to make any progress we must capture these strong-points. Portal describes the anniversary of Waterloo as " one of the most disastrous days we have had " though the initial stage savoured of comic opera.

" The cavalry," he writes, " under Lord George Paget went up to the front at 1 a.m. and formed a long line to keep the crowd of amateurs and sightseers from showing themselves. At dawn the French with about 24,000 men under General Mayran carried out an attack on the Malakoff. They could make no headway against the Russian batteries, however, and having tried for an hour to take the place, they retired, as also did the sightseers, very hastily. The action developed into a sorry affair enough. Lack of liaison with the French and the usual incompetence of the allied High Command were the chief causes of the débâcle."

He continues :

" One General vied with another in stupidity, General Airey being as stupid as any, which was only to be expected. His brigade hoping to get into the Redan, advanced without support to the cemetery (a well-chosen rendezvous) and there they are now (10 p.m.) ; they cannot go on or get out. Poor Colonel Yea of the 7th Fusiliers was wounded and taking off his cap and putting it on the top of his sword, shouted to the 7th to come on, whereupon a Russian rushed at him and blew his brains out. He is a great loss, as we looked to him as a rising man ; he had only the day before received the new Order of Merit from the Queen. Our fleet did nothing to-day ; they are too much afraid of losing a ship."

Portal was genuinely grieved at Lord Raglan's death on the 28th ; for though he was critical of his leadership, he had a great respect for him as a courteous and kindly man, as indeed had all who came in contact with him.

" Poor Lord Raglan's remains are escorted to-morrow from Headquarters to Kamiesh. Our men carry the body as far as the French lines and they take it on. All his staff go home with the body ; I only wish I was on that staff ; an odd wish, perhaps, to be on the staff of a dead Commander, but I am thinking only of leave."

Portal did in fact get three weeks' leave, as he wanted " to go anywhere to escape deaths, funerals and heavy guns." Constantinople was the only available leave resort, and writing on board the *Robert Lowe* on 8th July he says :

" George Sullivan and I put ourselves on board this very indifferent transport full of sick and wounded officers ; a case for Panmure. There is no medical officer on board ; it is really too bad. There are two of the hospital nurses from Balaklava on board ; such creatures, ah Lud, excellent good souls, I have no doubt, but drab to a degree ; Lord George says they are most of them like that, as otherwise all their officer friends might pay them too frequent visits."

Constantinople was " hot, dirty and stinking, and the streets were infested with mangy scavenging dogs." The notabilities, however, appear to have made themselves very comfortable ; and Portal was made welcome at Lord William Paulet's house on his arrival and refreshed himself in his large rooms with iced brandy and water. Lord William himself seems to have been hard to please ; for he was " quite sick of the whole thing and talks of giving up his appointment as Military Commandant." The Duke of Newcastle was staying in the same hotel as Portal, but was not a very lively companion, being laid up with diarrhoea and other complaints. Portal says : " No one knows why he is here, perhaps not himself, but I suspect he wishes himself home again."

Lord Stratford was of a different calibre, complacent and unperturbed, and the parties at the Embassy were a source of continual gratification to the gay English colony. Lord and Lady

George Paget, of course, entertained in their usual magnificent way and contributed largely to the gaiety of the proceedings. Portal thoroughly enjoyed this pleasant interlude, where " at least," he says, " one saw civilized beings and heard music and singing."

The campaign pursued its dreary course, made more dreary for the English army by its uninspiring commander, Simpson, whom Portal describes as " a commonplace man with no confidence in his own judgement and less in that of others, except possibly General Airey, by whom he is likely to be entirely ruled." Whether this latter supposition was correct or not, Simpson appears to have been quite incapable of taking any effective action himself, on any occasion. The French victory at the Tchernaya on 16th August somewhat lifted the gloom, and Portal says it was a great set-off against the 18th June and cheered up the troops considerably. Portal had an unpleasant reminder of a former experience in this battle, and he describes it in a letter written the day after :

" We got the order to advance all the cavalry into the valley of the Balaklava Charge to attack if necessary. We therefore marched down this valley till we almost got within range of the Russian guns. Six regiments of the Chasseurs d'Afrique were with us. Here we watched with intense interest the approach of the Russians, who under cover of their guns advanced steadily across the plain against the Sardinians, whose steady fire and that of our artillery drove them back with heavy loss. Meanwhile the Russians also attacked the bridge across the Tchernaya, which was held by the French, who however retired, and we thought the day was lost. Suddenly the French re-formed and charged in most brilliant fashion, retaking the bridge and routing the Russians completely. Then came a horrible moment ; our Brigade was ordered with the Chasseurs to cross the Tchernaya and charge the Russians. I am thankful to say that General Pélissier, who was there in person, thought better of it, and it was well he did, for it would have proved as mad an act as our former exploit at Balaklava."

Portal, like everyone else, was delighted when Sebastopol fell, but was disgusted at the English army's contribution to the victory, though he gives high praise to the French. In a letter to his mother, written on 10th September, he again writes of the attack on Sebastopol :

" Sebastopol is gone at last, thanks to the French, whose magnificent attack on the Malakoff nothing could withstand. I wish I could say the same of our attack on the Redan, which was shamefully conceived and carried out, or rather not carried out, for we failed signally to take it. In fact, so badly did we perform our part of the operation that it became a question of some interest whether the French would be able to hold the Malakoff. However, in the middle of the night a Highland officer crept up to the Redan and to his joy and astonishment found it empty. I suppose the bells in every parish in England are commemorating the fall of this great city which the Russians have so kindly evacuated."

The campaign was virtually over, and after some delay Portal, with Lord George Paget and the Light Cavalry, or what remained of them, moved to Eupatoria on 14th October. Lord George was "in no good humour" on the day of embarkation ; for he had just arrived from headquarters, where a somewhat un-profitable argument had taken place between himself and General Simpson, "which of course," says Portal, "led to nothing, like most of the General's plans." Now, however, the course of events took a pleasanter turn and Lord George recovered his spirits, as did the Light Cavalry ; for they learnt that they were free from the dismal domination of a carping and inefficient disciplinarian and were to take part in a last gay adventure under the auspices of an inspiring French general who knew his job. Portal gives a short summary of the proceedings :

" General d'Allonville called on Lord G. Paget yesterday and stayed a long time. He intends going out with all his cavalry and ours and the Turks on 22nd October to make a reconnais-sance and find out what the Russians are really about. George

Paget was highly delighted and fell in with the plan at once. He and I are in a house in the town which would be comfortable enough if we were not eaten by fleas all night."

The reconnaissance, or excursion, as Portal calls it, was a great success so far as the handling of cavalry was concerned. "General d'Allonville handled us capitally, and our system of drill met with his decided approval ; his good opinion is infinitely superior to any of our own Generals, as he knows so much more about it, I am sorry to say." The excursion occupied a very pleasant three days by the shores of a lake close to Eupatoria, but the results obtained about the intentions of the Russians do not appear to have been very notable. Portal writes :

" Nothing much was achieved ; we came up with a large force of Russians in order of battle, which we at once put ourselves into, but as General d'Allonville, being a cavalryman, had forgotten about our infantry, which did not turn up as expected, we did nothing, the Russians retiring first, we following suit and retiring on Sak. It was a magnificent sight to see the two armies drawn up looking at each other, with the Bashi-Bazouk devils performing extraordinary antics ; and when we changed position, the Russians did the same. It made a most beautiful field-day."

As a fitting climax to this inter-allied patrol and to show his appreciation of English co-operation, General d'Allonville, on behalf of the French cavalry officers, gave a farewell party. Portal, who liked to amuse Eliza Taylor, tells her in a chatty letter what took place :

" *8th November*. Last night General d'Allonville invited the officers to ' un Punch D'adieu ' at seven o'clock. The name sufficiently informs you that it was a ' swigging party,' nothing more or less. At the appointed hour G. Paget and I sallied forth ; on arriving within 200 yards of the place of entertainment an officer asked who we were, and on being told, shouted at the top of his voice, ' General Lord Paget,' upon which the military band struck up some lively tunes. General d'A. then appeared, took George Paget's hand and led him to the centre of the banquet hall. The tables groaned with punch and every conceivable wine. In about an hour General d'A. proposed the health of the Queen, and the band played the National Anthem. George Paget then, in a very neat speech, proposed the health of the Emperor of the French. After this a number of beautifully dressed vivandières came in with cakes, etc., and were much admired, especially by the Cornets. Soon after General d'A., George Paget and myself retired, none too soon as we heard afterwards. Those who remained got lively, and the fumes of the punch made them feel uneasy about their heads next morning."

At the end of November the 4th Light Dragoons underwent a dreary period of waiting for embarkation orders at Eupatoria. Portal writes: "I dined on board the *Valorous* with General Scarlett who was a major in General Taylor's old regiment, the 6th Dragoon Guards, and now commands all the cavalry in the Crimea. The next day I rode all round the fortifications with him and showed him everything. He hopes we may get off soon." It was not until February 1st, however, that owing to contrary winds and the dilatoriness of the navy the 4th Light Dragoons embarked in the *Golden Fleece* which sailed for England. Portal writes: "We are all very wrath with the navy, who, when for a few hours the sea was smooth in the mornings, which it seldom was, knocked off work to give the sailors their dinners, which lasted till 2 p.m. Had it not been for these sacred two hours for dinner, we might all have been embarked several days ago." Portal, however, was in high spirits as he had proposed to and been accepted by Eliza Taylor. He lost no time in writing to her and telling her that he really hoped at last that he was on his way home.

Chapter Twenty-Three

WEDDING BELLS

ELIZA TAYLOR was staying with her sister at Haccombe and had received her fiancé's letter from Eupatoria, saying that he was sailing any day in the transport *Golden Fleece* and that he would probably land at Plymouth. He did not, however, give any date. It was the beginning of March 1856 and the Rev. Fitzwilliam Taylor was retailing extracts, in the dreary monotone habitual to him, from a two days old *Western Daily Mercury* to an unappreciative audience seated round the breakfast table at Haccombe. Sir Walter Carew had finished his second mutton chop, which to him was a necessary preliminary to a day's hunting, and was about to leave when the Rev. Fitzwilliam alighted on a paragraph of some interest.

"'It is reliably reported,'" he read, "'that at the Peace Conference held in Paris on 25th February an armistice until 31st March was agreed upon.'" The Rev. Fitzwilliam after a pause said, "That means that the war is off." Sir Walter, whom the war had not afflicted unduly while it was on, replied, "Well, so am I," and left the company to their deliberations.

Lady Carew and her daughter Bessie were thrilled at the news, and her sister Eliza could hardly contain herself.

The climax came when Dally the butler, with his usual lugubrious expression, entered with an orange envelope. Dally mistrusted orange envelopes as harbingers of ill-omen, and with an air of distaste handed it to Lady Carew.

" A telegraphic despatch, m'lady, just arrived on horseback from Newton station."

The message, which was from Sir William Parker, the naval Commander-in-Chief at Plymouth, ran as follows : " Transport *Golden Fleece* signalled off the Lizard, will probably arrive Plymouth March fifth. Pray take up your quarters in Admiralty House."

It was decided that Lady Carew and her sister should go to welcome the homecoming warriors, Bessie and B, much to their disgust, being left to look after their father. The ladies could not, of course, go unaccompanied by a male escort, and the Rev. Fitzwilliam volunteered his services.

On arrival at the Plymouth terminus the disadvantages of crinolines, which had come into fashion in the previous year, became apparent. The fly chartered by the Rev. Fitzwilliam had evidently not been designed for these articles of wearing apparel, and difficulty was experienced in getting the ladies in. But with the aid of the flyman at one door and the Rev. Fitzwilliam at the other, they were eventually pulled and pushed into place. The Rev. Fitzwilliam, not fancying the musty interior, seated himself on the box, where the red-nosed flyman, as the former records, " breathed a benediction of stale spirits over me."

The *Golden Fleece* had been sighted from Plymouth Hoe far out to sea early on 6th March, and just before noon came to her moorings to the accompaniment of blasts from ships' whistles and music from the band of the Royal Marines. There were many West Countrymen among the troopers of the 4th Light Dragoons, and the Corporation of Plymouth had decided to give them a West Country welcome. Memories went back to the summer of 1854 when they had sailed from Plymouth in the *Simla*. " The girl I left behind me," which was a suitable air for that occasion, now gave way to " See the conquering hero comes." This, as it happened, was particularly appropriate ; for it was learned that General Williams, " the hero of Kars," was on board. For Eliza Taylor, of course, there was only one hero in the ship, Captain Robert Portal, of whom there was as yet no sign. Shepherded by the Admiral and his flag lieutenant, the Admiralty House party made their way on board, and into the saloon, through a seething mass of women waiting to greet their menfolk with bottles of porter.

The saloon was insufferably stuffy, the atmosphere redolent with the fumes of cigar smoke and sherry. A knot of be-whiskered officers and a few civilians appeared to be celebrating their return from the war, and the arrival of the ladies was for the moment not noticed. The Rev. Fitzwilliam writes:

" We came unheralded on a crowd of military swells who did not take the slightest notice of us. There was no sign of Robert, and Eliza was getting fidgety. Just then three gentlemen entered; the first, to my surprise, was Lord Palmerston, who at once recognized us, and introduced Sir Charles Wood, the First Lord of the Admiralty. Then came Lord Fortescue, Lord George Paget, and last, but by no means least in Eliza's eyes, Robert. Lord Palmerston told us that he had looked in at his consti-tuency at Tiverton and had come on to welcome General Williams, to whom we were all introduced. The General is a sour-faced individual with a moustache like a walrus, to whom I did not take much. After thanking the Admiral for his hospitality, we managed to slip away, and Robert, who had palmed off his duties on someone else, came with us. He and Eliza, rather to Ann's disapproval, went in a fly by themselves to the station whilst Ann and I followed in another."

There was a good deal of excitement in the village of West Ogwell over the wedding of Captain Robert Portal and Miss Eliza Taylor. It was to be expected that a large number of the military were to be present, seeing that the bridegroom was a member of " the gallant six hundred." The vanguard, a dozen N.C.O.s of the 4th Light Dragoons, who were to act as the guard of honour, had already arrived. They had played sad havoc with the supply of beer in the Plow Inn and, it must be confessed, with the girls of the village, to whom the brilliant uniform was a source of unfailing attraction. It had been decided by the mother of the bride, in spite of the Rev. Fitzwilliam's protests, that the Bishop of Exeter, Dr. Phillpotts, should perform the ceremony. Sir Walter Carew, who disliked the Bishop for his high-church proclivities, took the Rev. Fitzwilliam's part, and threatened to absent himself if " that Romanizing clown in leggings " took part in the proceedings. Lady Carew, who secretly thought that the Bishop would give tone to the wedding, smoothed things over. It was finally arranged that the Rev. Fitzwilliam should give his sister away ; Lord George Paget was to be the best man. Sir Walter Carew, who thought that Mrs. Taylor "kept a poor sort of table at West Ogwell House and like all women a worse cellar," insisted on the wedding breakfast being held at Haccombe. Miss Bessie and B, much to their delight, were selected as bridesmaids.

It was a distinguished assembly that attended the wedding breakfast on 3rd May. The Prime Minister, Lord Palmerston, was the principal guest. Miss Bessie, who had constituted herself press reporter for the occasion, writes in her diary :

" There were a lot of old Crimean friends at the breakfast. Lord Cardigan, who no-one particularly wanted to see, he probably came to atone for the ' mistake ' at Balaklava ; Sir Colin Campbell, who everyone was delighted to see ; Admiral Lyons, who as usual was very breezy ; Mr. Augustus Stafford, who was such a help to Miss Nightingale, and lots of others. Funnily enough, Papa and Lord Cardigan seemed to get on very well, I think mostly because they both liked champagne. At the end of breakfast, Lord Palmerston proposed a toast to the bride and bridegroom, making a very nice little speech. He wished them happiness and told Aunt Eliza that she was fortunate in her choice of one of the heroes of the Light Brigade of whom England is proud. Lord Cardigan said, ' Hear, hear,' as if Lord Palmerston was including him. As the carriage with Aunt Eliza and Uncle Robert was going away, Papa, who I think must have been excited by the champagne, blew his horn, cracked his whip, and shouted hark away. The horses were off

like a flash and broke into a gallop with Keller the coachman
shouting, 'Hold hard, Sir Walter.' We all thought it very
amusing, except Aunt Eliza and Uncle Robert, whose furious
faces appeared at each window."

Miss Bessie was a little off the mark in supposing that Lord
Cardigan's presence at the wedding was an atonement. On the
contrary, he had come to smooth things over with Lady Carew's
brother-in-law, Colonel Morris, who had commanded the
17th Lancers in the charge at Balaklava and with whom he had
had an acrimonious correspondence. The letters they had exchanged related to an incident which had occurred on the ridge
on which the Light Brigade were drawn up just prior to the
charge, and is in fact an interesting fragment of history. Had
Colonel Morris's advice been acted upon, it is more than likely
that the virtual destruction of the Light Brigade would have
been averted.

There were three eye-witnesses to this dispute between Lord
Cardigan and Colonel Morris on the Balaklava ridge on 25th
October 1854 : Lord Lucan, Captain White, the acting adjutant
of the 17th Lancers, and Trumpeter John Brown of the same
regiment, whose sworn testimony finds a place among the letters.
Briefly the facts were as follows : the Heavy Dragoons had
broken through the Russian cavalry and Colonel Morris rightly
considered a heaven-sent opportunity presented itself for his
regiment to attack the right flank of the Russian cavalry. He
requested permission from Lord Cardigan, who categorically
refused it. Captain White then said to Colonel Morris : "If I
were in command of the regiment, I would attack by myself
and stand a court martial. There is a C.B. staring you in the
face as you cannot fail."

The statement of Trumpeter John Brown presents a clear
picture of what occurred. He says :

"When the regiment [the 17th Lancers] was drawn up in
line on the brow of the hill previous to the Heavy Dragoon

charge, the advance of the Russian cavalry attracted Colonel Morris's attention and he ordered the regt. to go threes right in order to attack the right flank of the Russian cavalry when Lord Cardigan rode up and said, ' What are you doing, Col. Morris, front your regiment' (or words to that effect). Col. Morris answered, ' Look there, my Lord,' pointing with his sword to the enemy advancing. Lord Cardigan answered, ' Remain where you are, Sir, until you get orders.' I remember sounding the Trot by the Commanding Officer's orders when he ordered the regiment to go threes right, and I think my sounding attracted Lord Cardigan's attention. I also remember Colonel Morris saying to Lord Cardigan, ' Let me take the regiment on to the attack.' "

Lord Cardigan solemnly declared in the House of Lords that no such interview ever took place. Lord Lucan, on the other hand, told Colonel Morris when he met him in London that he perfectly recollected the incident. Lord Cardigan evidently considered that a wedding party assisted by champagne offered a suitable background to make his peace with the injured party.

The Portals' honeymoon was spent in Paris, under very favourable auspices. Captain Portal had received an invitation from General d'Allonville, under whom he had served in the Crimea, to be his guest at his home in Versailles. General d'Allonville was in attendance on the Emperor, who, when he heard that Captain Portal was a survivor of the famous charge, was most forthcoming to him and his wife. The Emperor had become quite the family man since the birth of the Prince Imperial in March, and insisted on Mrs. Portal viewing the young prodigy. The royal family were in residence at the palace of St. Cloud and Mrs. Portal was conducted by the Emperor himself to the royal nursery, where she met the Empress and the infant. Eliza Portal writes in her diary :

" The Empress Eugénie was the most lovely person I have ever seen and very amiable. The Prince, who was nearly two months old, was a dear little baby, and the Emperor and Empress were overwhelmed with joy at his arrival. The Emperor told us how much he had enjoyed the visit of our Queen and Royal Family last year to Paris. He pointed out that it was the first time an English Sovereign had beheld Paris for four centuries, since the infant Henry VI was crowned there in 1422. I thought it very clever of him to remember his history so well."

It took a good deal to move Sir Walter Carew, unless it were to go on a yachting trip, and it needed the united efforts of Lady Carew and her two daughters to persuade him that it was essential for them to see the peace celebrations in London on 29th May. Two cogent arguments were put to Sir Walter to induce his acceptance of the proposal : one was that Miss Bessie deserved a treat, since she had just celebrated her seventeenth birthday ; the other, that it would be the only opportunity of seeing the newly wedded couple before they returned to garrison duty at Lichfield. The second reason was rendered invalid by a letter from Eliza Portal : " We are staying to see the illuminations in London on the 29th," the letter ran, " and then we want you all to come for a house-warming in our new house. Robert says tell Walter that William Palmer the poisoner is to be hung at Stafford, which is quite near, on 14th June." It was this last tit-bit which faintly interested Sir Walter, and somewhat unwillingly he agreed to the expedition.

The transport of Sir Walter, his family and servants to London, and arrangements for their lodgings on arrival, constituted a considerable undertaking. The Portals were to join them at the Hanover Hotel, of which about half had been engaged for the party. Sir Walter insisted on the Rev. Fitzwilliam's accompanying him to share a smoking-compartment.

Victorine, Lady Carew's French maid, was permitted to travel in a second-class carriage, while Henry, the second footman, who acted as Sir Walter's valet, had to content himself with a third-class open truck. This form of transportation was, if the truth were known, more enjoyable to Henry than any other ;

for his view was restricted for most of his time by the frosted-glass windows of the servants' quarters at Haccombe, which Sir Walter had installed after the abolition of the window tax in 1851, adopting the motto that servants should be neither seen nor heard.

Chapter Twenty-Four

CRIMEAN AFTERMATH

THE Portals joined the party at the Hanover Hotel, arriving in a carriage lent them during their stay in London by Lord George Paget. Young Walter Carew, now a subaltern in the Blues, infuriated his father and delighted Miss Bessie and B by driving up in a private hansom complete with " tiger." Sir Walter strongly disapproved of " this new-fangled shut cab," and considered that it was no vehicle for a man to drive in. Miss Bessie and B, however, considered that it was eminently suited as a conveyance for ladies, and having received permission from Lady Carew, persuaded Walter to allow his tiger to take them on a shopping expedition with Victorine. It ended in disaster. Miss Bessie, describing their experience, writes :

" We started off from the hotel at a spanking trot, scattering a little crowd of cads who jeered and hooted us. It was a wet day, so we had to have the glass down against the rain, which made it rather stuffy but which Victorine thought très confortable. All went well until the middle of Piccadilly when the horse slipped up on the wet pavements ; we heard a terrific crash behind and the next thing we knew was a peeler sitting on the horse's head. Another peeler let us out and we then saw that the tiger's seat at the back had broken off and the tiger was sitting in the street still holding the reins. No one was hurt except Victorine, who had cut her head when the front glass broke. We had to go home in a smelly four-wheeler."

During the spring of 1856, many distinguished Frenchmen were visiting London for the celebration of the Queen's birthday on 29th May : others were there for more practical reasons. Among the latter was that voluble and enterprising engineer, the Vicomte de Lesseps. Captain Portal had met him while serving under General d'Allonville, and had heard de Lesseps explain his scheme for cutting a canal from the head of the Red Sea to the Bay of Sineh. The Vicomte was in process of forming a company, and having received little satisfaction from the Queen, whom he had just visited, and still less from Lord Palmerston, was casting round for other adherents. The house of Portal, he knew, had the monopoly of the manufacture of bank notes, of which his company was in need, and he considered that a renewal of his friendship with a member of that family would be an advantageous step. He therefore became a frequent visitor at the Hanover Hotel. No bank notes were, however, forthcoming, Robert Portal making it clear that at present he had no control in the business. Sir Walter, whose ideas were limited to a cut in the income tax and who had no interest in cutting a canal, told the Vicomte that he should apply to that "miserable feller, Cornewall Lewis." Sir George Cornewall Lewis, who was now Chancellor of the Exchequer, had succeeded to the baronetcy in 1855. He had been at Eton with Sir Walter and had had a varied career. He was now M.P. for Radnor Boroughs and had been a Financial Secretary to the Treasury. From 1852 to 1855, he was editor of the *Edinburgh Review*, and was something of an author. Any man who became Chancellor of the Exchequer and had the power to impose taxes was in Sir Walter's view " a miserable feller " and so in this case it was merely a matter of speech which had become a habit. De Lesseps, answering Sir Walter, with some truth said :
" You English are all the same ; you cannot see beyond your noses." Victorine was more impressed with her fellow-countryman and told Miss Bessie that " M. le Vicomte was a true aristocrat with waxed moustaches the most *ravissant*."

There was a great flutter in the dovecotes at the Hanover Hotel on 27th May, for on that day the Queen held a Drawing Room at Buckingham Palace. Captain and Mrs. Portal had been commanded to attend to be presented on the occasion of their marriage and as an honour to one of the survivors of the charge of the Light Brigade. Lady Carew considered that it was a favourable opportunity for her two daughters also to be presented, and at the last moment, after certain intricate manœuvres, succeeded in obtaining an invitation through the medium of Lord Palmerston. Sir Walter, who regarded the ladies' decking themselves out with frills and furbelows as so much waste of time, said that nothing would induce him to go. Miss Bessie gently reminded her father that he had not been asked. The Drawing Room party left in Lord George Paget's carriage, and Miss Bessie has a few words to say about the proceedings :

" The barouche was very roomy, which was lucky as Mama's and Aunt Eliza's crinolines took up most of the room. Uncle Robert, B and I sat with our backs to the horses. B and I being debutantes wore pre-raphaelite white dresses with feathers and felt very bird-like. When we got out of the carriage we were taken charge of by Prince Edward of Saxe Weimar, the Queen's A.D.C. He and Uncle Robert had served in the Crimea and had lots to talk about. The Prince looked very like a German ; I suppose he is one really. The Queen who looked very happy, was dressed in a lovely grey moiré silk. The Prince was on her left and looked very handsome though rather stern. Mama, who had been presented before, presented B and I. B was rather awkward and tripped over her dress while curtseying ; I saw some of the ladies in attendance smiling, but Mama looked very angry. Uncle Robert and Aunt Eliza were presented by Lord Panmure, the Secretary-at-War."

On 29th May, the Queen's birthday was kept and London was illuminated in celebration of peace. Neither function seems to have interested Sir Walter, who detailed the Rev. Fitzwilliam " to take a look round Tattersall's " with him, and afterwards,

" B. " CAREW, BESSIE CAREW AND LADY CAREW

feeling the urge for fresh air, they decided to take a penny trip on the steamboat to Greenwich for a whitebait dinner. Young Walter was on duty for an inspection of the Household Cavalry and the Foot Guards by Prince Albert. Miss Bessie gives an account of the major items of the day:

" Aunt Eliza was disappointed because he could not come with us but very excited that Uncle Robert had received a message from Lord Panmure to go in uniform as the Prince was going to present the Crimean medal to him and General Williams who the Queen has made Baronet of Kars, so Uncle Robert trotted off by himself. Mama, Aunt Eliza, B and I drove to the Horse Guards, arriving there at 10. The Prince arrived on horseback escorted by a detachment of the Blues commanded by a Captain and a subaltern who to our delight we found was Walter. We had very good seats and were amongst the high and mighty, Lord Palmerston, Lord Panmure, Lord Clarendon, Sir George Grey, and Lord Hardinge, the Commander-in-Chief. Lord Hardinge is like Lord Palmerston to look at, except that he has no whiskers, and seems to be very seedy, which Lord Palmerston certainly is not. Lord P. is to be invested with the Order of the Garter. He told Mama that the war saved him from getting the order of the boot and that the Queen had been very kind to him. In the evening we drove along the Mall and watched a grand display of fireworks, which was most beautiful. They came from Hyde Park, the Green Park, and Victoria Park. The Queen, Prince Albert, the Prince of Wales, Prince Alfred, and Princess Alice came on to the balcony at Buckingham Palace and watched. The Royal children got very excited and skipped about like young goats. When we got back, we found Papa and Uncle Fitz both very cross ; Papa because he had a bad attack of gout which he said the whitebait had given him, but Uncle Fitz put down to the '45 port ; Uncle Fitz was furious because his pockets had been picked on the steamboat. He reported the theft to Sir Richard Mayne, the Commissioner, who said all clergymen were careless, and did nothing, which made Uncle Fitz more furious. I think we had a more exciting day."

The next day the Rev. Fitzwilliam considered the picking of his pockets a minor disaster to the shock he received on reading a letter, forwarded from Haccombe, which put him on the ecclesiastical mat. He had been reported by the Bishop of Exeter to Dr. Sumner, the Archbishop of Canterbury, for "aiding and abetting the Patron of the Living in refusing to allow the Rural Dean to perform the rightful duties of his office." Sir Walter, who regarded Haccombe Church as his private property, had consistently refused the right of entry to the Rural Dean and had on several occasions seen him off the premises. Dr. Phillpotts, now that the war in the Crimea was over, determined to take action, and the archpriest in the person of the Rev. Fitzwilliam was summoned to appear at Lambeth Palace to answer to this act of indiscipline.

Sir Walter, whose attack of gout had rendered him more irascible than usual, shouted, "Let me get at the feller and I'll learn him a thing or two." Whether he referred to the Bishop of Exeter or the Archbishop is not clear, but unfortunately he was unable to get at either and the responsibility fell on the Rev. Fitzwilliam who duly appeared before Dr. Sumner.

The Rev. Fitzwilliam was of a peaceable nature and had no wish to be involved in Sir Walter's peccadilloes. By a process which he called "hedging and ditching" he escaped with a reprimand. He was astute enough to realize that the three livings with their not inconsiderable stipends, of which he had the cure, were well worth preserving. His feelings towards the Bishop of Exeter, however, were decidedly unchristian.

The Glorious First of June was not forgotten in the aftermath of the war, and was celebrated in traditional fashion in Trafalgar Square. The Rev. Fitzwilliam and Sir Walter sat in a stilly silence in the hotel, the former nursing his reprimand and the latter his gout, which was on the mend. The remainder of the party entered into the spirit of the day. Miss Bessie writes :

" We were invited by Sir Charles Wood to watch a march past of bluejackets in Trafalgar Square. Walter brought a friend, a Mr. Evelyn Wood, who was in the Naval Brigade at Sebastopol and was invalided home. He then thought he preferred the army and joined Uncle Robert's regiment as a Cornet ; he is a fine-looking young man and very amiable. Uncle Robert thinks he will make a good soldier."

Uncle Robert was something of a prophet ; for in 1858 Evelyn Wood gained the V.C., and after a distinguished career was promoted Field-Marshal in 1903. Miss Bessie continues her journal of the day's events :

" We all decided to enjoy ourselves in the evening ; Mama and I were determined to hear the Swedish Nightingale who is visiting England and is singing in a concert at the Italian Opera House. Aunt Eliza was rather tiresome and said she wanted to see the Italian, Madame Ristori, who is making her first appearance as Medea at the Lyceum, so she, B and Uncle Robert went together. I think Mama and I had the best of it. Jenny Lind's singing was divine and the Queen, who was with the Prince in the Royal box, kept clapping her hands in applause. Papa has not much musical ear, for when I told him about the Nightingale singing, he said, ' I'd sooner hear a cock pheasant.' Walter and Mr. Wood went to a rather vulgar exhibition by Mr. Barnum of his three midgets, of which the chief was General Tom Thumb. However, we all enjoyed ourselves in our different ways."

The Portals had taken a house called Murley Grange, between Lichfield and Cannock, and the party left London the next day by the London and Birmingham Railway ; this involved a change to the Trent Valley line, and an unfortunate contretemps occurred. Miss Bessie makes a note of it in her journal :

" Papa, who still had a felt boot on, was being wheeled in a chair by Henry to the Trent Valley train when a gentleman who seemed to be in a great hurry collided with Henry, giving Papa a nasty jar. Papa let out a roar like a bull, and was really very rude to the gentleman, who came up and peered into Papa's face. ' Pardon me, sir,' he said, ' but surely I meet an old school-fellow. Sir Walter Carew, is it not ? ' Papa looked at him and said, ' By Gad, it's Gladstone ; next time look where you're going, or I may use my boot on you as I did thirty-four years ago.' Papa told me that Mr. Gladstone had been his fag at Eton, and was always top of his form while Papa was at the bottom."

The Murley Grange establishment came up nearly, if not quite, to Sir Walter's ideas of comfort. Captain Portal's servant Hodge, who had been with him in the Crimea, had collected a full staff of indoor and outdoor servants. The butler was a most superior person, and having been a footman in the Duke of Argyll's household was still infected by an atmosphere of nobility. He addressed Sir Walter as " your Grace," which infuriated him. " Tell your Jackanapes," he said to Robert Portal, " to do away with his airs and graces and call me plain sir, like my father, grandfather and great-grandfather."

The parade duty roll of the 4th Light Dragoons must have been somewhat depleted ; for Robert Portal, who had now been promoted Brevet Major, had a permanent detachment of the regiment employed as grooms and on other household chores. The soldiers at all events had the merit of keeping the indoor maid-servants happy and contented, and Victorine confided to Miss Bessie that life would be very dull were it not for *les cavaliers*. The Rev. Fitzwilliam, as Miss Bessie records, " was made Clergyman to the army," and under protest conducted morning prayers for the household. This, the Rev. Fitzwilliam said, was his penance for absenting himself from his parish. The Rev. Fitzwilliam's ministrations would appear also to have been a penance for the army and the household staff, for they entailed a good deal of hanging about. Miss Bessie, who was in sympathy with the sufferers, writes : " We all got very hungry waiting for Papa and Uncle Fitz, who were always late.

Mama got very cross with Uncle Fitz and said all he did was to gabble prayers and gobble breakfast."

Two more guests arrived in the persons of Lord George Paget and Mr. Russell, who as *Times* correspondent had become very friendly with Robert Portal in the Crimea. There was a good deal of light badinage over incidents in the campaign, and Portal twitted Russell with the incident of his being chased by Cossacks.

The trial of William Palmer, the Rugeley doctor, for murder, and his being sentenced to death, had excited extraordinary interest. In view of the crowds expected to attend the execution, and the fear of disorders that might occur, two squadrons of the 4th Light Dragoons had been detailed to assist the civil power. Major Portal had in any case to be on duty, and Sir Walter was determined to accompany him as an onlooker. They stayed for the night of the 13th June at the Vine Inn at Stafford, where Calcraft, the executioner, was also installed. Calcraft was inclined to be discursive, and regaled Sir Walter with his experiences as hangman dating from 1828. Sir Walter apparently found these macabre recollections entertaining, and after a bottle of his favourite '45 port, which he shared with Calcraft, he became genially somnolent.

Major Portal, in his journal describing the day's events, writes :

" The execution took place outside the jail ; there was a crowd of about 50,000 and near the scaffold there were several old hags knitting, which brought to mind the *tricoteuses* of the French Revolution. It seems that in this year of grace 1856 we have not advanced much since then. When Palmer was turned off, there was a deep-seated roar in the mob, which for a moment got out of hand. The Peelers were quite useless, and I gave the order to draw swords. We made a sort of half charge, and after some belabourings with the flats of the sabres, we restored order. This sort of work sickens one and I was thankful when the duty was over."

The house-party broke up on 16th June for the usual summer cruise in the *Beatrice*. Sir Walter was getting restive and wished to be captain of his own ship again. He had been frankly bored with the social life and the aftermath of the Crimean War, but being presumably heartened by Mr. Calcraft's reminiscences and having been an eyewitness of an execution, he was moved to declare that the expedition "might have been worse."

EPILOGUE

AND so in the summer of 1856, we take leave of the family party as they set off for their cruise to Norway in the *Beatrice*. There were the usual passengers aboard, all of Sir Walter's choosing as being amenable to his will and pleasure. Lady Carew was nearly forty, but bore her years well and was as attractive as ever, in spite of having put up with Sir Walter's tantrums for nearly twenty years. Miss Bessie, who had become quite a travelled young lady and exceedingly sure of herself, was as keen on sailing as her father and knew far more about the technical details than he did. Miss B. took after her mother, and was becoming a very pretty girl. Then there were Harriet Fortescue and her husband, the latter having become somewhat indolent as he neared his fifties. Lord and Lady Willoughby de Broke were also in the party; they had uprooted themselves from Warwickshire as Lord Willoughby hoped to get some fishing in Norway. Young Walter of the Blues had got two months' leave; he was now the heavy Household Cavalry man and had cultivated a luxuriant crop of whiskers, which satisfied Miss Bessie's fastidious taste. Finally, there was the Reverend Fitzwilliam, who had again torn himself away from his parish and now talked of getting married. Colonel and Mrs. Morris were unable to be present, as the Colonel's old wound was causing him trouble. The other absentees were Major and Mrs. Portal. Robert Portal, for his services in the Crimea, had been promoted to command the newly-raised 5th (Royal Irish) Lancers, which while pleasing him immensely, precluded him from taking a yachting trip. Dally and Henry were still officiating as steward and under-steward, and M. Perron, who had become quite an old-time retainer, was apparently giving complete satisfaction in charge of the culinary department.

Altogether the omens were fair for a prosperous voyage and so far Sir Walter, who had not fallen out with anyone, was on his best behaviour. Mr. Dove, over a glass of grog with the mate, reflectively wondered how long this happy state of affairs would continue.

Within five years Lady Carew, the beautiful Rose of Devon, had ceased to play her part in the amusements, wrangles and small cares of the Carew household. She died in 1861, the same year which saw the death of the Prince Consort, still a comparatively young woman.

She did not keep a diary, like other members of the family, and her letters do not seem to have been preserved, but one would have liked to know whether she was happy and whether the brilliance of her social life compensated her for twenty-four years of marriage with Sir Walter.

Twelve years later, catastrophe overtook her only son. Young Walter Carew who, at the age of thirty-two, was a captain in the Blues, with every appearance of a successful life ahead, and who had become engaged to a girl of whom his father greatly approved, had a bad fall when out hunting and suffered severe head injuries. Careful and devoted nursing seemed to have restored his health and his wedding took place in 1872. But in the year following his wedding, Walter Carew shut himself in his room and committed suicide.

Sir Walter died the following year, leaving his Haccombe and Marley properties to his two daughters.

Miss Bessie and Miss Beatrice never married. One wonders if a lifelong experience of an ill-mannered domestic tyrant had discouraged them from matrimony. They both lived to be very old ladies and died soon after the end of the first World War.

INDEX

INDEX

INDEX

J7